# *Daniel*

## Prophet
## to the
## Nations

John M. Oakes

# *Daniel*

## Prophet
## to the
## Nations

Illumination Publishers International
www.ipibooks.com

*ipi*

# Daniel
Prophet to the Nations

ISBN: 978-0-9776954-8-5

*Book design: Toney C. Mulhollan*

Illumination Publishers International
**www.ipibooks.com**
6010 Pinecreek Ridge Court
Spring, Texas 77379-2513

# Dedication

To
Jan
Benjamin
Elizabeth
Kathryn
and Ruth Oakes, my mother

# Table of Contents

# Table of Contents

### Part Two
### Daniel: Prophet of Comfort

# Acknowledgements

Thanks go to my wife Jan who has always supported my efforts to study and to write.

I owe a debt to those who have given input into the text and editing, including my mother Ruth Oakes, Andrew Lamb, and J. Brian Craig. A special thanks to Elizabeth Thompson and Jerri Newman for their thorough editing and advice.

In addition, I want to express a much-deserved thanks to Gordon Ferguson and Douglas Jacoby, both of whom, as Christian ministers and writers, have been model and inspiration to me.

# Foreword

It is a privilege to write this foreword for John Oakes' new book on Daniel. I have known John for many years and respect him so much as a disciple of Jesus Christ. John and Jan were on the San Diego ministry staff for a period when Gregg Marutzky and I were leading the church there. John was a very competent minister and a very supportive, encouraging friend. For all of his intellectual capacity and academic training (with a Ph.D. in chemical physics), he is a very down-to-earth, practical man and a very humble one. Therefore, my first thoughts about commending the book to you come through the avenue of being able to commend the writer as a great brother in Christ. He is not just good at writing—he is good at living what he writes about, and he personally sets the example that he calls others to follow.

But now to the book I am commending. Several things stand out in reading the book, which will make it a very valuable addition to any library. One, John writes in a very practical and challenging way. As Daniel and his friends face the spiritual battles of their day, the readers find plenty of direction to examine our hearts and lives as we face similar temptations in our day. For example, as John writes about the temptation of Shadrach, Meshach and Abednego to bow down to the king's idol in order to save their lives, he posed some probing questions by which to evaluate our level of idolatry in a number of areas. Then he added this little story from his own life.

I can vividly remember the day when, as a graduate student, my adviser called me into his office to share a concern. He said it was really obvious that pursuing a Ph.D. and a career as a professional scientist was not my first priority. He said in all sincerity that if I did not intend to make the pursuit of science my life, I might need to consider doing something else. What could I say in response to this? In my heart I was saying, "Yes! It is working! My boss has noticed that my commitment to God is far more important to me that getting a Ph.D." I hope that my colleagues would make the same sort of comment about me today. If not, I must ask myself if I have not begun to be at least a part-time worshiper in the church of academia.

Those convictions, coming from a college professor, definitely earn my respect for him. They force me to take a closer look at my own temptations to compromise in subtle ways to avoid having others think badly about me. This book will have that kind of effect on you.

Another outstanding part of the book is John's ability to blend his knowledge about the history, culture, language and political situations of Daniel's day, to set the stage well for us readers. Even if we are quite uninformed in these areas, we will end up really understanding subjects that before were mysteries, as these things are brought to life in a manner that grabs our attention. John knows these subjects well, and without such knowledge being passed on to us, our intellectual grasp and appreciation of Daniel would be lessened considerably.

Yet another outstanding area of John's writing is the straightforward, thorough manner with which he addresses the book's symbolism. Writers are sometimes tempted to skim over the harder issues of interpretation and focus mainly on the easier ones, especially those that are more easily applied. John covers the practical applications well in the narrative sections of the book, but wades right in to identify the meaning of the signs and symbols that occupy a fair segment of Daniel. You will not put this exposition down without knowing what the "beast with three ribs in its mouth between its teeth" (Daniel 7:5) symbolizes or what the other key symbols represent. As the meaning of all of these symbols is unfolded for you, your faith in the Bible and in the present kingdom of which we are a part will increase dramatically.

To this end I commend this new book and its author—to increase our knowledge, our faith and our commitment to live our lives as committed disciples of Jesus. May God add his blessings to accomplish these things for all who read the book, and may it find a wide audience. Its potential impact on individuals and the kingdom deserves that exposure. And to God be the glory!

Gordon Ferguson
Phoenix, Arizona

# Introduction

Daniel occupies a distinctive place among the characters of the Old Testament. Although the book of Daniel fits neatly into the fabric of the Old Testament writings, its subject and style are unique. What other prophet had the non-Jewish world as his primary sphere of ministry? What other book (except maybe Esther) focuses primarily on happenings in the Gentile world, rather than in Israel? What other book in the Old Testament talks about angels and the resurrection so much—or provides such a vivid prophetic picture of the future history of the world?

Because of this unique setting, the book of Daniel is packed full of practical examples of how to live a life for God while living in a non-believing world. At the same time, the book can be very helpful in building the faith of those who read it because of its amazingly accurate prophecies of the future.

The content of Daniel is easily divided into two parts. One part of the book comprises the historical accounts of events in the life of Daniel and his friends Shadrach, Meshach and Abednego; the rest of the book depicts Daniel's prophetic visions of the future. These two types of material are interspersed throughout the book. In order to illustrate how the prophetic and the historical material are distributed, consider the outline of Daniel below.

## Outline of the Book of Daniel

**Chapter I** – Nebuchadnezzar chooses Shadrach, Meshach, Abednego and Daniel for service. They refuse to compromise with "the world."

**Chapter II** – Nebuchadnezzar's first dream: a huge statue. Daniel's interpretation of the dream describes the four world empires.

**Chapter III** – Shadrach, Meshach and Abednego refuse to bow down to a giant idol: Their adventure in the fiery furnace.

**Chapter IV** – Nebuchadnezzar has a dream of a great tree and Daniel interprets the dream. The interpretation comes true and Nebuchadnezzar worships God.

**Chapter V** – Daniel interprets the writing on the wall. Belshazzar, grandson of Nebuchadnezzar, is overthrown, and the nation of Babylon comes to an end.

**Chapter VI** – Daniel is thrown into the lions' den.

**Chapter VII** – A vision of the four beasts, the ten horns and the little horn.

**Chapter VIII** – A vision of a ram (Media/Persia) and a goat (Greece), along with the stern-faced king (Antiochus IV Epiphanes).

**Chapter IX** – Daniel's prayer and God's answer: 490 years until the Messiah comes.

**Chapter X** – Daniel's final vision: Daniel is overcome and helped by angels.

**Chapter XI** – Daniel's final vision, continued: The kings of the South (Egypt) and the kings of the North (Syria), then the abomination of desolation in Jerusalem.

**Chapter XII** – The resurrection of the dead and the time of the end.

The historical/practical parts of Daniel are found in chapters one, three, five and six, while the prophetic visions are contained in chapters two, four and seven through twelve. When Daniel wrote the book (or when the editor who collected his writings put them into their final form), the material was arranged chronologically, rather than thematically. However in this book, Daniel will be studied thematically, rather than chronologically. In other words, after introductory material, we will cover the historical/practical parts first, followed by the visions and their interpretations.

Whether in its historical aspects or in its prophetic writings, the book of Daniel has one overriding theme: *God rules the nations—do not fear*. Given this Biblical truth, the primary lesson to be learned by the readers of Daniel is that they must be faithful to their commitment to the Lord God, regardless of their circumstances. No matter what happens in their lives, if followers of God will put their faith in the unseen but all-powerful God of heaven, they will be considered righteous and will receive their reward on that great Day in the future. Through Daniel, God is telling his people that no matter what happens in the economic world, the religious world, the political world, or the social world, God is in control. God knows his people. He is watching over his righteous servants. Anyone who puts his or her trust in God will ultimately be vindicated. The reader will see this theme developed throughout the book often and in various ways.

The book of Daniel is a varied collection of accounts, visions, dream interpretations, letters, and prayers taken from the different stages in Daniel's long life.[1] However, God is the ultimate author of the book of Daniel (2 Timothy 3:16), so it is not surprising that the book has a unifying theme and purpose running through its potpourri of material. The original purpose of the book of Daniel was to prepare God's people for the times of great tribulation and persecution that lay ahead. God wanted his people both then and now to remain righteous no matter what the world might throw at them. More specifically, the book was written to help the nation of Israel remain faithful through the terrible persecutions under the Seleucid king Antiochus IV Epiphanes (more on that in the historical overview in chapter one).

In Daniel, one finds a great number of parallels with the New Testament book of Revelation. The implicit purpose of Revelation was to prepare disciples of Jesus Christ for the great persecutions under Nero, Domitian, Trajan, Hadrian, Marcus Aurelius, Diocletian and other Roman emperors.

The early church was encouraged with the knowledge that God is in control, not only of the nations in the physical world, but also in the heavenly realms. It is easy to see the parallel to the theme of Daniel.

Readers of the New Testament are usually more familiar with the historical background of the persecutions of the early church under Rome than they are with the persecutions of the Jews in the period between the Old and New Testaments. The Jewish persecutions under the Greek kingdoms are the primary subject of the prophetic parts of the book of Daniel. One of the goals of our study is to better acquaint Bible readers with Jewish history, thus making the book of Daniel more accessible to them.

It is impossible to reach a complete understanding of Daniel's message without having a general understanding of the history of the Jews from the Babylonian period until the time of Jesus Christ. The first chapter of our book provides a historical overview of this period, which will set the stage for both the practical lessons and for understanding the prophetic visions of Daniel.

**Part One** of this book will cover the sections of Daniel that involve events in the lives of Daniel and his friends Shadrach, Meshach and Abednego. One will find a recurring theme in these chapters. Through many difficult and challenging situations, Daniel and his friends had to learn how to conduct themselves in a godly way while living in a ungodly society and political system. We can all relate to this challenge. When the Jews suffered under intense persecution, especially during the reign of Antiochus IV Epiphanes—an event the book of Daniel was preparing them for—they were able to look back to Daniel's example. They could see Daniel remain steadfastly faithful despite ~~the fact that~~ he had little support from other godly men and women. They could see clear and practical examples of the way God rules the nations. Daniel, Shadrach, Meshach and Abednego serve as dramatic examples of how to live for God. It is God's desire for us that "those who are wise will shine like the brightness of the heavens, and those who lead many to righteousness, like the stars for ever and ever" (Daniel 12:3).

Part Two of the book will cover those sections of Daniel that are primarily prophetic in nature. Where the lives of Daniel and his friends (Part One) provide the practical example of how to live a righteous life in an ungodly world, the prophecies of Daniel (Part Two) will predict actual future events that Israel and the church will have to endure in order to remain faithful to God. For a reader in the twenty-first century who is able to look back and see how these amazingly specific prophecies were realized, the validity of the message of Daniel will be proven in a convincing manner. The faith and deep convictions thus gained should help the student of Daniel to put the book's great practical examples of righteous living to work in their own lives.

To summarize, keep in mind the theme of Daniel, *God rules the nations—do not fear.* Also remember that the purpose of Daniel is to prepare God's people to remain faithful and righteous in times of great trouble. The theme and purpose of Daniel will be revealed throughout the book's practical/historical accounts and its examples of prophetic visions. Prepare yourself to be challenged to live a righteous life for God "in a crooked and depraved generation, in which you shine like stars in the universe" (Philippians 2:15). Also, prepare yourself to be greatly inspired as Daniel proves through its amazing and specific prophecies that the Bible truly is the inspired word of God.


John M. Oakes, Ph.D.
San Diego, California

## Notes

[1] In 605 B.C., after Nebuchadnezzar's first campaign against Judah, Daniel was taken to Babylon, probably as a young adult. Daniel survived long enough to be an official under Cyrus ("So Daniel prospered during the reign of Darius and the reign of Cyrus" Daniel 6:28.), implying that he lived a few years past 538 B.C. Therefore, Daniel almost certainly lived for more than eighty years.

# Chapter One

## Historical Background to the Book of Daniel

The historical and political background to the book of Daniel is extremely important both to understanding the message of the book and to interpreting the visions and prophecies of Daniel. This is perhaps more true for Daniel than for any other book in the Bible. There are several reasons for this fact.

First, Daniel lived in a Gentile world. The entire background of his life is different from that of all other major OT figures. Esther and Ezekiel are exceptions, as they lived in Gentile nations, but even they lived among fellow Jews. Daniel had to deal with a radically different culture and political climate from that of other characters in the Bible. Some Bible readers are at least somewhat familiar with the customs and politics of the Jews during Old and New Testament times. But attempting to interpret Daniel from the usual Old or New Testament historical and cultural perspective will only lead to confusion. When reading Daniel, one requires a different cultural education and understanding—that of 6th century B.C. Babylon. Therefore, understanding the historical and cultural setting of the book will prove very useful as we interpret the book of Daniel.

Another crucial reason for understanding the historical and political setting of Daniel is that Daniel himself was an important political figure. He rose to a high advisory position in the Babylonian Empire, a great world power in its time. In fact, he was "chief of the magicians, enchanters, astrologers and diviners" (Daniel 5:11). In Babylon, which was famous for being heavily influenced by its magi, this was a very high post for Daniel to occupy.

When the Medes and Persians took control under Cyrus and destroyed the Babylonian Empire, Daniel did not lose his political influence; instead, he was raised to an even higher position. Darius the Mede planned "to set him [Daniel] over the whole kingdom" (Daniel 6:3). In fact, "Daniel prospered during the reign of Darius and the reign of Cyrus" (Daniel 6:28). Cyrus ruled an empire of greater size and grandeur than any previous ruler in the recorded history of mankind, and Daniel was a chief administrator in his empire. Surely a thorough knowledge of the political and historical setting will help us better understand Daniel's influence and place in the the the ruling hierarchy.

But most importantly, one must understand the historical setting of the book of Daniel because of the amazing predictive prophecies found in it. Daniel contains in outline form the history of the "known world" of the Jews over a period of about six hundred years. This would not be so spectacular if it were not for the fact that Daniel tells the history of the world before it happens. He wrote a history book of the future! Many of the visions (such as that of the ram with two different horns, or the goat with the prominent horn, or the bear with three ribs in its mouth) can only be understood in light of the historical setting of the 5th–2nd B.C. century Near East. As you read this book, you will gain ample historical background information to be able to understand these very unusual visions of Daniel.

In order to describe the historical background of the book of Daniel, we must turn back over four hundred years of history to the beginning of the nation of Israel under Saul and David. But before doing this, it will be helpful to describe the geography of the neighboring regions of Israel (also known as Palestine), an area known as the Near East, or by a nearly synonymous term, the Middle East.[1]

## The Geographical Setting of Daniel

The nation of Israel lies in a narrow, fertile belt aligned in a north-to-south line along the eastern end of the Mediterranean Sea (see maps in the first appendix). Israel was then (and remained so throughout its history) at the crossroads of the much greater empires and nations surrounding it. To the southwest lay the fertile and heavily populated Nile valley—home of the ancient empire and culture of Egypt. To the west was the Mediterranean Sea, but to the northwest of Palestine/Israel was Asia Minor (modern-day Turkey), home to the Hittites, the Lydian Empire and later to the Greek and Ottoman Empires. To the east and south of Palestine was a desert region, home to the primarily Bedouin peoples known in the Bible as the "Arabs," the "Sabeans" (i.e., Sheba), the "Edomites," the "Nabateans" and others.

Most important of all to Daniel was the fertile Mesopotamian valley that lay to the northeast of Israel. Actually, if one looks at the map, the valley of the Tigris and Euphrates Rivers lies more to the east than to the northeast. However, in order for travelers or invading armies to reach Israel from Mesopotamia, they had to travel up the river valleys and descend into Israel through Syria to avoid traveling through the desert. So to the Jews, Mesopotamia is to the northeast.[2]

Daniel spent his entire adult life in Mesopotamia, living in Babylon and Susa (one of the capitals of Persia). Mesopotamia, in the northeast, was home to the ancient Babylonian Empire (famous as the home of Hammurabi and his first recorded system of laws), the Akkadian Empire, the Assyrians, the neo-Babylonians, the Persians and Medes.

*Figure 1. Assyrian King Ashurnasirpal II killing lions in a relief from Nimrud, dated 850 B.C., now in the British Museum.*

Israel itself was constantly caught in a squeeze play between the empires to the southwest (Egypt), to the northwest (the Hittites and the Greek Empires), and to the northeast (Assyria and Babylon, for example). One can readily see, then, why the geography and the history of Israel are intimately connected.

## Historical Prelude

Our historical sketch will begin with the foundation of the kingdom of Israel under Saul the Benjamite (about 1050-1010 B.C.). Saul established the Israelite monarchy, but because of his pride, the kingdom was taken from him (1 Samuel 13:13-14). Saul's successor was David (about 1010-970 B.C.), from the tribe of Judah. David was a man "after God's own heart" (1 Samuel 13:14). David was one of the most revered political figures in the history of Israel. He defeated all the traditional enemies of Israel: the Philistines, Ammonites, Amorites, Edomites and Moabites, to name a few. His son Solomon (about 970-930 B.C.) increased the territory of Israel and established Jerusalem as one of the great economic, political and cultural capitals of the world. These were the glory days of Israel. When Daniel points forward to the reestablishment of God's kingdom (Daniel 2:44-45 and 7:18), surely his Jewish readers assumed it would be a return to glorious times like those under David and Solomon.

*Figure 2. Akkadian Bronze Head of Sargon, c. 2300-2200 B.C., in Iraq Museum in Baghdad, Iraq.*

*Figure 3. Black Obelisk of Shalmaneser III that pictures Jehu, the King of Israel, c. 841 B.C.*

The period of the united kingdom of Israel ended with the reign of Solomon's son Rehoboam. After a coup attempt by Jeroboam, Israel was permanently divided. Israel in the north (the "Northern Kingdom") had Samaria as its capital, while Judah in the south (the "Southern Kingdom") had Jerusalem as its capital.

The Northern Kingdom became much more deeply involved in pagan worship. The populace began to follow the practices under the cults of Baal, Ashtoreth and others. For this reason, God brought Israel into judgment. The Northern Kingdom was attacked and destroyed by the Assyrian

*Figure 4. Assyrian Nineveh Royal Palace relief showing King Ashurbanipal, c. 669 to c. 630 B.C., on his royal chariot with Parasol.*

Empire under Sennacherib. Samaria was defeated, sacked and leveled in 722 B.C. Here one sees for the first time kings "from the north" coming down in judgment of Israel. At this time, Judah was almost destroyed, but thanks to the faith of Hezekiah, Jerusalem was saved, but only temporarily.

The Assyrians, with their capital in Nineveh, were well-known for their fierceness and ruthlessness. When they conquered a nation, they killed a large proportion of the inhabitants. In order to prevent the subjugated nation from rebuilding and later rebelling, they had the practice of deporting en masse the remaining population and dispersing them throughout other parts of their empire. This was the fate the occupants of the Northern Kingdom suffered.

Thus the "ten tribes"[3] were scattered in various eastern provinces of Assyria. The small remnant of Jews left behind intermarried with other peoples who had been brought into northern Israel as exiles from their own countries. This intermixing eventually led to the nation/culture/religion called "the Samaritans" in Jesus' day, who were considered unfaithful by the Jews for marrying into the other races and engaging in false worship.

Relatively more faithful kings ruled the small kingdom of Judah. The Southern Kingdom was kept in line to some extent by virtue of having Jerusalem, the center of religious orthodoxy, as its capital. Judah was able to continue as an independent power for more than one hundred years after the destruction of the Northern Kingdom. In the meantime, the Assyrian kingdom was completely destroyed by the combined armies of Cyaxares II of the Medes and Nabopolassar, king of the Babylonians. Nineveh, the capital of Assyria, was destroyed in 612 B.C. when the allied armies of Media and Babylon diverted the river and threw open the river gates, exactly as prophesied by Nahum (Nahum 2:6). Nabopolassar gained ascendancy over most of the former Assyria, including all of Mesopotamia. Our historical outline has now reached the time of Daniel, Prophet to the Nations.

## Historical Background During the Life of Daniel

Nabopolassar's son, Nebuchadnezzar, is a major figure in the book of Daniel. He continued the exploits of his father, even exceeding them. In 605 B.C., he succeeded his father on the Babylonian throne. At this time, the king of Judah, Jehoiakim, submitted to Nebuchadnezzar after being subjugated (2 Kings 24:1). The "captivity" of Jerusalem could thus be dated from 605 B.C. The initial date of the Babylonian captivity will be an important reference point for understanding some of the visions of Daniel. Nebuchadnezzar took a number of captives to Babylon with him at this time. Among those captives, apparently, were Daniel, Hananiah

*Figure 5. Ishtar Gate from Babylon, now in the Berlin Museum.*

(later Shadrach), Mishael (later Meshach) and Azariah (later Abednego). This is seen from Daniel 2:1, which mentions Daniel and his associates already in Babylon in the second year of Nebuchadnezzar's reign.

    While all these events were transpiring with the Jews, Nebuchadnezzar fought several battles with the Egyptians, the most famous being the battle at Carchemish. This conflict took place in northern Palestine. In this epic battle, Nebuchadnezzar devastated the army of Pharaoh Necho. Eventually, Babylon came to rule the entire former

Egyptian territory in Palestine. Jehoiakim died and was succeeded by his son Jehoiachin. However, before he died, he took the consequential step of rebelling against Babylon.

Therefore, in the eighth year of his reign, 597 B.C., Nebuchadnezzar attacked and defeated Jerusalem. He took Jehoiachin and a large number of the leading men of Judah into captivity in Babylon, but he spared the city itself. The "captivity" of Judah can thus be dated either from 597 B.C. or from the 605 B.C. date mentioned previously.[4] This will be important in understanding the chronology of Daniel. It is interesting to note that the exact sequence of events of 597 B.C. were prophesied by Isaiah almost one hundred and fifty years before they occurred, at a time when Babylon was a minor political power (Isaiah 39:5-7).

Nebuchadnezzar set up a puppet king in Jerusalem to serve as his vassal. He chose Jehoiachin's uncle, Zedekiah. Eleven years later, Zedekiah foolishly rebelled against Nebuchadnezzar, despite being advised by God through Jeremiah to remain in submission to him. The armies of Babylon returned, this time occupying, burning and razing the city of Jerusalem in 586 B.C. This is one of the most compelling moments in the history of God's people. Many more captives were carried off to Babylon at this time as well. Thus the period of the kings of Israel came to an ignominious end. (These events are recorded in 2 Kings 24:8-25:22, Jeremiah 51:1-30, and 2 Chronicles 36:15-20.)

Nebuchadnezzar's son Evil-merodach succeeded him but proved to be a much weaker leader. Eventually, Nabonidus came to power through a coup. In order to legitimize his rule, he married the daughter of Nebuchadnezzar. He was a mystic—seemingly more interested in cultic worship than in keeping control of his large empire. His son, Belshazzar (grandson of Nebuchadnezzar through Nabonidus' wife) shared the throne with his father after 553 B.C. This is the Belshazzar of Daniel chapter five.

Weakness in Babylon gave an opening to a rising power to the east of Babylon. The Median Empire, allies of the Babylonians when they had defeated Assyria, was now eyeing the Mesopotamian valley. However, in the meantime, Cyrus the king of the Persians threw off his overlords the Medes in 550-549 B.C., becoming the uncontested ruler of the Persia/Median dual Empire.

Cyrus "the Great" is a very important figure both in the prophecies of Daniel and in the events of Daniel's life. He was truly a unique ruler for his time. Breaking with the pattern of cruelty to defeated rulers and nations, Cyrus showed great restraint when he defeated the Medes. He did not destroy their capital, Ecbatana. Neither did he attempt to impose Persian religion (which later became Zoroastrianism, a religion still practiced today, especially in parts of India and Iran). Rather than deporting the peoples he defeated, he actually instituted the practice of allowing exiles to return to their homelands. This practice was to play a decisive role in the history of Israel.

The three other great powers of Cyrus' day were Babylon, Lydia (whose center of power was in Asia Minor) and Egypt. Cyrus eventually defeated the first two, while his son Cambyses defeated the Egyptians. First, Cyrus attacked Lydia. The king of Lydia was the fantastically wealthy Croesus, whose name is synonymous with wealth. Lydia fell in 546 B.C. Next in line was Babylon, which fell virtually without a fight in 539 B.C. This is an important date, because soon after overcoming Babylon, Cyrus issued the decree allowing the Jewish exiles to return to Israel. This decree is recorded in 2 Chronicles 36:23:

> The Lord, the God of heaven, has given me all the kingdoms of the earth and he has appointed me to build a temple for him at Jerusalem in Judah. Anyone of his people among you—may the Lord his God be with him, and let him go up.

*Figure 6. Cyrus Cylinder Cuneiform, fulfillment of Isaiah 45:13, in c. 536 B.C. It is now in the British Museum.*

This is truly a remarkable decree from Cyrus. Lest anyone think this is just a story the writers of 2 Chronicles made up, it is virtually identical to a decree which was discovered carved into a stone cylinder called the "Cyrus cylinder." On this Persian cylinder, Cyrus is quoted as saying, "All of their peoples I assembled and restored to their own dwelling places." A similar statement, actually from Darius, is also recorded in the famous Behistun inscription—carved into a huge cliff in the desert regions of southern Persia. The Cyrus cylinder records the bloodless overthrow of Babylon as described in Daniel chapter five. In addition, Cyrus also had a policy of returning plundered "gods" to their native peoples. Although the Jews obviously had no such idols, the decree was applied to the stolen items from the temple in Jerusalem—the same items which were used in the idolatrous drunken feast by Belshazzar the night Babylon was captured (Daniel 5:1-5). Cyrus decreed that the utensils be sent back to Jerusalem (Ezra 6:3-5).

In one of the most astoundingly specific prophecies in all the Bible, Isaiah had predicted this occurrence. Writing somewhere around the year 750 B.C., more than two hundred years before the events took place, Isaiah prophesied (Isaiah 45:13):

> I will raise up Cyrus in my righteousness: I will make all his ways straight. He will rebuild my city and set my exiles free, but not for a price or reward, says the Lord Almighty.[5]

Perhaps Daniel influenced Cyrus to be protective and sympathic toward Israel for he occupied a high position in the government of Cyrus. Presumably, Daniel died some time during the reign of Cyrus.

## From Daniel's Death to the Close of the OT

Cyrus' son, Cambyses (also called Artaxerxes in Ezra 4:6) succeeded him in 530 B.C. (see the chart on page 31). Artaxerxes brought the rebuilding of the temple to a stop. He also conquered the empire of Egypt. Despite his successes, he later committed suicide, bringing his son Darius I to the throne in 521 B.C. During his rule, Darius allowed the completion of the temple under the leadership of the governor Zerubbabel and the prophet Haggai.

Darius turned his attention to the Greeks in Asia Minor. In one campaign, he even crossed into mainland Greece, where he was defeated in the famous battle of Marathon. Darius and his successors Xerxes I (Ahasuerus in the book of Esther), Artaxerxes I Longimanus, Darius II, and Artaxerxes II all used up the power of Persia in vain attempts to subdue the Greek mainland for the next one hundred and fifty years. This fruitless expense of Persian power ultimately allowed for the destruction of Persia by Alexander. Xerxes won the famous battle at Thermopylae in 480 B.C., but this was truly a hollow victory, as he lost almost his entire army defeating three hundred Spartans in a strongly held mountain pass. This is the same Xerxes "who ruled over 127 provinces stretching from India to Cush" (Esther 1:1). His son Artaxerxes I Longimanus is the ruler who gave permission to Ezra to return to Jerusalem in 458 B.C. and also issued the decree to rebuild Jerusalem, which he sent with Nehemiah in 445 B.C. This date will be a very important one in interpreting the prophecies of Daniel.

## Between the Testaments

With Nehemiah's last return to Jerusalem in 432 B.C., the Old Testament draws to a close, but our story does not. To the Bible neophyte, the preceding account may be almost entirely new. For those who have studied the Bible for a long time, the preceding outline may be at least somewhat familiar. However, as the historical summary continues below, it will cover events "between the testaments."[6] A good majority of Bible readers, even long-time Bible students, will be learning about this part of the history of Israel for the first time, because the events are not recorded in the Bible. The really amazing thing about all this is that Daniel was very familiar with this material, even though it occurred hundreds of years after he died.

## The First Six Kings of Persia

| Persian King | Yrs. of Reign | Major Events |
| --- | --- | --- |
| Cyrus | 550-530 B.C. | Babylon conquered |
| | | Decree to restore Jerusalem |
| Cambyses | 529-522 B.C. | Egypt conquered |
| Pseudo-Smerdis | 522-521 B.C. | |
| Darius I Hystaspes | 521-486 B.C. | Temple rebuilt |
| | | First attack on Greece |
| | | Defeat at Marathon |
| Xerxes I | 486-465 B.C. | Attempted conquest of Greece |
| | | Disaster at Thermopylae |
| | | Esther |
| Artaxerxes | 465-424 B.C. | Decrees to rebuild Jerusalem |
| | | Ezra and Nehemiah |

By the middle of the fourth century B.C., it was not just the power of the once-mighty Persian Empire that had been dissipated. In the Peloponnesian wars, the two great city-states of Greece—Athens and Sparta—had been bled nearly dry as well. The once-overwhelming fleet of Athens was destroyed. The famed Spartan blood had been spilled several times too many to be replenished. Onto the scene burst Philip of Macedon. He seized the throne of the obscure and relatively uncivilized state of Macedonia in 359 B.C. Philip marched down from his mountain stronghold to defeat the city of Amphipolis in the same year, changing the name of this famous city to Philippi.

*Figure 7. Darius I and Xerxes I give audience, c. 490 B.C.*

*Figure 8. Ruins of the Persian Royal Residence at Persepolis, Iran, begun by Darius I and completed during the reigns of Xerxes I and Artaxerxes I, Achaemenian period, 6th-4th Centuries B.C.*

Philip recognized the greater civilization of the Greeks. He therefore made a decision that changed the history of the world. He sent his son Alexander to Greece to study under Aristotle, who was perhaps the greatest intellect in all the history of Greece. Alexander eventually combined the great military genius of his father with a zeal for spreading Greek culture throughout the entire known world. Alexander carried copies of the Odyssey and the Iliad with him wherever he went. He was truly the apostle of Hellenism (a common term for Greek culture).

In 338 B.C., Philip defeated Athens, and the entire region of Greece was open to his armies. In 336 B.C. he was murdered, and his twenty-year-old son Alexander ("the Great") succeeded him. In the same year, Darius III became emperor of Persia. Alexander crossed the Straits of Dardanelles in 334 B.C. with a small army, mostly of Macedonians. In a symbolic gesture, he had all the transport boats burned when they landed in Asia. In a series of decisive battles (Granicus in Asia Minor in 334 B.C., Issus in Syria in 333 B.C., Gaugamela in Mesopotamia in 331 B.C.), Alexander completely destroyed the power of Persia. Darius III died in 330 B.C., making him the last ruler of ancient Persia. Alexander also conquered Tyre (332 B.C.) and Egypt (332 B.C.). He continued on through all the eastern provinces of Persia, all the way into the valley of the Punjab, on the border of India. The way to conquer even India lay open to Alexander,

*Figure 9. Battle of Alexander and Darius III at Issus with detail of the Roman mosaic from the Casa del Fauno, Pompeii, late 2nd Century B.C. in the Museo Archeologico Nazionale, Naples, Italy.*

but his army refused to go on. Alexander married a Bactrian princess named Roxana and fathered a child through her. Very soon after she conceived his only son, Alexander died in Babylon of a fever at the age of 35 (323 B.C.).

The question of succession came up immediately upon his death, but Alexander's son was still an infant. His succession to rule Alexander's empire proved impossible. Instead, several of Alexander's generals seized power in various parts of his huge realm. By 315 B.C., four outstanding generals remained to found four Greek dynasties. These were Ptolemy (Egypt), Antigonus (Mesopotamia all the way to India), Lysimachus (Thrace) and Cassander (Macedonia and Greece).

Ptolemy had a very successful general named Seleucus who attacked Antigonus' armies and won northern

Syria and Mesopotamia. He eventually rebelled against Ptolemy Lagi, establishing his own dynasty. The Ptolemaic rulers and the Seleucid successors are the kings of the South and kings of the North of Daniel chapter eleven. The history of the battles between these two kingdoms will be described in detail later in this book when Daniel eleven is discussed. However, one extremely important figure in this history must be mentioned at this point. This is Antiochus IV Epiphanes, one of the Seleucid kings, who came to power in 175 B.C. In the back-and-forth struggle between the Ptolemaic and the Seleucid kings, Antiochus occupied Jerusalem and began a very intense persecution of the Jews, making both circumcision and the worship of God punishable by death. He was attempting to "Hellenize" the Jews by completely eliminating their unique culture. This period will be extremely important in the study of Daniel. Much more will be said about Antiochus IV Epiphanes and his persecutions.

The Jews under the Persians as well as the Greek Ptolemaic Dynasty had been passive—submitting to relatively benign foreign rule, seemingly without a great deal of bitterness. However, the persecutions of Antiochus IV Epiphanes inspired a revolt by the Hasidim (an orthodox sect of Judaism). An aged priest named Mattathias was ordered to make a sacrifice at a pagan altar. Instead, he killed the apostate Jew demanding the sacrifice. Mattathias fled to the hills with his sons. He died soon thereafter, but his son Judas Maccabeus continued the guerilla war tactics of his father. Eventually, in 164 B.C., Judas, founder of the Maccabean Dynasty of the Jews, took Jerusalem and re-consecrated the temple. Antiochus IV Epiphanes had desecrated the temple three years earlier. He had placed a statue of himself in the temple and even sacrificed a pig on the altar. The re-consecration of the temple is remembered in the Jewish festival of Chanukah, noted as the Feast of Dedication in John 10:22 and the NIV footnote with it.

The Maccabees were able to achieve a tenuous independence for the Jews, at least for a short period. Judas Maccabeus' brother Jonathan succeeded him, another brother Simon succeeded Jonathan. His son John Hyrcanus I later ruled in Jerusalem. Under John Hyrcanus I, Judah reached a size almost as great as that of the kingdom under Solomon about 900 years earlier. John Hyrcanus I defeated the Idumeans (Edomites in the Old Testament) and forced them to be circumcised. A series of brutal, irreligious successors followed John Hyrcanus I on the Maccabean (also called the Hasmonean) throne. Ultimately, the Roman general Pompey entered the city of Jerusalem in 63 B.C., bringing to an end the brief independence of the Jewish nation and ushering in the long period of Roman rule in Palestine.

During all the events described here, to the west a new power had been growing steadily over the previous three centuries. Beginning as a sleepy town on the banks of the Tiber River, the city-state of Rome gradually gained ascendancy over the entire Italian peninsula. In a series of decisive battles, commonly known as the Punic wars, the Romans eventually defeated the Carthaginians, the greatest power in the West, successors to the power of Tyre. Carthage, the capital of the Carthaginian Empire, was in modern-day Tunisia, on the north coast of Africa. The most famous general of the Carthaginians was Hannibal, who crossed the Alps with an army including a great number of elephants. In 146 B.C., the Romans destroyed the city of Carthage, covering the ruins with salt in order to prevent the site from being reoccupied.

Having disposed of the Carthaginians, who had controlled the western Mediterranean Sea, the Roman republic set about the systematic elimination of the former Greek dynasties. In 133 B.C., they gained Pergamum, setting up the province which came to be called Asia. Rome began to interfere in Egypt as well. As mentioned before, the Roman general Pompey took Jerusalem in 63 B.C. Soon after this, Julius Caesar seized power in Rome. When he was killed, Mark Antony came to power. For a brief period, the Parthians (successors to the Persian power) controlled Jerusalem, but in 41 B.C., Rome regained Jerusalem, which she ruled for more than four hundred years. Mark Antony appointed Herod (an Idumean) "king" over Judea in 37 B.C. This is the first Herod of the Bible (Herod the Great), who rebuilt the temple in Jerusalem.

Octavius (nephew of Julius Caesar, also known as

Octavian) chased Mark Antony out of Rome. Octavius was later known as Augustus Caesar, the first emperor of Rome. This is the same Augustus mentioned in Luke 2:1. Mark Antony fled to Egypt, where he formed an alliance with the very last of the "Greek" Ptolemaic rulers, Cleopatra. He was defeated at the battle of Actium in 31 B.C. by Octavius. Thus Egypt passed to Rome.

In the time of those (Roman) kings, a peasant from the small town of Nazareth, located in the obscure district of Galilee, began a spiritual movement that ushered in the kingdom of God on earth; the church of Jesus Christ. Within one generation, this movement was to spread throughout the Roman world, becoming a kingdom that would never be destroyed (paraphrasing Daniel 2:44). Daniel foretold these events more than five hundred years before they occurred.

*Figure 10. Octavius (Augustus Caesar, who reigned 27 B.C.-14 A.D.).*

One last event that occurred soon after the establishment of the kingdom of God is quite significant to the study of Daniel. Due to the unwise and insensitive policies of the Roman emperors, especially those of Caligula, a smoldering Jewish rebellion developed into a full-blown rebellion to throw off the Roman government in AD 66. In order to put down this insurrection, Nero sent his general Vespasian. When Nero died, Vespasian went to Rome to be declared emperor, and his son Titus took over the siege of Jerusalem. In 70 A.D., Titus' troops breached the walls of Jerusalem, burned the temple and leveled the city. As foretold both by Daniel (Daniel 9:26-27) and by Jesus (Luke 21:6, 20-24), the Jewish temple and the Jewish practice of religious sacrifice came to an end forever. Truly, *God rules the nations!*

## Notes

[1] The distinction between the two is minor. Many would not include Persia, or modern Iran, in the Middle East, perhaps because it is a decidedly non-Arab country. Some would not include Egypt as part of the Near East, since it is in Africa, but Persia would certainly be part of the Near East.

[2] This explains the fact that when the Bible refers to nations, armies or kings "to the north," it is actually referring to nations which, when looking on the map, appear to be more from the east. For example, consider Isaiah 41:25, Jeremiah 4:6, 6:22, 16:15 and 46:6, Ezekiel 26:7 and Zechariah 2:6, to mention a few.

[3] Some people over-emphasize the number ten in talking about the ten "lost" tribes. There were thirteen total tribes from Jacob, including the Levites who inherited cities rather than land. In fact, the southern kingdom of Judah contained in its population the tribes of Benjamin and Judah, plus a majority of the Levites, who naturally left Samaria when worship of *Yahweh* was superseded by the cult of Baal. Besides these tribes, most of Simeon (whose tribal territory was in the south), along with a significant number from the other tribes who had fled as religious or political refugees, lived in the southern kingdom of Judah.

[4] Sir Robert Anderson, in his book, *Daniel in the Critics' Den*, (New York: Cosimo Classics, 2007—originally published in 1909), pp. 117-123, put forth an interesting theory concerning the seventy years. He claimed that there were seventy years of captivity, starting in 605 B.C., and a separate seventy years of desolation, starting in 586 B.C., when Jerusalem was destroyed. Both dates have a logical terminus seventy years later. The support from scripture for there being two separately calculated "captivities" seems weak. Nevertheless, Anderson makes some interesting points. The interested reader should consult Anderson's book.

[5] Cyrus is called "the Lord's anointed." Bear in mind that the word Messiah means "the anointed one." Perhaps just as interesting, the root meaning of the name Cyrus is "shepherd." The "shepherd" Cyrus, who watched over Israel, is a symbolic figure of Jesus Christ, the "Good Shepherd." Here one can see that God used Cyrus, a non-believer, but savior of Israel nevertheless, as a prefigure of Christ. There will be more on the subject of OT historical figures of Christ at a later point in the book.

[6] The words "between the testaments" are in quotes because this is the title of a very good little book of the same name: *Between the Testaments,* Charles F. Pfeiffer, (Guardian of Truth Foundation, 1959). Much of the material in this section comes from this book. Another helpful source is *The Book of Daniel*, Jim McGuiggan, (Montex Publishing Company, 1978), chapter one. Also useful is the book *Customs and Controversies*, J. Julius Scott Jr., (Baker Books, 1995). This book deals with the social and religious background of Judaism in the period "between the testaments."

# Chapter Two

## Daniel: Prophet to the Nations

The historical background to the book of Daniel is extremely important. In addition, the religious background of Daniel the book and of Daniel the man require some attention before proceeding into a chapter-by-chapter study of the book. This chapter of our book will provide some biographical information on Daniel himself. It will also explore the language of the book in some detail.

### Daniel the Man

First, consider the background of the author himself. Many liberal theologians would like to dispute the authorship of the book. They have a good reason for taking this stand. If one accepts that the historical person Daniel was the author of the book entitled *Daniel*, then this fact alone would provide incontrovertible proof that the Bible is the inspired word of an omniscient God. This is true because Daniel lived in the sixth century B.C.—long before the events prophesied in the book happened. Many people who call themselves theologians have a great stake in attacking the divine authorship of the Bible. Much more will be seen on this and how one can know from the evidence that the book of Daniel was written considerably earlier than would be asserted by the liberal theories.

Let us assume, at least for now, that the author of the book was Daniel. Actually, Daniel himself was most likely not the final compiler/editor of the book. Consider, for example, Daniel 4:19, "Then Daniel (also called Belteshazzar) was greatly perplexed," or Daniel 7:1, "Daniel had a dream," or Daniel 10:1: "In the third year of Cyrus king of Persia, a revelation was given to Daniel." The text contains many more examples in which Daniel is referred to in the third person.

On the other hand, consider Daniel 7:15, "I, Daniel, was troubled in spirit," or Daniel 8:1: "In the third year of King Belshazzar's reign, I, Daniel, had a vision." Perhaps most interesting of all is Daniel 10:2, in which Daniel refers to himself in the first person: "At that time, I, Daniel, mourned for three weeks." This is noteworthy because in the preceding verse, Daniel 10:1, Daniel is referred to in the third person .

The most natural way to understand all this is to assume that Daniel himself wrote down certain visions as God commanded him. Then, at a later time in his life, or more likely, at a time fairly soon after his death, a compiler/editor collected the visions Daniel had recorded. Presumably, the person who collected the visions also provided a historical narrative describing the most significant events in Daniel's life, as well as in the life of his companions Shadrach, Meshach and Abednego. Evidence to support this view is found in the fact that the historical chapters refer to Daniel in the third person, while in general, the visions are recorded by Daniel in the first person. Perhaps the best example of this occurs, as mentioned earlier, in Daniel 10:1-2. In these two verses, the compiler/editor gives the background to the vision in the third person (verse one), while the actual vision, as recorded by Daniel, begins in the second verse and is described in the first person.

Further support of the idea that the book was pulled together by an editor is indicated by the mixture of the Hebrew and Aramaic languages in the book. There will be more on this later.

Is all this important? For a person who is already convinced that the Bible is the word of God, it is not important. However, to the critic of the Bible, these are essential matters. If Daniel is to be used as irrefutable proof of the inspiration of the Bible, then its authorship, and more importantly its *date* of authorship, are significant issues.

Much research and thought has led this author to conclude that the book of Daniel was written by Daniel himself. More accurately, Daniel is the author of at least large parts of the book, while the rest was written and collected by someone very close to the events described. We will discuss more evidence supporting these conclusions as we progress through our study.

So who is Daniel? Not much is known about his background. Unlike Isaiah or Amos or other prophets, we do not know Daniel's father. We do know that he was one of the captives taken from Jerusalem. More specifically, he was from among "the royal family and the nobility" of Israel (Daniel 1:3). From this one can assume that he was most likely well educated even before Ashpenaz followed Nebuchadnezzar's orders and taught him "the language and literature of the Babylonians" (Daniel 1:4). One can be certain that Daniel was a very wise and intelligent person. The reader can conclude this from reading about his life throughout the book of Daniel, even without being told in verse four about his extraordinary education.

Daniel is clearly one of the spiritual giants of the Old Testament. Interestingly, Ezekiel, a contemporary of Daniel, lists Daniel with Noah and Job as among the best possible examples of men who, if it was possible for personal righteousness to save someone, could be saved by their own good lives (Ezekiel 14:12-14). Of course, even these three could not save themselves! Imagine a man whose spirituality and righteous life were so impeccable that a contemporary would dare to list him with Noah and Job. Would those who know you even be tempted to list you alongside Daniel, Noah and Job as a righteous person? Daniel is truly a figure to be studied and emulated.

But what exactly is the position of Daniel in the Bible? Two points come to mind. First, he was a prophet, but not a prophet in the "normal" sense, and second, he occupies a position as a historic/prophetic figure of Jesus Christ himself.

Daniel was a prophet. However, he was not a prophet in the most common sense of the word used by the Jews. It is interesting to note that in the Jewish Bible, the book of Daniel is not even grouped in the section of the "Prophets," but in the "Psalms" (known as the *"Hagiographa"* to the Jews, also called "The Writings"), along with Job, Proverbs and others. Actually, Daniel may have originally been grouped within the Prophets. For example, in about 175 A.D., Melito of Sardis put Daniel in the Prophet category when cataloguing the OT books. In many of the oldest Greek manuscripts, Daniel is among the books commonly referred to as the "Prophets," but then again, so was the book of Chronicles (there is only one book of Chronicles in the Hebrew Bible), so that does not prove much about the Israelites' view of him. Either way, there seems to have been at least some doubt in the minds of the Jews about whether Daniel held the position of a prophet.

One thing that makes Daniel unique among the prophets (with the partial exception of Jonah, who spent most of his career in Israel, but preached to the Assyrians in Nineveh) is that his ministry during his life was not to Israel, but to the pagan nations of Babylon and Persia. The general rule for a prophet was that he or she was a preacher of righteousness and repentance to the people of God. Even prophets such as Isaiah and Obadiah, who preached oracles against pagan nations (Isaiah 13, 28; all of Obadiah), delivered their messages to Israel. From Moses to Elijah, from Isaiah to Ezekiel and Zechariah, the prophets spoke to the people of Israel: "Thus says the Lord...". In the book of Daniel, one does not encounter a single "Thus says the Lord" spoken to his people. In fact, there is no really solid evidence that Daniel was a preacher at all. He was a righteous man, for sure, the recipient of many visions as well as the inspired interpreter of dreams. However, he was not one who held the recognized position of "prophet" to Israel in his lifetime. Jonah was called a prophet, and so were Nathan and Joel, but Daniel was not a prophet in that sense.

The Hebrew word for "prophet" carries with it the denotation of one who speaks forth, as well as the connotation of one who is the messenger of God. That is what men like Jeremiah and Elisha were. In the case of Daniel, it was primarily his life itself that spoke forth, rather than his preaching—at least during his lifetime. His prophecies, if they can be called that,[1] were primarily about the distant future. One simple way to describe the person Daniel is not as a prophet, but as one who prophesied about the future for God.

The second point about the man Daniel is that he serves as a symbolic picture of the Messiah. There are several other men who God uses as prophetic figures of Jesus Christ. Among them are Joseph, Moses and David. These pre-figures to Christ collectively serve as one of the great bodies of evidence, not only that Jesus Christ is the Messiah, but also that God inspired the Bible. In the persons of Daniel, Moses, Joseph, David and others, God created living prophecies of Christ, rather than written prophecies. The very events of these men's lives mirror those of Jesus Christ in very interesting ways.

Consider Joseph: He was sent off into Egypt as a young man, just as Jesus was. He was betrayed by jealous brothers, as was Jesus. He too was sold for a small price.[2] He lived a very righteous life. Because of his righteous life, he was able to "save" God's people, in his case from starvation, when he called them to Egypt. Many other analogies can be made between the life of Christ and of Joseph.

Moses, like Joseph and Daniel, serves as a prefigure of Jesus. A jealous king wanted to kill him when he was an infant. Moses was sent away from God's people as a young man. He was an extremely righteous man who saved God's people, calling them out of slavery in Egypt, providing an obvious analogy to the Messiah. The Bible even describes how the people were "baptized into Moses...in the sea" (1 Corinthians 10:2). He was the giver of the OT Law as Jesus was the giver of the "Law of Christ." These are only a few of the many parallels between the lives of Moses and Jesus Christ.

David serves as a historical prefiguring of Jesus as well. Like Jesus, David also had to leave his country to wander, in his case among the Philistines. He too saved God's people by bringing them political freedom and by establishing a physical kingdom, which was itself a figure of the spiritual kingdom of God. Many of the details of David's life were echoed in the life of the Messiah, as can be seen, for example, by reading Psalm 22. God promised that salvation would come through David (Psalm 89:19-37)—and indeed it came, not only during David's reign as king, but also through Jesus as one of David's descendants.

Daniel, then,[3] is one among many. He too led a life that was a living prophecy of the coming Messiah. Like the others, he was taken away from the people of God as a very young man. Like Joseph, Moses and David before him, as a young man Daniel lived a nearly impeccable righteous life among ungodly people. He proclaimed the release of God's people from captivity by the Babylonians (Daniel 9:1-3), and saved many from death when he successfully interpreted Nebuchadnezzar's dream.

It is truly inspiring to consider how God used the lives of these men to serve as templates for the life of Christ. According to the wisdom of the world, our lives are shaped by luck or by our environment, or perhaps by the "gods." In the case of these great figures of the Bible, God worked to make the actual events of their lives serve as living prophecies of the coming Messiah. Can it be argued that mere luck resulted in a repeating pattern in all these men's lives, which was carried out to fulfillment in the life of Jesus Christ? Perhaps, but for any but the most hardened skeptic, this evidence serves as another amazing proof of the inspiration of the Bible and of God's work in sending his Son as the Savior of the world.

So, then, Daniel is a prophet (sort of) and a prophetic figure of Christ. More could be said about how his life is a pre-figuration of the Christ. It would be a good exercise as you study the book to consider for yourself other ways in which the life of Daniel parallels the life of Jesus.

## The Language of Daniel

The language of Daniel is another element that makes the book unique among the Bible's various books. First and foremost, Daniel is written largely in Aramaic. Daniel 2:4 states, "Then the astrologers answered the king in Aramaic." The ensuing speech and all that follows, all the way through

Daniel chapter seven, is written in Aramaic. Virtually the entire Old Testament was originally composed in Hebrew, so why is part (and more specifically, why only these five chapters) of Daniel in Aramaic? And more specifically, why are these five chapters in Aramaic, but not the others?

First, it might be useful to consider a few facts about the Aramaic language. Aramaic was the *lingua franca* (i.e., the common language) of the Babylonian Empire. The language began as the native tongue of the Arameans, one of the peoples commonly referred to in the Old Testament. The Arameans lived in a region equivalent to modern-day Syria as well as parts of northern Iraq and southeastern Turkey. This region corresponds roughly to the area now occupied by the modern-day Kurds. Because the Arameans were in the region bridging Mesopotamia and Egypt, their language gradually came into widespread use, especially for commerce. By the time of Daniel, it was the predominant language in Mesopotamia and Palestine, as well as in Syria. When the Persians corresponded with their representatives in Palestine, they apparently wrote in Aramaic, as evidenced by Ezra 4:8-6:18. Here one finds the text of letters written in Aramaic. In Jesus' day, several hundred years after Daniel, Aramaic was still the predominant language of Palestine. In fact, several Aramaic idioms crept into the original Greek NT manuscripts (for example, Matthew 27:46). Jesus grew up speaking Aramaic.

Daniel was a child of the nobility or at least of the aristocratic class of the Jews. One can therefore assume that he could speak Hebrew. Because he eventually became a high official in the Persian Empire, it can also be assumed that he could speak Persian. However, the language most familiar to Daniel was probably Aramaic. Most likely, the final editor who pulled the book of Daniel together also used Aramaic as his primary language. Therefore, it is reasonable to assume (but not conclusively) that the original copy of Daniel was in Aramaic.

The more difficult question, then, is why approximately half the book as it has come down to us is in Hebrew. This will call for some speculation. It seems likely that at some point someone translated the book into Hebrew. Perhaps the same compiler/editor who brought the writings of Daniel together, as speculated above, did the partial translation into Hebrew. Either way, for some unknown reason, this person left part of the book in its original Aramaic and translated the rest into Hebrew. It is worth noting that copies and fragments of Daniel are among the Dead Sea Scrolls. These copies were made in the first century before Christ. The versions of Daniel found in the Dead Sea Scrolls have the same Hebrew-Aramaic-Hebrew split found in the much later Hebrew manuscripts, confirming that the mixture of Hebrew and Aramaic originated at a very early date.

Whether the original was in Hebrew or in Aramaic probably may not seem important to most English-speaking readers of Daniel, since they are likely reading the Bible in an English translation anyway. The average reader is not going to be very concerned with what the original language was. Nevertheless, there is a major reason that the original language of Daniel is very important to us: The theological liberals who would attack the authenticity of Daniel make their strongest argument based on the language of the book. For this reason, it becomes extremely important to consider both the date at which Daniel was written and the nature of the language in which it was written.

It is difficult to stress too strongly the importance of the argument over the date of the writing of the book of Daniel. It will be shown that if the book of Daniel was written by about 500 B.C., as is claimed in this book, then even the most hard-core skeptic will have to concede that there are undeniable marks of inspiration in the book. The prophecies are just too specific to be ignored. Given the strong evidence in support of an earlier date for Daniel, it becomes apparent that a good number of liberal theologians,do not want to accept the simple fact that the Bible is a product of God, rather than man. Their tactic is to claim that the book must have been written somewhere in the second century B.C., after the greatest share of the incredibly specific prophecies had already been fulfilled.

The originator of this attack on Daniel was the third-century neo-Platonist philosopher Porphyry. Porphyry was a pagan and definitely not a Christian. He is the first recorded writer to assert a second-century B.C. date for the writing of Daniel. This pagan attack on the authenticity of Daniel appears to have disappeared in history, only to be revived by supposed Christian theologians in the eighteenth century with the rise of so-called "higher criticism."

I think it is important to note that there are many with their Th.D. degrees—people who claim to be religious experts—who would attack the authenticity of Daniel. Why? Because to accept it to be what it claims to be, i.e., written entirely or in part by the historical figure Daniel in the sixth century B.C., would be to accept that the Bible as a whole is the production of an all-powerful God rather than of man. In the spirit of 1 Peter 3:15-16, this issue should be investigated and considered carefully.

There are a few reasons commonly given to support the claim that the book of Daniel is a fake document, written in the second century B.C. Some of these arguments will be addressed where they naturally come up in the context of this book, but the (seemingly) strongest and most consistent argument for a late date of the writing of Daniel is based on its language. The argument is as follows, to quote from S. R. Driver:[4]

> The verdict of the language of Daniel is thus clear. The *Persian* words presuppose a period after the Persian Empire had been well established: the Greek words *demand*, the Hebrew *supports*, and the Aramaic *permits* a date *after the conquest of Palestine* by Alexander the Great (332 B.C.). (emphasis is Driver's)

As it turns out, this, the strongest argument for the late date of the writing of Daniel (at about 150 B.C.) is a weak one indeed. This is made particularly true since even the critics admit that their argument only supports a date some time after 300 B.C., which certainly is a long way from 150 B.C. Driver says that the inclusion of Greek words in Daniel demands a date of writing some time after 300 B.C. Unfortunately for Driver's opinion, this simply cannot be supported by the facts. The argument is that Greek influence in Mesopotamia only became significant after the time of Alexander the Great. In other words, assuming that there was very little Greek influence in Persia in the time of Daniel, the Greek words in the book would reflect a much later date of authorship. However, the claim that there was very little Greek influence in Babylon/Persia in the sixth century is simply not true. In fact, records exist that describe Greek captives being sold into slavery in Mesopotamia as early as the time of the Assyrian ruler Sargon (722-705 B.C.). The Greek poet Alcaeus, writing about 600 B.C., mentions that his brother served as a mercenary in the Babylonian army. There is a large body of evidence of major cultural and political contact between the Greek states and the Mesopotamian powers before the time of Daniel. So why does Driver make the claim recorded above?

Let us look more closely at the claim that the Greek words in Daniel *"demand"* a composition date in the second century B.C. The argument is based on a paltry three Greek words contained in the entire book of Daniel. There are only three Greek words and all are words for musical instruments (*kitharis, psalterion* and *symphonia*, contained in Daniel 3:5). One should ask at this point: What words are first borrowed from a foreign language? For example, consider the influence of the Chinese language on the English. Would we be likely to borrow the Chinese word for water? No, because our English word is far too common and familiar. What if we used a musical instrument of Chinese origin for which we had absolutely no word in English? Obviously we would use the Chinese word for this instrument. Not suprisingly, the Chinese word for guitar is "guitar." How did the Spanish word *bolo* (that funny thing with two stones attached to a rope used by Argentine cowboys to rope horses) get into the English language? The explanation is simple: We had no word for a bolo in English. This is the kind of Greek word contained in the language of Daniel.

Is this evidence that Daniel was written around 150 B.C.? Absolutely not. In fact, the Greek contained in Daniel is actually strong evidence that it was written *before* the time of Alexander the Great, because after this date, when Greek influence in the Mesopotamian region became dominant, one can assume that more Greek words would have crept into the book of Daniel than just three words for musical instruments.

The same sort of argument from facts about the history of languages can be applied to all the linguistic claims of Driver and others of the liberal theological school. The full argument would be too long for the purposes of this book. The interested reader should look into the references quoted for a fuller treatment. However, to sum up, consider a quote from a noted author in the field, R. D. Wilson, regarding the claim that the Aramaic of Daniel allows for a second century B.C. date for the writing of Daniel:

> We claim, however, that the composite Aramaic of Daniel agrees in most every particular of orthography, etymology, and syntax, with the Aramaic of the North Semitic inscriptions of the 9th, 8th, and 7th century B.C. and of the Egyptian papyri of the 5th century B.C., and the vocabulary of Daniel has an admixture of Hebrew, Babylonian and Persian words similar to that of the papyri of the 5th century B.C.; whereas, it differs in composition from the Aramaic of the Nabateans, which is devoid of Persian, Hebrew or Babylonian words, and is full of Arabisms, and also from that of the Palmyrenes, which is full of Greek words, while having but one or two Persian words, and no Hebrew or Babylonian.

Here, Wilson uses the Nabatean and Palmyrene Aramaic as the closest Aramaic to what one might assume was used in Palestine in the second century B.C. To summarize, every linguistic argument supports the claim that Daniel was written somewhere in the sixth or fifth century B.C. If this is true, then ultimately it will lead to the conclusion that Daniel is undeniably inspired by God. There will be much more to be said on this subject.

## Notes

[1] I say "if they can be called that" because the prophets in general were involved in "forth-telling"—in other words, preaching about righteousness and judgment. For all the prophets, with the very noticeable exception of Daniel, "foretelling," or predictions of the future, were only a relatively small part of their writings.

[2] It is interesting to apply Zechariah 11:12-13, which is a predictive prophecy of what Judas did to Jesus, to Joseph's life as well. In the case of Joseph, he was symbolically sold by "Israel" when the eleven other sons of Israel, the progenitors of the tribes of the nation of Israel, sold him into slavery (see Genesis 37).

[3] Adam, Noah, Joshua, Solomon, Zerubbabel and Melchizedek could be added to the list of those whose lives God used as historical pre-figurations of the Messiah. For more on this, see John Oakes, *From Shadow to Reality* (Illumination Publishers Intl., 2005), pp, 56-83.

[4] I would like to acknowledge as sources for this section, *The Book of Daniel*, Jim McGuiggan, (Montex Publishing Company, 1978), pp. 11-21 and *Daniel in the Critics' Den*, (New York: Cosimo Classics, 2007—originally published in 1909). Both are to be recommended to the reader interested in pursuing the subject further.

# PART ONE

## Daniel: A Righteous Man in an Unbelieving World

The lives of Daniel and of his friends Shadrach, Meshach and Abednego serve as powerful and practical examples of how to live day-to-day life as a disciple of Jesus Christ. In part one of this book (chapters 3-6) we will see these men of great godly character and conviction facing similar kinds of trials and temptations to those we face on a daily basis. The trials of Daniel and his friends are like our own, except they occur on a much more intense level than most of us typically experience. We will see Daniel and his friends stand up to the most gut-wrenching pressure the world has to offer, but remain faithful until to the end to the God who could save them. As God said to Daniel (Daniel 12:3), "Those who are wise will shine like the brightness of the heavens, and those who lead many to righteousness, like the stars for ever and ever." These words could very well have been applied to Daniel and his friends. It is my hope that they can also be applied to your own life, and even more so for having read this book.

# Chapter Three

## Conviction or Compromise?

Our story starts with Daniel and his friends Hananiah, Mishael and Azariah as very young men in the great pagan city of Babylon. They have been ripped from their ancestral home in Jerusalem, more than a thousand miles away. Have they been stolen away from their families as well? Or did the Babylonians kill their parents? We are not sure. At this point Jerusalem has not been destroyed yet, but the political power of the Jews has been completely eliminated. A puppet king rules in Jerusalem. Jehoiakim, the former king, has been captured and blinded. The treasures of the temple in Jerusalem have been looted and now lie in the treasury of King Nebuchadnezzar.

All these events are an exact fulfillment of the prophecy left behind by Isaiah about one hundred and fifty years beforehand. In Isaiah 39:6-7, we find the prophecy given by Isaiah to King Hezekiah concerning the future of his family and of Israel:

> The time will surely come when everything in your palace, and all that your fathers have stored up until this day, will be carried off to Babylon. Nothing will be left, says the Lord. And some of your descendants, your own flesh and blood who will be born to you, will be taken away, and they will become eunuchs in the palace of the king of Babylon.

Could there conceivably be any greater evidence that God is in control of world events, or that his Word is inspired?

The lesson of this prophecy and its fulfillment must have had a great impact on the captives as they were carried on their several-month journey in chains from Jerusalem to Babylon. We can only speculate about their personal thoughts, but I'm sure they were shocked by the consequences of their nation's lack of repentance. Unfortunately, it was too late to avoid the destruction of their lives and heritage.

Not only have our protagonists lost their homeland; they have had their names taken away as well. Presumably, this is an attempt to alienate them from their Jewish background and assimilate them into the Babylonian culture. Daniel is given the name Belteshazzar by the chief chamberlain, while Hananiah, Mishael and Azariah are called Shadrach, Meshach and Abednego. The name Belteshazzar means literally, "may Bel protect his life." Bel was the chief god of Babylon. This name change would appear to be a deliberate attempt to "paganize" Daniel. Fortunately, like all the attempts of the Babylonians to paganize Daniel and his friends, it failed miserably.

The taking of captives from a conquered city is a tactic that had been practiced by the Assyrians as well. The purpose was two-fold. First, it was an attempt to break down the social, political and economic fabric of a conquered people by taking away the strongest leaders in the society. This would make them much less likely to resist the economic domination of the conquerors. Second, it was a way to build up the base of intelligent, well-educated, talented people at the disposal of the king of the conquering nation. This is what one finds occurring in chapter one of Daniel. There is a brain drain from Israel to Babylon as Nebuchadnezzar employs the most talented captives from Israel as officials in his government. Third, the taking of the children of the ruling elite as captives provided a strong incentive for the conquered people to remain in submission to the conqueror. To rebel could mean to have their hostage children killed as a result.

One can assume that the Israelites, Daniel and friends included, would have resented losing their homeland, their wealth, their position of power and countless other things.[1] It might be said that they have lost everything. To God, however, Daniel and his friends stand to lose something else of far greater worth. Loss of wealth and power counts for nothing in God's eyes. The greatest danger in the eyes of God is that they might abandon their commitment to Him. Relinquishing cultural distinction is one thing, but losing a heart-felt devotion to the one true God is certainly another.

It is an interesting historical fact that the Jewish people have resisted cultural and religious assimilation more tenaciously than any other nation in the world for the past three-and-one-half millennia. What other fairly small nation has maintained a definite identity for as long as the Jews have? Is there any other example of a people being completely scattered many thousands of miles from their homeland, yet maintaining much of their culture and language for hundreds of years? Consider the nation of Israel today: The people speak a language that they have revived, even after it was not used as a primary language for more than two thousand years. Indeed, the book of Daniel is part of God's plan to help his people maintain their religious distinction, even as a persecutor attempts to stamp out the distinct Jewish culture. The history of Israel is the saga of repeated attempts by other nations to eliminate the powerful cultural and religious force we call Judaism. The Egyptians, Assyrians, Babylonians, Greeks (of special interest to the book of Daniel, as we will see), Romans and Arabs, as well as the Roman Catholic Church and most recently the Nazis have all tried to eliminate Jewish distinctiveness, but without success.

In Daniel chapter one, we see on a very personal level an attempt to assimilate the Jewish leadership into Babylonian culture. God uses Daniel and his friends as an undying example of how to remain holy (meaning "set apart") even as the world pressures godly people to become like the rest.

Let us go back to the story. Daniel is offered the chance for wealth, comfort, position and power. The regimen he must follow to prepare for his tryout before Nebuchadnezzar includes consuming "the royal food." We can assume that this is pretty good food—probably the greatest delicacies available anywhere. Daniel should go for it, right? Wouldn't we go for it too? It is not a sin to eat good food, is it? Surely God has nothing against success, right? The answer is no—as long as wealth, comfort, position and power do not interfere with our being close to God and doing his will. The problem is that the great majority of people are not up to the task of receiving these great blessings without compromising their faith.

The book of Daniel is getting very practical for us right away, isn't it? The crisis in Daniel's life, and in the lives of Shadrach, Meshach and Abednego, is the same crisis we face every day of our lives, especially for those who are a part of the American culture, where the predominant faith is in the god of wealth and comfort.

There is an interesting point to the age-old argument over whether wealth is a good thing or not. Money, like power and pleasure, is not bad in itself. It is a question of who controls whom. Does our money control us, or do we control our money?

In Daniel's case, would he allow comfort and wealth to dictate his conviction and lifestyle, or would he follow God's commands? Daniel and his friends recognize the great seriousness of the issue at hand immediately. Recognizing the seriousness of the decision, we can assume that the four Jewish youths prayed to God. It seems a wise course for Daniel to be willing to accept service to the king. This appears to be a gift from God, a way to assure positive treatment of his fellow Israelites. So how can Daniel and his compatriots pursue a good career, while at the same time making absolutely sure their pursuit is God's will? And how can they provide themselves a rock to stand on, to ensure they will not allow their blessings to compromise their primary commitment to God?

Daniel chooses a wise path. He decides not to "defile himself with the royal food and wine" (Daniel 1:8). Instead, he accepts the offer to prepare for service to the king—but in a way that proves to himself and to his potential employer that, whether he gets the job or not, God comes first. If only we could follow the example of Daniel, Shadrach, Meshach and Abednego in this matter. How can we provide a specific reminder to ourselves at work that, even though we may pursue a successful career (a good thing), we would rather give up all opportunity for advancement, or even the job itself, if it ever seemed to threaten our primary commitment to our Lord God?

In Daniel and his friends, one can see a living example of the motto, "In matters of opinion, go with the current, but in matters of principle, stand like a rock." They did not legalistically reject all things Babylonian. They did not refuse to accept service to a pagan king out of some sort of "holier-than-thou" attitude. However, they maintained throughout their lives a very sharp line that they refused in the most stubborn fashion to cross. If career or position or comfort or popularity were to come in the way of total dedication and devotion to God, they would absolutely refuse to compromise. It will be seen that this occasionally got them into some hot situations!

Verse nine is the key verse in chapter one: "Now God had caused the official to show favor and sympathy to Daniel." Here one can see the theme of the book: *God rules the nations—do not fear.* This theme will be emphasized again and again in Daniel. God is trying to tell the Jews that if they will stay true to their commitment to remain holy and to obey the Law of Moses, he will work powerfully on their behalf. Throughout the book of Daniel, God is always working behind the scenes to support those who are dedicated to Him. This is reminiscent of 2 Chronicles 16:9:

> For the eyes of the Lord range throughout the earth to strengthen those whose hearts are fully committed to him.

The response of Nebuchadnezzar's chief chamberlain Ashpenaz is absolutely typical of how God works in our lives: "Now God had caused the official to show favor and sympathy to Daniel, but..." There is that "but..." God is definitely working behind the scenes to cause Daniel and friends to be supported, but even in helping Daniel, he still allows the prophet's faith to be tested. Ashpenaz responds to Daniel, in essence, "I want to help you, but I am afraid of the king." It is quite reasonable for Ashpenaz to fear the wrath of Nebuchadnezzar. In fact, if the king were to hear that Ashpenaz had not followed his orders to the letter, the chamberlain could very well forfeit his life.

Since Ashpenaz is a pagan, Daniel cannot appeal to his trust in God, so instead he devises a plan. If the plan works as Daniel has in mind, it will result in him and his friends being able to work for King Nebuchadnezzar, and it will also bring glory to God. Daniel's instinct in time of extreme pressure is to put his faith in God, not in himself. Is that your instinct? Daniel's plan is to allow Ashpenaz to conduct a test: "Please test your servants for ten days: Give us nothing but vegetables to eat and water to drink. Then compare our appearance with that of the young men who eat the royal food, and treat your servants in accordance with what you see" (Daniel 1:12-13).

It is God who said, "Do not put the Lord your God to the test" (Deuteronomy 6:16, Matthew 4:7). Is Daniel sinning here? The answer is no. One can probably assume that Daniel is not even sure what God's will in this situation is. Daniel chooses a strategy that simultaneously allows him to test his own faith and, he hopes, to determine what the Lord's will is. It is interesting to speculate how Daniel and his companions would have reacted if the verdict had been negative. What if, after ten days, they actually looked worse than the "control group" (to use the scientific term)? From what one can see of Daniel, Shadrach, Meshach and Abednego, it can be assumed that they would have said something like, "It is the Lord's will: We will not compromise. Do with us as you will. If we must drop out of contention for this great job opportunity rather than compromise our holy commitment to God, then let God's will be done."

It would also be fun to speculate about what they did during those ten days. Did they "pump iron" in an effort to look more buff? Did they oil their skin like competitive body-builders? Maybe or maybe not. Given what we know of their spirituality, undoubtedly they spent a significant amount of time crying out to God. Perhaps their prayer went something like this: "God, if it is your will for us to take on this responsibility, then help us to look ten times as great as these other men, but if you do not want us to get into this situation, we pray you make us look terrible as we go before

*Figure 11. Persepolis relief of a procession of Persian nobles.*

Ashpenaz, so we will know for sure what your will is."

I once encountered a situation that was somewhat similar to the one faced by Daniel, although the import of the decision was certainly not as significant as it was in Daniel's case. I was in graduate school at the University of Colorado, and a few of us in the campus ministry group were trying to get good dorm rooms for the following year. The idea was to live on campus, where we could hold Bible study groups in our rooms. On the morning when we had to line up, I got in line very early to be sure to get a room. One of the women in our campus group came running in quite a bit later and ended up so far back in line that it appeared unlikely she would get the dorm room she wanted. As we snaked past one another in the line, I asked her what had happened. She said that she and another friend had stayed up late praying—among other things, they had prayed specifically that they would get the room God wanted them to get. I said to her, somewhat chidingly and sarcastically, that she would have done better by going to bed on time so that she could have gotten up early enough to get in line.

God chose to humble me in my pride that day. I learned that when the young woman reached the front of the line, the rooms in the dormitory she wanted to live in had long before run out. However, at the moment she reached the front of the line and asked for a room, the woman behind the counter just happened to find one more application that had fallen off the table onto the floor. She said to my friend, "Well I guess this is your lucky day." I am convinced that God answered the prayers of my sister in Christ, that day, and he humbled me at the same time.

Similarly, at the end of the ten-day trial period, Daniel, Shadrach, Meshach and Abednego all "looked healthier and better nourished than any other of the young men who ate the royal food" (v. 15). God's young servants had the answer to their prayer in a convincing manner.

Is this God's way of telling us that the vegetarian diet is to be preferred in order for us to live a healthy life? It is a big stretch to press that conclusion out of this passage of scripture, especially because the miraculous working of God is being stressed, rather than the advantage of eating vegetables. It is interesting to note, however, that because of the experiment with Daniel and his friends, Ashpenaz ordered all the other candidates off the king's food and onto a strict vegetarian diet (v. 16). One can guess that this did not exactly make Daniel or his companions very popular.

And not only did God bless the four young men with physical health; because of their faithfulness, God granted to them "knowledge and understanding of all kinds of literature and learning" (v. 17). Besides that, to Daniel he gave the gift of understanding visions and dreams, a talent which will prove decisive in our story. Here one finds another spiritual principle at work. It has already been shown that God ranges over the earth seeking hearts that are fully committed to him, so that he might strengthen them. Because these young men had proven themselves to be faithful—relying on their Father in heaven rather than on their own strength, even in intense trial—God was looking for ways to pour additional blessings on them.

This brings to mind two parallel passages in the Bible. The first is from the life of Solomon when he was appointed king. At the beginning of his reign, God said to him in a dream, "Ask for whatever you want me to give you" (1 Kings

3:5). This was quite an offer, to say the least. Rather than asking for wealth or fame or military victory, Solomon asked for wisdom and an ability to discern good from evil as he governed his people. The key to understanding Solomon's heart is found in his statement, "But I am only a little child and do not know how to carry out my duties" (v. 7). Because of Solomon's humility and faith in his God, he was blessed with even more than he asked for. God not only granted him great wisdom; he also gave Solomon wealth and honor beyond that of any other king of his day. It is extremely unfortunate that Solomon later worshipped some of the gifts, instead of the giver of those gifts, and eventually lost his humility. He listened to his foreign wives more than to God.

A second parallel passage to the last part of Daniel chapter one is found in Jesus' parable of the talents (Matthew 25:14-30). To quote from the master in the story, "Well done, good and faithful servant! You have been faithful with a few things; I will put you in charge of many things. Come and share your master's happiness" (v. 21). Here we find a general spiritual principle that is also illustrated in the life of Daniel: God is waiting for his people to ask him for things that will allow them to serve other people, rather than asking him to meet their own needs. Not only is God pleased to answer this kind of prayer, he will want to bless such faithful people in ways they had not even asked or imagined when making their original requests. To those people God says, "Come and share your master's happiness."

This is truly great news. However, given the sinful nature common to all people, a great caution must be added. Solomon got caught up in the gifts and forgot the giver. What about you? Have the blessings God has poured into your life become a curse because they have distracted you from the one who gave you those blessings in the first place? Unfortunately, even with true disciples of Jesus, many cannot handle great riches, success, fame etc. without letting it go to their heads, causing them to lose their faith. Be careful what you pray for![2]

Praise God that, as far as we know, this was not the fate of Daniel or his companions. They remained faithful to God even after receiving his great blessings. For them, the key was humility and a true reliance on God.

At the close of the first scene in Daniel, the four protagonists are finally presented to Nebuchadnezzar. Despite their faith, it can be assumed that they are very nervous as they are brought before the most powerful man in Babylon. Even a faithful prayer does not completely rid a person of all vestiges of fear. However, due to their humble and faithful request to God, he is able to pour abundant blessings on them. They pass the test with flying colors. In fact, "in every matter of wisdom and understanding about which the king questioned them, he found them ten times better than all the magicians and enchanters in his whole kingdom" (v. 20). This is a great testimony to the four young men and to their God.

It has been shown from Daniel chapter one that God is in control of persons and circumstances, and in some cases, he even guides the thoughts of ungodly men. The message to the Jews of the second century B.C. while undergoing a terrible persecution is: Do not fear, God is in control. Even if events get truly scary, if you will humbly continue to put your faith in the God who can save you, he will take care of you. *God rules the nations—do not fear!*

As mentioned previously, this book will first cover the chapters that depict events in the lives of Daniel and his friends, followed by the chapters that contain the visions and prophecies received by Daniel. Because Daniel chapter two involves the great prophetic dream of the statue of gold, silver, bronze and iron, we will now turn our attention to the third chapter of Daniel.

## Notes

[1] Could it be that Daniel, Shadrach, Meshach and Abednego were forcibly made into eunuchs? There is no mention of wives or children for Daniel or his friends in the text of Daniel. This was not an uncommon practice for servants of kings in ancient times. Almost certainly the four were "made eunuchs in the palace of Nebuchadnezzer" (Isaiah 39:6-7).

[2] For further study, consider 1 Corinthians 4:7, Deuteronomy 9:4-6 and especially Deuteronomy 8:10-20.

# Chapter Four

## The Fires of Persecution

The second scene in the conflict between righteous men and a pagan world is found in Daniel chapter three. What an spectacular scene! What a frightening circumstance for youths who have dedicated their lives to serving God and God alone.

The events of Daniel chapter three occur a few years after Daniel and his friends have entered the service of the Babylonian government. It also comes after Daniel had interpreted the king's dream of a giant statue, representing the great earthly kingdoms, which were destroyed by the hand of Jehovah (see Daniel chapter 2). In chapter three of Daniel, Nebuchadnezzar has set up his own huge statue. Could this statue be an attempt, conscious or unconscious, to thwart the prophetic dream of the giant statue, which Daniel had already interpreted for him?

Nebuchadnezzar's statue is an image of gold ninety feet high and nine feet wide, set up in the plane of Dura. The town of Dura was located in the center of a large valley plain on a mound six miles southeast of Babylon. This statue must have been an awesome sight. Skeptics and even liberal theologians have attacked the historical authenticity of Daniel based on the claim that it would be impossible to build this statue. They argue that it would require too much gold, and besides, the dimensions are too large to make it possible to build such a large, imposing statue. There is a valuable practical lesson in there for us.

First of all, one can almost certainly assume that the statue was not made of solid gold. Surely it was only covered with gold foil. Gold, being the most malleable of all metals, can be pounded into very thin sheets. Most state capitol buildings in the United States have a gold dome. When people say that their state capitol has a golden dome, do they mean it is solid gold? Of course they don't. And who can say that it was impossible for a ninety-foot (sixty-cubit) statue to be built using Babylonian technology? It is not even known if it was built as a monolith or in the shape of a human or of an animal. Besides, a large part of the ninety feet could very well have been taken up by a pedestal on which the statue was placed: a common practice even today.

In any case, it seems more reasonable to accept the word of the author of Daniel, who presumably saw the statue himself, rather than accept the criticism of skeptics who are so closed-minded that they can read Daniel and still deny the obvious marks of inspiration in the book.

The statue is erected on the plane of Dura. This is probably so that large numbers of people can be involved in worshipping the statue out in an open area. Much of the religion of Babylon involved mystery rites and rituals performed by the priestly class (later known as the magi), behind the scenes, out of the way of the general public. Nebuchadnezzar has decided to put on a public religious ceremony for the masses, not just for the religious elite, so he needs a large open area; something not available within the walls of Babylon. Nebuchadnezzar is going for what amounts to public emperor worship. It is not difficult to guess how God feels about that.

Imagine the thoughts of one of those who had helped build the statue and cover it with gold as he stands in the crowd at the opening ceremony. This person might be saying to himself, "Here I helped build this statue with my bare hands, and now we are being asked to bow down to it as if it is a god!" Can something made by man be a god? First God made man, and now man is seeking to make God. Surely in our sophisticated, technology-driven age, we have gotten beyond this tendency to worship what our own "hands" have made. Surely not!

We can only imagine the intensity of the scene. Nebuchadnezzar assembles the "satraps, prefects, governors, advisers, treasurers, judges, magistrates and all the other provincial officials" (Daniel 3:2) to come to the dedication ceremony. It would be safe to assume that many others not specifically mentioned were there as well, probably numbering in the thousands. Guess who is among the "invited" guests: Shadrach, Meshach and Abednego! We do not know where Daniel is, but perhaps he is off on a mission for the king to one of the provinces of Babylon. Whatever he is doing, one can assume that for some reason he is not at this dedication ceremony, because he is not mentioned in the account, and surely, had he been present, he would have acted as his friends did.

A herald shouts out to the assembled crowd:

This is what you are commanded to do, O peoples, nations and men of every language: As soon as you hear the sound of the horn, flute, zither, lyre, harp, pipes and all kinds of music, you must fall down and worship the image of gold that King Nebuchad-nezzar has set up. Whoever does not fall down and worship will immediately be thrown into a blazing furnace (Daniel 3:4-6).

Did our heroes know ahead of time that this was to be the decree? If so, then they had plenty of time to consider what they would do in response to the order. More likely, this announcement hit them completely by surprise. Satan likes to use the element of surprise to get us to compromise our faith. If Peter had had time to consider his response to the question he was asked as he stood in that fateful court-yard, he possibly might have avoided denying being a fol-lower of Jesus. But being caught alone and unprepared, he denied even knowing Jesus.

Imagine the fear racing through the minds of the three young Hebrew men. Here God has gotten them this great job, and now look what it has gotten them into. At this point, they must be tempted to wonder if it really was God's will for them to get this great job after all. Imagine the scene when the band strikes up and thousands of people bow. This is the most incredible kind of peer pressure one could conceive. Talk about sticking out in a crowd! And experience tells us what everyone is going to do the instant the music starts. The people do not take this religious charade seriously. They will look around to see if anyone has the nerve to remain standing.

Thoughts are beginning to race through all three of our protagonists' minds in the moments between the issuing of the decree and the sounding of the instruments. Thoughts that may have come to mind might have included, "Is it really that big a deal if I just bow my body but not my mind to the statue? God knows my heart. What good can I do for God if I die right now? Couldn't I do more for God by performing this little ritual and then devoting myself to him anyway? Doesn't the end justify the means? What will Meshach do? What about the effect on my family?" Praise God and praise God again that Shadrach, Meshach and Abednego are able to say a resounding "no" to the temptations implied in these thoughts!

The inspiration of God can absolutely be seen in this account. Remember that, although the book of Daniel is for all readers in all ages, it was most specifically written for the Jews, living under the incredible persecution of Antiochus IV Epiphanes. Antiochus IV Epiphanes placed many of the Jews in a very similar situation to that experienced by Shadrach, Meshach and Abednego. They had to choose between a "small" compromise with the world, and death. This is a true story. This actually happened. What a great living, breathing example of faith under the pressure of a persecutor. Surely those who remained faithful under the brutal attacks of Antiochus, even to the point of death, remembered well the faith of Shadrach, Meshach and Abednego. And what about our brothers and sisters who suffered the great persecutions at the hands of Emperors Nero, Domitian, Trajan, and Hadrian; at the bloody hands of Marcus Aurelius, Septimus Severus, Maximinus, Decius, Valerian and Diocletian? When they were ordered by Diocletian to sacrifice to the emperor deity, they were in a very similar situation to that of Shadrach, Meshach and Abednego. It is an historical fact that many Christians compromised their conviction when threatened by the Roman authorities with a choice between

*Figure 12. Persecutor Marcus Aurelius* c. A.D. *173 in the Piazza del Campidoglio, Rome, Italy.*

*Figure 13. Roman Emperor and persecutor Hadrian (c. 117-138* A.D.*) from the National Archaeological Museum, Naples, Italy.*

offering a sacrifice and death or imprisonment. A number made the sacrifice to a false idol. Many of those who compromised their faith later attempted to be accepted back into the fellowship of believers as true disciples of Jesus. Thanks in part to the example that can be found in Daniel, many had the faith not to deny Jesus, even to the point of death. Did those who offered the sacrifice to the Roman idol lose their salvation for this unfaithful compromise? We have to assume that those who compromised their faith did not lose their salvation if they truly repented. God's grace is bigger than this. However, their testimony was seriously compromised, and God was definitely not glorified.

At this point, it would be prudent to consider how to apply the principle just described to daily life. In what way has the world around us tried to intimidate us into bowing down to its idols? Have you felt the tug to bow down to the idol of work? Have you (supposedly) bowed your head but not your heart to the idol of public opinion? What about the gossip shrine, or the home/boat/vacation statue? Are you giving in to the peer pressure to love the things of this world?

*Figure 14. Roman Emperor and persecutor Diocletian (c. 284-305 A.D.) in the Capitoline Museum, Rome, Italy.*

The astrologers who denounced the Jews probably did not really care one way or another whether the Jews bowed to the idol. The problem the astrologers had was that the righteousness of Shadrach, Meshach and Abednego made the astrologers themselves look bad by comparison. Anyone who is willing to stand up for their convictions makes hypocrites look bad. Unfortunately, the most common response of hypocrites is not to gain conviction and begin to imitate the righteous lives they observe. Most often, the response of the world to those who live by strong moral conviction is to try to bring the righteous down to their own uninspiring level. If one does not actually tell off-color jokes in the chapel of unwholesome talk, its priests and priestesses will happily settle for a person simply chuckling lightly. "Bowing your head, but not your heart" is good enough for them. But are we really just bowing our head...?

I can vividly remember the day when, as a graduate student, my adviser called me into his office to share a concern. He said it was really obvious that pursuing a Ph.D. and a career as a professional scientist were not my first priorities. I was a very hard and dedicated researcher, probably more focused that most, but in the final analysis, my boss and fellow graduate students knew my commitment to God came before the pursuit of scientific discovery. My adviser said, in all sincerity, that if I did not intend to make the pursuit of science my chief focus in life, I might need to consider doing something else. What could I say in response to this? In my heart I was saying, "Yes! It is working! My boss has noticed that my commitment to God is far more important to me than getting a Ph.D." I hope that my colleagues would make the same sort of comment about me today. If not, I must ask myself if I have not begun to be at least a part-time worshiper in the church of academia. As Jesus said, "No servant can serve two masters. Either he will hate the one and love the other, or he will be devoted to the one and despise the other. You cannot serve both God and Money" (Luke 16:13). It is not that disciples of Jesus should be less than the best they can be at work. God commands his followers: "Whatever you do, work at it with all your heart, as working for the Lord, not for men" (Colossians 3:23). It is a question of the heart. What is our first love?

At the moment of truth, the three young Jews remain standing while everyone else bows down to the statue. Many do so in total hypocrisy, knowing that this is just a lump of rock covered with a paper-thin layer of gold. Our heroes' fellow-advisers/astrologers immediately point out the recalcitrants. They remind me of my children who catch their siblings not bowing their heads when the family prays together. How do they know their sister is not closing her eyes while praying unless they are peeking as well? "They neither serve your gods nor worship the image of gold you have set up" (Daniel 3:12). What hypocrites! They are not serving Nebuchadnezzar's gods either. They are serving and worshiping themselves.

Nebuchadnezzar is absolutely livid! Perhaps he thought to himself, "How dare one of my advisers—people I raised from nothing to be advisors in the greatest empire in the world—defy my command to worship the idol? Who do they think they are? Are their gods greater than mine? Why, then, was I able to conquer their pitiful little nation?" The king gives them one more chance to repent and worship the idol. But having taken their initial stand, and now standing together before the king, this time the three Jews' decision is confidently stated. There is no way they will give in now. The king snarls out those fateful words: "If you do not worship it, you will be thrown immediately into a blazing furnace. Then what god will be able to rescue you from my hand?" (v. 15).

The response of Shadrach, Meshach and Abednego is one of the great highlights of the Bible. It reminds us of Stephen standing before the Greek Jews in Acts 7. It bears a complete quotation:

> O Nebuchadnezzar, we do not need to defend ourselves before you in this matter. If we are thrown into the blazing furnace, the God we serve is able to save us from it, and he will rescue us from your hand, O king. But even if he does not, we want you to know, O king, that we will not serve your gods or worship the image of gold you have set up (Daniel 3:16-18).

If this was an attempt to mollify the anger of Nebuchadnezzar, it was a poor attempt indeed. If it was calculated to stir his anger to the greatest possible heights, it succeeded wonderfully.

Look at the faith of the three young Jews: "Our God is able." Even better is the phrase, "but even if he does not...." Nebuchadnezzar, the worst you can do to us is to kill us! Remember that for the ancient Jews, the idea of an after-life or of being in heaven with God was a somewhat ill-formed concept. What courage! Bear in mind that at this point, Shadrach, Meshach and Abednego have no idea what God's will is. They do not know whether God will save them from the flames or whether they will experience an unimaginably horrible death. Probably, they assumed that their decision meant death. There was no precedent in the history of Israel of God saving a person from raging flames. Yet, they did not back down on their conviction. They chose to give honor and glory to God. It seems that God does not hesitate to allow us to be in situations where we must put our faith in him, not knowing what the outcome of our principled stand will be. As Peter explains it, "These have come so that your faith—of greater worth than gold, which perishes even though refined by fire—may be proved genuine and may result in praise, glory and honor when Jesus Christ is revealed" (1 Peter 1:7). If one knows what the outcome will be, faith is not needed.

The phrase, "but even if he does not," was a very important one for the Jews facing persecution under the Seleucid Dynasty four hundred years later. Under the Seleucid king Antiochus IV Epiphanes, a law was passed declaring that if a male child were circumcised, both the parents and the child would be killed. First they killed the child in front of the parents, then the mother, and last of all the father. Those who would be faithful to the Law of Moses had to decide whether to bow to the idol of Hellenism or to face a painful death. The Jews facing execution for their faith at the hands of their Greek persecutors had little reason to believe that, once arrested, God would save them from death as he had in the case of Shadrach, Meshach and Abednego. If the three youths had been sure that God was going to save them from death, they would not have served as nearly so powerful an example for those who would in the future be threatened with death for their faith. Those words,

"But even if he does not, we want you to know, O king, that we will not serve your gods..." were able to ring through the centuries as a call not to compromise with the world, even on pain of death.

As it was for the Jews in the second century B.C., so, in a milder form, it is for us. If we refuse to sacrifice to the career idol—by working sixty hours a week, missing family or church commitments—our careers may be threatened. But then again, they may not. Like Shadrach, Meshach and Abednego, we can only say to our boss, "My God is able to cause me to have a successful career despite your attempts at intimidation, but even if he does not, and I end up with a lesser position, I will not bow down to the almighty career god." There are many other practical applications of this concept that I will leave to the reader to discover.

As mentioned previously, Nebuchadnezzar is absolutely livid. One can assume that he is used to being able to intimidate people at will because he has the power of life or death over all his subjects. The stubborn faith of these Jews incites him to order that the furnace be heated seven times hotter than usual. One should take this example as a warning from God that when we stubbornly stand up for what is right, those in the world may take our righteous behavior as a personal attack. Those who are used to using intimidation to get their way may even turn to violence. Like Nebuchadnezzar, they may turn up the heat against the righteous seven-fold. Fortunately, it is difficult to measure the level of stubbornness of a true disciple of Jesus when it comes to matters of faith.

It is interesting (and ironic) to note that Nebuchadnezzar's attempt to get revenge on Shadrach, Meshach and Abednego for their stubbornness by turning up the heat is really quite foolish. If one wants to exact revenge by torturing someone in a fire, turning up the heat is definitely not the best approach. A much hotter flame would presumably end their tortures almost instantaneously, compared to the much more gradual and painful death they would face in a cooler furnace. But as the Proveb 29:11 says, "A fool gives full vent to his anger, but a wise man keeps himself under control."

The executioners obviously could not make the flames literally seven times hotter (skeptics have even tried to attack the book of Daniel on this point, saying the writer was obviously mistaken to believe the fire could be seven times as hot), but one can assume that under the witheringly angry look of Nebuchadnezzar, they stoked and fueled that furnace to the hottest temperature it had ever seen.

Shadrach, Meshach and Abednego are bound hand and foot. In their hurry to carry out the order of Nebuchadnezzar, the executioners do not even take time to think about how to protect themselves from the engulfing flames. As they approach the white-hot furnace, the door is opened and the three helpless young men are hurled through the opening. The fire is so hot that those who throw them in are overcome and killed. What were the thoughts of Shadrach as he was tied and carried up to the furnace? Did Meshach say a quick prayer asking God to forgive Nebuchadnezzar? Were Abednego's thoughts overwhelmed with terror, or was he able to control his fear enough to have one last thought of his family? It is still not too late. All Abednego has to do is raise his hand while being dragged to the furnace. "Stop! Okay, yes, I will bow to the statue. Only do not throw me into the fire." No such plea is heard. What heart and courage!

And what were the last-minute thoughts of the Apostle Paul as he was led to the executioner's chopping block? He left us with a clue in 2 Timothy 4:6-8: "The time has come for my departure. I have fought the good fight, I have finished the race. I have kept the faith. Now there is in store for me the crown of righteousness, which the Lord, the righteous Judge, will award to me on that day."

Imagine the thoughts of some unknown disciple in the second or third century, condemned to die by burning at the stake because she refused to offer sacrifices to the Roman gods. As the flames began to lick at her feet, did she think to herself, "I wish I had just given in and made the sacrifice to the emperor?" That thought might have flickered through her mind—and who could blame her for having such a thought?—but perhaps she then remembered the comforting words in the book of Daniel. As this unknown disciple stood tied to the stake, she could take much-needed comfort in the knowledge that God would be with her in those flames, just as he did with Shadrach, Meshach and Abednego.

And do not forget the nameless Jews who suffered under the persecutions of the Greeks. The murderous attacks of the Seleucid kings were no less terrifying and deadly than those our brothers and sisters endured under the Roman persecutors. They may not be recorded in the Bible because they occurred "between the Testaments," but should we honor these men and women any less? And it is worth remembering that as Shadrach, Meshach and Abednego were thrown into the fire, they did not have the level of assurance of eternal life that readers of the New Testament have. The concepts of salvation, the resurrection and heaven were only vaguely revealed in the Old Testament. (At least that was true until the book of Daniel was written, as will be shown). How much more should disciples of Jesus hold up under pressure from the world, knowing that they have an eternal home waiting for them in heaven?

King Nebuchadnezzar strains to look into the furnace to see the men consumed in the fire, when to his utter amazement, he sees four figures walking around in the flames. The bonds of Shadrach, Meshach and Abednego have been burned away, but they are unharmed. Nebuchadnezzar sees one who "looks like a son of the gods" (v. 25). It would appear that an angel was in the furnace with the three youths. The angel must have glowed with a brilliant white light, even brighter than the flames in the furnace, in order to inspire Nebuchadnezzar's description that he appeared as one of the gods.

The angel in the flames gave encouragement to Shadrach, Meshach and Abednego, for sure. Even without the angel, they probably would have been fired up (excuse the pun) at being preserved from the flames, but the assurance and encouragement of God's messenger must have been a great blessing. The angel is a visible reminder to future generations of believers that God is with those who are persecuted for their faith.

In utter amazement, King Nebuchadnezzar unwisely approaches the opening of the fiery furnace. Perhaps his excitement caused him to temporarily forget what happened to those who threw the three in the furnace in the first place. In words reminiscent of those spoken by Jesus outside Lazarus' tomb, Nebuchadnezzar calls out, "Shadrach, Meshach and Abednego, servants of the Most High God, come out! Come here!" (v. 26). Not only are the youths unharmed, but their hair and clothing are not even singed, nor is there even a smell of fire on them!

God has truly brought about one of the greatest miracles recorded in the Bible. As a result, Nebuchadnezzar praises "the God of Shadrach, Meshach and Abednego" (v. 28). It is interesting that he respects the courage and conviction of the three Jews even though they had been defying him. God may not have appreciated the king's decree that any people "who say anything against the God of Shadrach, Meshach and Abednego be cut into pieces" (v. 29), but we can certainly appreciate Nebuchadnezzar's zeal for the God of Israel. As a result of the men's courage and of God's work in saving them, Nebuchadnezzar promotes Shadrach, Meshach and Abednego to higher positions in his service.

It is worth looking carefully at Nebuchadnezzar's change of heart. Is God assuring his people that if they take a strong stand under the pressure of persecution they will see their persecutors saved? Probably not. Besides, one should be very skeptical of these sorts of "conversions," which come on the heels of a miraculous event. God certainly can use intense events in people's lives to cause them to wake up and turn to him. However, it is wise to wait and see if these sorts of sudden changes are genuine or fickle. In the parable of the rich man and Lazarus (Luke 16:19-31), the rich man begs for an opportunity to go back and warn his family about the coming judgment, saying, "If someone from the dead goes to them, they will repent" (v. 30). Abraham replies in the parable, "If they do not listen to Moses and the Prophets,[2] they will not be convinced even if someone rises from the dead" (v. 31). It can be concluded, then, that a life-shaking event in someone's life may open him or her up, but the ultimate test is how he or she will respond to the Bible. It is not a question of whether a person can get excited about a religious experience, but of whether they are willing to repent, and lead a righteous life for God from that point forward.

Returning to the story, Nebuchadnezzar has a religious experience but not a true conversion, as can be seen in Daniel chapter four, for he has already returned to giving himself glory rather than God. The lesson to be learned is that we have no guarantee that our faithful actions under persecution will lead to salvation for our persecutors or for those who observe our persecution. A believer should hold up faithfully under persecution because it is the right thing to do—because he or she loves God, rather than man. Still, it is an encouragement to know that one's acts of faith and courage are a form of evangelism to the lost world.

In conclusion, Daniel's friends' refusal to give in to the fiercest possible kind of peer pressure provides a great example of how to remain righteous in a world that does not acknowledge the sovereignty of God. In Daniel chapter three, God uses Nebuchadnezzar as a symbol of those who would persecute the righteous throughout the ages. The flames of the furnace represent for us the means of those persecutions. The deliverance of Shadrach, Meshach and Abednego from the flames is symbolic of the ultimate deliverance of the righteous from those who persecute them.

As God tells his people in Isaiah 43:1-2:

Fear not, for I have redeemed you; I have summoned you by name; you are mine. When you pass through the waters, I will be with you; and when you pass through the rivers, they will not sweep over you. When you walk through the fire, you will not be burned; the flames will not set you ablaze.

God is telling his people to be faithful to him, even unto death, and surely, he will be with them always.

Because Daniel chapter four involves a dream and a prophetic interpretation of that dream by Daniel, it will be addressed in part two of the book. It is time, then, to move on to the story of the writing on the wall.

## Notes

[1] Asa H. Craig, *Christian Persecutions*, (The Burlington Publishing Company, 1899), 57-67.

[2] In other words, "If they do not listen to the Old Testament..."

# Chapter Five

## Party Animal Meets Man of God

Daniel chapter five opens with King Belshazzar giving a great banquet for a thousand of his nobles. It might be more accurately referred to as a great drinking party. But who is Belshazzar? How did he get into this scene? It turns out that there is a space of many years between the end of Daniel chapter four, which occurred somewhere near the end of Nebuchadnezzar's reign, and the events recorded in chapter five. It is worth remembering that the events covered in the book of Daniel span a time period of close to seventy years, from the time of Daniel's youth until he reached senior citizen status.

Let us go back to our antagonist, Belshazzar. The critics of the book of Daniel have attempted to attack it at this point. "Who," they say, "is this Belshazzar?" It turns out that when the kings of Babylon are listed in the traditional order, Belshazzar is not even on the list. Herodotus, for one, makes no mention of Belshazzar when he lists the kings of Babylon in his *Histories*. The liberal theologians and agnostics loudly proclaim that they have further evidence that the Bible contains a number of fictitious stories made up by people hundreds of years after the supposed events occurred. They claim that the Bible places on the throne a fictional character as the king.

There is a problem with this claim that the kingship of Belshazzar is fiction: The claim does not stand up to the facts. It is wishful thinking on the part of people, some of whom would prefer that the demands of God in their lives simply go away. In point of fact, an inscription was discovered recently on the massive Ziggurat in Ur which makes it plain that Belshazzar ruled Babylon as co-regent with his father Nabonidus. Nabonidus carried out a palace coup against Evil-merodach in 556 B.C. In an attempt to legitimize his rule, he later married Nitocris, the daughter of Nebuchadnezzar. His son, Belshazzar, was therefore the grandson of Nebuchadnezzar. Soon after gaining power, Nabonidus turned to a fascination with philosophy and mysticism. He spent most his reign at the desert shrine of Tema in Arabia, devoting himself to the moon god Sin. This unpopular ruler lost much of his interest in ruling his great empire, turning effective rule over to his son. Archaeological evidence found in Ur has shown that Belshazzar became official co-regent in 553 B.C. In the absence of his father from the capital, and his near absence from governing in general, Belshazzar was the de facto king of Babylon. He ruled Babylon until October 12, 539 B.C. This fateful date in the history of the Near East, as well as in the history of God's people, is the subject of Daniel chapter five.

Consider the scene in Daniel before us: Belshazzar calls for a great banquet for his nobles and officials at a time when his empire is falling apart. He represents to us the end of an oft-repeated pattern in ancient history. A great empire was built on the personality and character of Nebuchadnez-zar (with some credit to his father as well). Upon his death, the power of the empire is left to a son unworthy of the po-sition. The lack of strong leadership leads to rebellion and civil war. A breakdown in discipline, joined with the natural tendency of man toward dissipation when tempted with all the trappings of wealth and power, leads to further decline in the moral and civil power behind the empire. Within cen-turies, or sometimes in just a few generations, the last rul-ers sit in a fortress, enjoying the privileges but forgetting the responsibilities that come with power. Finally, a new person or nation comes onto the scene to sweep the old away. In the case of Babylon, that new man is the person known to his-tory as Cyrus "the Great."

The time for regime change has come to Babylon. While Belshazzar prepares his banquet, the army of Cyrus is already approaching the city. As they say, the writing is already on the wall. Well, not quite, but it will be shortly.

As Belshazzar drinks his wine, he becomes a bit inebriated. We can assume that he is most likely reflecting on how great a ruler he is as he sits among a bunch of sycophantic nobles and officials. This reminds him of one of his grandfather's great victories, when he humiliated the once-proud Jews, carrying off as captives the entire class of nobles and aristocrats, as well as the famous temple treasures. Belshazzar makes the fatal mistake of calling for the cups taken from the temple in Jerusalem.

What Belshazzar fails to take into account is that the temple treasures are from the temple of the almighty God—the same God who had already publicly humbled his grandfather Nebuchadnezzar. God had humbled Nebuchadnezzar first in the event already described in Daniel chapter three, and second in the events from chapter four, that we will examine later. It was Belshazzar's grandfather who had issued the decree that no one should say anything against the God of the Jews, on pain of death by dismemberment. Ironically, this was the same grandfather who had declared about the Lord Jehovah, that "those who walk in pride he is able to humble." This statement by Nebuchadnezzar about God is going to be proved true in the case of his grandson Belshazzar, and in very short order.

Belshazzar gives the orders "to bring in the gold and silver goblets that Nebuchadnezzar his father[1] had taken from the temple in Jerusalem, so that the king and his nobles, his wives and his concubines might drink from them" (v. 3). Is he ignorant of the blasphemy he is committing against God? Or is he well aware that taking a drunken toast to the gods of Babylon using these holy items is a direct affront both to Jehovah and to the memory of his father? Here he is using the same vessels formerly used in the temple to serve the one true God—creator of the entire universe—to get himself and his guests drunk. To add insult to injury, he is using the sacred vessels to celebrate his own worldly power. We can assume that the Jews in subsequent centuries who read this account had an even greater sense of outrage at this arrogant blasphemy than modern readers do.

One can see God's powerful yet subtle hands behind this scene. God is using Belshazzar as a historical symbol of all that is prideful in man, especially in the rich and arrogant. The whole time, Belshazzar is totally unaware of the significance of the scene in which he is taking part. He is simply acting the way which is natural to him. This is reminiscent of the way God used Pharaoh in the time of Moses. God made Pharaoh into a powerful symbol of Satan and of sin's power to enslave our lives. Pharaoh was only acting as himself the entire time, yet God was working behind the scenes, using Pharaoh and his relationship with Moses, the "savior" of Israel, as part of his scheme to prepare the way for the ultimate Savior, Jesus Christ. In his sovereignty, God declared to Pharoah, "I raised you up for this very purpose, that I might display my power in you and that my name might be proclaimed in all the earth" (Romans 9:17).

Similarly, in the book of Daniel God says concerning Belshazzar, "I have put you in your position as king of Babylon for this very purpose: that I might declare to the nations that anyone who defies me and attacks my people will be humbled." It is almost as if Belshazzar is acting out a part in a play, with God as the invisible director.

To add blasphemy to insult, as they drink the wine from the temple goblets, Belshazzar and his guests offer toasts to "the gods of gold and silver, of bronze, iron, wood and stone" (Daniel 5:4). No matter how much reverence people offer to their gods, that is all they are: chunks of metal, carvings of wood or stone, or pieces of paper. When will we learn to revere the creator, rather than created things?

In Daniel 5:5, we read, "Suddenly the fingers of a human hand appeared and wrote on the plaster of the wall, near the lampstand in the royal palace." Notice the historical detail concerning the plaster and the proximity to the lampstand. This kind of detail could only come as the testimony of an eyewitness or of someone who spoke to an eyewitness. Notice as well the word suddenly. As they are making one of their toasts, suddenly the hand of God appears before their very eyes. God enters the scene in a way calculated to have the greatest possible effect. As the account records, the king actually watches the hand write on the wall.[2] He turns very pale and his knees begin knocking. The all-powerful king is reduced to a frightened, shaking puppy. He is shaken out of his drunken stupor more effectively than could be accomplished by any ten cups of coffee.

The king sees right away that he is dealing with a power much greater than himself! Seeing only a tiny part of God (his "hand") tells him what we all instinctively know: We will come before our Creator in judgment some day. So he calls for his enchanters, astrologers and diviners to unravel the situation. Is it not typical that our true nature—be it good or bad—comes out in times of extreme stress? Belshazzar struts around the palace like the lord of the earth, until he is confronted with the hand of God. Then what does he do? He calls for the astrologers! Supposedly, we live in a time when in our great technology and sophistication we have moved beyond reliance on such superstitions as astrology. (Yet, Ronald and Nancy Reagan were reported to have had an astrologer advising them in areas of schedule and travel.)

At this point, rather than simply pointing the finger at Belshazzar or at a neighbor or coworker, we ought to turn the finger around at ourselves. In what ways are we like Belshazzar? The theme of Daniel, and more specifically, the theme of Daniel chapter five is: *"God is in control—do not fear."* God is telling us not to focus on outward circumstances. Ultimately, God is the power "behind the throne." Be patient. Trust in God. Ultimately, the prideful, arrogant, persecuting enemies of God will be dealt with, and dealt with in a very convincing manner. Let us continue to give glory to God.

We can also learn a lesson about how we ourselves approach confusing or overwhelming situations. In what ways do we turn to the "enchanters, astrologers and diviners" when faced with a situation that seems out of our control? And do not be deceived; we all will face circumstances beyond our control.

So Belshazzar calls in his enchanters, astrologers and diviners, and he declares, "Whoever reads this writing and tells me what it means will be clothed in purple and have a gold chain placed around his neck, and he will be made the third highest ruler in the kingdom" (v. 7). One might ask, why the third highest ruler, rather than the second highest ruler? Who is the second highest ruler? Much to the dismay of those who would attack the Bible, the answer to this question reveals once again the uncanny historical accuracy of this great book. The fact is that Belshazzar himself was the second highest ruler in Babylon. Remember that his father Nabonidus was still alive. Although Belshazzar had been the effective ruler of Babylon for fourteen years, his father was still officially the head of state. Officially, until his father died, Belshazzar was considered the regent, despite the fact that he had long been used to the title "king."

This is one of a great number of incidental historical details in the Bible that proves to anyone whose mind is the slightest bit open that the Bible is truly an accurate record of historical events. If Daniel was a mainly fictional account written around 150 B.C. (as claimed by those who are unwilling to accept its divine inspiration), then how could one explain that a writer, supposedly writing a fictional account four hundred years after the events in question, could get the detail about "the third highest ruler" right? Four hundred years after the events, it is extremely unlikely that an author would be aware of the co-regency of Nabonidus and Belshazzar. The skeptic could argue for luck or coincidence, but how many times does the Bible have to be "lucky" before it becomes obvious to any neutral observer that there is much more than luck involved here?

The "wise" men cannot read the writing and Belshazzar is even more frightened. His bottom-line faith is in the magicians, and they have failed him. Actually, his bottom-line faith is probably in himself, but he is painfully aware that he cannot help himself in this situation.

At this time, his queen, or, more likely, his mother,[3] having heard about the commotion, enters the hall. She remembers that there is one man in the kingdom who, unlike those posturing fakes Belshazzar relies on, really can interpret dreams and visions: Daniel. She reminds Belshazzar that Nebuchadnezzar had appointed Daniel as "chief of the magicians, enchanters, astrologers and diviners" (v. 5:11).[4]

On the advice of his mother, the desperate Belshazzar calls for Daniel. Isn't that just like us at times? Sometimes we try everything else within our power to deal with a crisis until, in desperation, when no other choice presents itself, we finally turn to God. Do we need to be in a desperate situation before we turn to God, or can we train ourselves to habitually rely on God in every situation? Belshazzar makes the same offer to Daniel as he made to the others: If he can interpret the writing, he will receive a purple robe (symbolic of royal authority), a gold chain and the third position of authority in the kingdom.

So Daniel enters the scene. He is now (in 539 B.C.) somewhere in his seventies, at least. Where has he been these past several years? Apparently, when Nebuchadnezzar died, Daniel was soon forgotten and pushed off into relative obscurity. Belshazzar had completely forgotten him. More accurately, he had chosen to forget him (Daniel 5:22). There has truly been a huge change between Daniel 4:37 and Daniel 5:1. The God of Israel is out of the picture in Babylon. At least, that is how those who do not know God would see it. The reality, of course, is that God is always working behind the scenes. Daniel has seen the heights of power and the depths of obscurity. When he is offered the greatest temptation in the world,[5] his faith in God, as well as the wisdom he has gained with age, allow him to defiantly declare, in another of the classic lines in Daniel:

> You may keep your gifts for yourself, and give your rewards to someone else. Nevertheless, I will read the writing for the king, and tell him what it means (Daniel 5:17).

I can only pray that as I grow older, I will have the kind of character that allowed Daniel to make such a statement to King Belshazzar.

Now that he has an absolutely captive audience, Daniel proceeds to deliver a sermon that is a stinging rebuke of Belshazzar: "The Most High God gave your father Nebuchadnezzar sovereignty and greatness and glory and splendor" (v. 18). Again, we see the theme, *God rules the nations.* Jehovah gave the kingdom to Nebuchadnezzar. It did not come from Nebuchadnezzar's own greatness.[6]

To paraphrase the rest of Daniel's speech: And you, Belshazzar, are no different. But there is one very big difference between you and Nebuchadnezzar, O king. When Nebuchadnezzar's heart was hardened by his pride, God was able to humble him (as we will see when we cover chapter four).

But your heart is beyond humbling. You actually had the nerve to drink wine in the goblets from the temple of the Almighty God to give praise to the gods of silver, gold, bronze, iron, wood and stone. Your crime, Belshazzar, is that of the vast majority of humanity: "You did not honor the God who holds in his hand your life and all your ways" (v. 23).

Next, Daniel interprets the writing on the wall. One can assume that the common expression "the writing is on the wall" comes directly from this story. According to verse 25, the inscription reads:

MENE, MENE, TEKEL, PARSIN

The hand wrote on the wall using Persian words. The word *mene* means "numbered." The name for the monetary unit the mina comes from this root word. Perhaps for emphasis, God tells Belshazzar twice that his life has been evaluated and that his time has been numbered and come to an end. The word *tekel* means "weighed." Belshazzar's life has been counted and weighed in the balance. Unfortunately for him, his life has been found wanting. Are we prepared to have our deeds numbered, and to have our life weighed on God's scale?[7] Finally, God pronounces judgment on both Belshazzar and on his kingdom Babylon by using the word *parsin* (or the word *upharsin*—there is an insignificant variation in the Hebrew manuscripts here). The word *upharsin* in Aramaic means "torn" or "divided." There may be a double meaning in the word, which sounds very much like the word "Persian." Babylon is to be divided and given to the Medes and Persians. God will endure our pride and idolatry only up to a certain point. Eventually his great patience will give way to judgment.

God is about to judge both Belshazzar and his kingdom. It is a bit difficult for most people to identify with the emotion of looking forward to God's judgment on his enemies. This statement of personal judgment on Belshazzar is intended as an expression of comfort to those undergoing the great persecutions under Antiochus IV Epiphanes and under the Roman emperors. God's nature as judge is something most believers tend to avoid thinking about. Perhaps only those experiencing persecution to the point of death have a right to say, along with the martyrs in Revelation 6:10, "How long, Sovereign Lord, holy and true, until you judge the inhabitants of the earth and avenge our blood?"

It is difficult to understand how, after hearing this scathing pronouncement from Daniel, Belshazzar still is willing to fulfill his promise to put the robe and gold chain on Daniel and declare him the third in the kingdom. Despite the terrifying implications for himself, Belshazzar gives honor to Daniel. Perhaps he is experiencing a form of emotional anesthesia due to the shock of the events.

There is a great irony in Belshazzar's gift. As is faithfully recorded both in secular history and in the book of Daniel, the kingdom of Babylon was in fact overthrown that very night. Daniel's disdain for the gifts the world has to offer proved to be fully justified. Being third in command in Babylon suddenly became a very dangerous position. As Jesus so aptly put it, "The thief comes only to steal and kill and destroy; I have come that they may have life, and have it to the full" (John 10:10). Only God can give us a life that is truly valuable, truly meaningful. If only people could learn the lesson that the gifts the world has to offer in exchange for our honor and integrity are empty shells with no value at all.

It is interesting to point out that history records the event of the overthrow of Babylon in dramatic agreement with the Biblical record. For example, Cyrus himself had an inscription made recording the fall of Babylon. An inscription found on a clay barrel goes as follows:

> Marduk, the great lord...ordered [Cyrus] to march against his city Babylon....he made him set out on the road to Babylon...going at his side like a real friend. His widespread troops—their number, like that of the water of a river, could not be established—strolled along, their weapons packed away.

Without any battle, he made him enter his town Babylon...sparing Babylon any calamity.

Another account is that of Herodotus, the greatest of
ancient Greek historians. Herodotus produced a record of
the overthrow of Babylon that sheds light on the Biblical
account.

Cyrus...then advanced against Babylon. But
the Babylonians, having taken the field, awaited his
coming; and when he had advanced near the city,
the Babylonians gave battle, and, being defeated,
were shut up in the city. But as they had been long
aware of the restless spirit of Cyrus, and saw that
he attacked all nations alike, they had laid up provisions for many years, and therefore were under
no apprehensions about a siege. On the other hand,
Cyrus found himself in difficulty, since much time
had elapsed, and his affairs were not at all advanced.
Whether, therefore, someone else made the sugges-
tion to him, in his perplexity, or whether he himself
devised the plan, he had recourse to the following
stratagem. Having stationed the bulk of his army
near the passage of the river where it enters Babylon,
and again having stationed another division beyond
the city, where the river makes its exit, he gave order
to his forces to enter the city as soon as they should
see the stream fordable. Having stationed his forces
and given these directions, he himself marched away
with the ineffective part of his army; and having come
to the lake, Cyrus did the same with respect to the
river and the lake as the queen of the Babylonians
had done; for having diverted the river, by means of
a canal, into the lake, which was before a swamp,
he made the ancient channel fordable by the sinking
of the river. When this took place, the Persians who
were appointed to that purpose close to the stream
of the river, which had now subsided to about the
middle of a man's thigh, entered Babylon by this passage. If however, the Babylonians had been aware of

it beforehand, or had known what Cyrus was about, they would not have suffered the Persians to enter the city, but would have utterly destroyed them; for, having shut all the little gates that lead to the river and mounting the walls that extend along the banks of the river, they would have caught them as in a net; whereas, the Persians came upon them by surprise. It is related by the people who inhabited the city, that, by reason of its great extent, when they who were at the extremities were taken, those of the Babylonians who inhabited the center knew nothing of the capture (for it happened to be a festival); but they were dancing at the time, and enjoying themselves, till they received certain information of the truth. And thus Babylon was taken for the first time (Herodotus I:190-191).

This history of Herodotus provides striking confirmation of the Biblical account, including the fact that the Babylonians were caught unaware because they were having a great party at the time. It also suggests that when the writing appeared on the wall, for all practical purposes, the overthrow of Babylon may literally have already occurred.

On the night recorded in Daniel chapter five, Cyrus' armies were already approaching the city of Babylon under the generalship of Gubaru. Although Babylon had already been weakened in earlier battles, Cyrus certainly did not expect the city to fall without a fight. When his armies arrived at Babylon, they found a city virtually undefended. This is the same city with the famed walls thick enough to drive three chariots side by side on top of them. Perhaps it was just "luck" for the army to attack the city on the same night that all the leaders were getting drunk at a banquet with Belshazzar. Or perhaps God is working behind the scenes. Cyrus may have had had spies in the city informing him about the circumstances. Either way, one can clearly see the hand of God at work in allowing great historical events to show one more time that truly, *God rules the nations.* The mighty city of Babylon fell without a fight. "That very night Belshazzar, king of the Babylonians, was slain, and Darius the Mede took over the kingdom, at the age of sixty-two" (Daniel 5:30).[8]

Thus, on October 12, 539 B.C., the Babylonian Empire came to an ignominious end, in fulfillment of the prophecies in Daniel chapters two and seven, as will be seen. This event will serve as a type[9] for the destruction of any world power that in its pride sets itself up against the kingdom of God. It is a foreshadowing of the destruction of both the Greek and the Roman persecutors of God's people. Daniel survived the fall of Babylon and its arrogant king to become a powerful official in the Persian Empire. This should serve as a vivid illustration to the faithful and righteous child of God that even as the Lord serves judgment on the world, he will protect and support those who serve him faithfully. The fact that the world's greatest city with its impregnable walls fell without a fight serves as a powerful reminder that God rules the nations.

*Figure 15. Bas relief from royal palace in Persepolis, Iran.*

# Notes

[1] As mentioned previously, Nebuchadnezzar was actually his grandfather. It was common practice in ancient times to call a person's male predecessor their "father," no matter how many generations existed between the predecessor and the person in question.

[2] The throne room in the palace in Babylon where this scene most likely occurred has been excavated. It is 56 feet wide and 173 feet long. Interestingly, there is a niche in the throne room along one of the long walls where the king most likely sat. At the back of this niche is a wall of soft plaster. This may very well be the same wall where God's finger wrote.

[3] The Hebrew can mean either "queen" or "queen mother" (the mother of the king). The more likely of the two is the queen mother, as she would remember well the time of Nebuchadnezzar.

[4] This is another point on which the critics have attempted to cut down the divine authorship of Daniel. They would criticize the book because it calls Daniel chief of the magicians, enchanters, astrologers and diviners. They claim that there is no way the Jewish people would accept as a great leader someone who was an astrologer, diviner or magician. This argument, like all the others, falls apart upon inspection. It is true that the Bible condemns the practices of divination, astrology, or any other form of magic (for example, see Deuteronomy 18:10-12 or 1 Samuel 15:23). If Daniel had been involved in any of these practices, he certainly would have set a bad example. However, the Bible never identifies Daniel as a practitioner of any of the "magic arts." Apparently, Nebuchadnezzar appointed him as chief over the magicians, not an unreasonable choice from the point of view of the king. One can assume that the Jewish readers of Daniel could easily see the difference between being over the magicians and being one of them. In fact, when Nebuchadnezzar's daughter (now the queen) recalls the title Daniel held, she reminds the people of what Daniel actually did do. She reports that Daniel had a keen mind, knowledge, understanding, the ability to interpret dreams, and the wisdom to solve problems and riddles (v. 12). These were the exact skills given to Daniel by God, as recorded in chapter one! Nowhere does she say that Daniel practiced divination, astrology or magic.

[5] Remember that Daniel is a historical picture/symbol of the Messiah. Note the parallel to Matthew 4:8-10.

[6] God had already proven, at least to the Jews, that he had given the empire to Nebuchadnezzar when he prophesied it to the Jews through Isaiah, approximately 150 years beforehand (Isaiah 39:5-7), as mentioned previously.

[7] A parallel passage is found in Revelation 6:6.

[8] Isaiah prophesied these events in even more graphic language. Concerning Babylon, he said, "See, the day of the LORD is coming—a

cruel day, with wrath and fierce anger—to make the land desolate and destroy the sinners within it. The stars of heaven and their constellations will not show their light. The rising sun will be darkened and the moon will not give its light...See, I will stir up against them the Medes, who do not care for silver and have no delight in gold. Their bows will strike down the young men; they will have no mercy on infants nor will they look with compassion on children. Babylon, the jewel of kingdoms, the glory of the Babylonians' pride, will be overthrown by God like Sodom and Gomorrah. She will never be inhabited or lived in through all generations; no Arab will pitch his tent there, no shepherd will rest his flocks there...Her time is at hand, and her days will not be prolonged" (Isaiah 13:9, 17-20, 22). Here God describes two hundred years before the events, in dramatic apocalyptic language, the destruction of the Babylonian power by the Medes and Persians. Babylon was to exist as a lesser city for a while, but just as Isaiah prophesied, it eventually became a desolate, deserted waste in the desert, the haunt of jackals and wild goats.

[9] A type, according to *Webster's Dictionary* is: "A person or thing regarded as the symbol of someone or something that is yet to appear."

# Chapter Six

## Thrown to the Lions

The story of Daniel in the den of lions is one of the most famous stories, not just in the Bible, but also in all of western culture. There are legitimate reasons for this. The story is simple yet compelling. The theme of courage and moral conviction is a universal one, accessible to all ages and types of people. It just so happens that the story also fits perfectly within the theme of Daniel: *God rules the nations—do not be afraid.*

Chapter six opens on a high note for Daniel. His great reputation as an interpreter of dreams, as a man of wisdom and insight, and especially as a government administrator, has caused Darius to place him in a very high position in the new government of the Empire of Persia/Media. At first glance, this is a very surprising turn of events. When Cyrus overthrew the Babylonian Empire (recorded in Daniel 5), the king, Belshazzar, was killed. One would expect that Belshazzar's second-in-command, Daniel, even though he was only very recently appointed, would have been killed right along with Belshazzar. Instead, Cyrus' lieutenant, Darius the Mede, actually promotes his former "enemy" Daniel to be one of the three chief administrators over his far-flung 120 satrapies (a Persian word essentially equivalent to a province).

The fact that Daniel was promoted, rather than destroyed, seems unexpected. This is surprising until one recognizes the unique policies of the empire-builder Cyrus. In a dramatic break with empires of the past, when Cyrus

*Figure 16. Dying lioness from Nineveh, 650 B.C., British Museum.*

conquered a nation, he showed extreme benevolence to the conquered peoples. The preceding two great powers in the Mesopotamian area, Assyria and Babylon, had a policy of brutally suppressing national cultures by killing large numbers of the elite outright. They also deported whole populations to distant lands in order to assimilate them into the governmental and religious system of the conquerors. The nation of Israel was very familiar with this pattern. The Northern Kingdom was destroyed and its people deported by the Assyrians, and the Southern Kingdom had undergone the same treatment under the Babylonians.

*Figure 17. Babylon wall relief of a griffin.*

Cyrus had the policy of allowing conquered peoples to maintain cultural autonomy. He also employed the existing aristocracy of a region in his government, as long as they be his loyal subjects. In a move unique to ancient history, he even had a policy of sending the deported peoples back to their native areas. This would prove to be a great boon to the people of God—allowing them to rebuild the temple in Jerusalem and reestablish sacrificial worship there. No wonder God had prophetically said of Cyrus:

> He is my shepherd and will accomplish all that I please; he will say of Jerusalem, "Let it be rebuilt," and of the temple, "Let its foundations be laid" (Isaiah 44:28).

Is it not absolutely astounding that the Bible recorded these words about Cyrus approximately two hundred years before he stormed onto the scene as the head of the Persian and Median armies? God, through Isaiah, predicted that a man named Cyrus would free the people of Israel to rebuild the temple and ultimately the city of Jerusalem.[1]

A few words must be said about Darius the Mede. Darius is described as the ruler of Babylon in chapter six of Daniel. Nebuchadnezzar, Belshazzar and Cyrus, the other major historical figures mentioned in Daniel, are well-known historical figures. However, Darius the Mede is not well known to history. The critics of Daniel have attacked the historical authenticity of the book more strongly on this point than any other. The bottom line is that current knowledge of history tells us nothing of certainty about this man Darius. The critics have at the very least a good question to pose about this man. So who is Darius the Mede?

Many opinions have been expressed about the identity of Darius the Mede. Those who believe Daniel to be a historical fabrication would claim that the writer of the book, because he wrote hundreds of years after the fact, confused Cyrus with the well-known Persian ruler Darius I. Darius I was already mentioned in the historical introduction. He ruled the Persia/Media Empire from 522-486 B.C., succeeding Cambyses, the son of Cyrus. In other words, these people would claim that in Daniel 5:30, the Bible is just plain wrong when it says that after Belshazzar was killed, Darius the Mede (rather than Cyrus) took over the kingdom at the age of sixty-two.

Those who believe that the Bible is the infallible word of God will obviously be uncomfortable with this conclusion. However, if the believer were to dismiss the charge without giving it a thought, they would be guilty of the same mistake others make when they dismiss the Bible without checking out the evidence. Let us not be accused of this intellectually dishonest approach to studying the Bible. Or if this is an accurate accusation, let us decide now to change our way of thinking!

There is a great volume of evidence to support the claim that the Bible is an inspired account, and therefore an accurate historical account. This ought to cause the believer not to ask, why did the Bible get it wrong?, but rather to ask, who is this man Darius the Mede? He has been identified as:

1. Cambyses, the son of Cyrus, because Cambyses did in fact rule over the former kingdom of Babylon under his father Cyrus, garnering the title "king of Babylon." However, Cambyses was a Persian, not a Mede, and he was ruler of Babylon for less than a year—both facts that do not fit with Daniel 6:2 and Daniel 9:1.

2. Gubaru (or Ugbaru), the general who actually captured the city of Babylon for Cyrus in 539 B.C. Gubaru was a Mede. Cyrus appointed him governor of Babylon for a time. However, Gubaru is never referred to in extra-Biblical sources as a king.[2]

3. Astyages, the king of Media who was overthrown by Cyrus. The theory is that Cyrus made him governor of Babylon, and that, being a former king, he was given the honorary title of "king." However, there is no direct evidence to support the idea that he was ever ruler over Babylon.

Other theories have been offered as well.[3] A reasonable conclusion would be as follows: At some point after Cyrus conquered Babylon,[4] he appointed as governor a man from Media (rather than from Persia) named Darius. Very likely he appointed a Mede to govern his most important province at least in part to placate the Medes, who were in theory co-rulers of the Persia/Media Empire. This man ruled as a client king, organizing his large territory into one hundred and twenty "satrapies." To support this idea that Darius the Mede was a client king, consider Daniel 9:1: "In the first year of Darius, son of Xerxes (a Mede by descent), who was made ruler over the Babylonian kingdom..." Here it specifically states that he "was made ruler." In other words, he did not inherit the throne, but was appointed (presumably by Cyrus). It is very unlikely that anyone would say of the other Darius (i.e., Darius I) that he "was made ruler." Darius I ascended to the throne of Persia as a direct heir in the year 522 B.C.

Historical study may or may not eventually bring to light extra-biblical evidence to support Daniel's claim about Darius. However, those who have attempted to claim the Bible is historically inaccurate because it mentions cities, nations and people not found elsewhere have been proven wrong time and time again. It would be wise to give the benefit of the doubt to the Bible, given its track record.[5]

But it is time to get back to the story. Eventually, Daniel distinguishes himself in such an exceptional way in service to the Persians and Medes that the king intends to "set him over the whole kingdom" as a kind of Prime Minister (Daniel 6:3). Ironically, this is essentially the same position Belshazzar had promised Daniel. Wouldn't it be great if, like Daniel, our government leaders achieved their position because of their distinguished and exceptional service, rather than because of political patronage and personality? The problem for Daniel is that the other administrators and satraps had become extremely jealous of him. Not only has he gained ascendancy over them, but he has done so without resorting to bribery, or the granting of special favors, or any of the other things that make for politics-as-usual. Therefore, in their own minds, they owe him nothing. In reality, what they owe Daniel is respect and honest, loyal service.

In their jealousy of Daniel these bureaucrats attempt to dig up some dirt on him. In what is surely a rare occurrence in any society of humans, they have in Daniel a very high government official who is absolutely blameless. He cannot legitimately be charged with corruption or even with negligence in any way whatsoever. What a great example Daniel is for us. Could your co-workers say of you what these hypocritical men reluctantly had to say about Daniel?

The satraps have a meeting, very similar to the one held by the chief priests and the Pharisees recorded in John 11:45-53, when they discussed what to do about Jesus. They want to find a legal way to get Daniel out of the way of their ambitions. They realize that the only way to pull down Daniel, short of murdering him, is to find a way to turn his faultless righteousness against him. They will use his devotion to Jehovah as means to undo him. These manipulators decide to use Darius' pride to set a trap for Daniel. And so they begin to unfold their plot: "O King Darius, live forever" (Daniel 6:6). Is there a hint of hypocrisy here? Knowing Darius well, they decide to use one of his biggest weaknesses—his great pride—against him. They propose to the king that he issue the following decree: "Anyone who prays to any god or man during the next thirty days, except to you, O king, shall be thrown into the lions' den" (v. 7). In this decree, Darius is demanding to be worshiped as a god. To seal the deal, they have Darius put it into writing.

What will Daniel do in response to this decree? Clearly he cannot pray to Darius. Perhaps he should continue praying to the true God, but in a way that is more private. What does a man of righteousness do when pressured by "the world" to put his religion in the closet? God promises in 2 Timothy 3:12, that "everyone who wants to live a godly life in Christ Jesus will be persecuted." Our co-workers or neighbors or fellow students may not use the lions' den approach, but we can be sure that those who see our righteousness but are unwilling to repent will attempt to find a way to still our voices. How will we respond when pressured to repress personal expression of our devotion to God?

Daniel is not stupid. He sees the situation for what it is: a trap. But he also sees the situation for what it is in

God's sight: an opportunity to let his light shine before men, so that they may see his good deeds and praise his Father in heaven (paraphrasing Matthew 5:16). Daniel goes home to his apartment and prays toward Jerusalem, just as his habit has been all along. Apparently his devotion to God is no secret (is yours?), as his enemies know exactly what to do. They wait in hiding for Daniel from a vantage point opposite his open window. Why doesn't Daniel close the window when he gets home? Is he looking for trouble? Is he a glutton for punishment? The answer is no. Daniel is human, just like us. Just like us, he would prefer that his persecutors leave him alone. However, as much as he fears his persecutors, he fears his own sinful nature more. Possibly Daniel reasons that if he were to close the window (clearly, closing the window would not be a sin), it would for him symbolize compromising with the world.

In any case, whatever his motivation, Daniel prays to his God openly, and the die is cast. Chuckling to themselves at their ingenious plan, the men return to Darius to complete their entrapment. They manipulate Darius into stating one more time before all of them that the decree stands "in accordance with the laws of the Medes and Persians, which cannot be repealed" (Daniel 6:12). Notice how these men say, "Did you not publish a decree...?" In fact, it was they who had written the decree, and simply asked Darius to rubber-stamp it. How could Darius have been so foolish as to not know that they were using him to get to his loyal Prime Minister? The answer is that they were extremely confident that they could use his over-inflated ego to distract him from their true intentions. "Pride goes before destruction, a haughty spirit before a fall" (Proverbs 16:18).

Similarly, those who seek to live a righteous life for God should not be deceived. Mark it down: Those who would oppose the work of God will use similar methods. Jesus admonished his disciples to "be as shrewd as snakes and as innocent as doves" (Matthew 10:16). In standing up for the truth, God's people need to be loving and kind at all times. However, there is no virtue in being foolish. Disciples of Christ should prepare themselves for likely areas of Satan's attack. Those who oppose the work of God will attempt to use a person's weakest point to get him or her off a spiritual track. We share similar traits to Darius and for the majority of us, our weakest point is our pride.

Daniel's enemies, confident that there is no way out for either Daniel or Darius, spring their trap. They inform Darius that Daniel has continued to pray three times daily to God. Darius is furious! He now realizes what a fool he has been. Daniel is his most trusted adviser and administrator, and now Darius has been trapped by his own foolishness into having him killed. He tries for the entire day to figure out a way to get out of the situation. The ungodly men remind Darius that "according to the law of the Medes and Persians no decree or edict that the king issues can be changed" (v. 15). This provides for another confirmation of the historical accuracy of Daniel. It is known from outside historical sources that in the Babylonian Empire, the emperor was considered to be above the law, whereas in the legal system of the Medes and Persians, even the ruler was considered to be under the law. He may have been worshiped as a god, but he was still bound to follow any published law. By Persian and Median precedent, Darius had to carry out the decree or risk the rebellion of his subordinates. This detail provides still one more confirmation of the historical accuracy of Daniel.

It is touching to see how Daniel's honesty and unselfish, loyal service have won Darius' approval and even affection. Through this story, God is encouraging us. Although our righteous deeds may inspire the opposition of many, there will always be a Darius who, despite his pride, will "see your good deeds and praise your Father in heaven" (Matthew 5:16).

In diametric opposition to his own desire, Darius throws Daniel into the den of lions and has a stone placed over the entrance. His last words to Daniel are, "May your God, whom you serve continually, rescue you!" (v. 16) Although Darius has not yet been "converted" to worship of Jehovah, Daniel's example of righteousness and faith has softened his heart toward faith in the true God. Darius endures a sleepless night. It is easy to imagine him spending the night admonishing himself for his foolish pride. Darius returns at the crack of dawn to the lions' den. In a sheepish voice, expressing hope against hope, he calls out to Daniel. His voice is tinged with guilt at having indirectly, through his own stupidity, caused his friend and trusted adviser to be killed. God has humbled Darius!

To Darius' great joy, Daniel answers in complete sincerity, "O king, live forever!" (v. 21) What was Daniel's night like? Daniel says, " My God sent his angel" (v. 22). Did Daniel get to talk with the angel? Did Daniel pray all night, or was he so trusting of God's providence that he was able to sleep the night away, right under the jaws of the hungry lions? What we do know is that Darius, in great joy, orders his men to lift Daniel out of the lions' den. Daniel is completely unharmed "because he had trusted in his God" (v. 23).

In his anger at his deceitful advisers, Darius has them thrown with their families into the lions' den. Just in case anyone doubts the hunger of the lions, they pounce on their prey before they reach the ground. So much for the wicked administrators' plan to bring down Daniel! When God decides to lift up Daniel, he accomplishes his will in spite of any human opposition. There is no denying that God has worked to protect Daniel. In his excitement at not losing his adviser, Darius issues a decree that the God of the Israelites must be honored throughout his kingdom. What an encouragement to Daniel that his righteous decision has been vindicated!

Once again, the message of Daniel to those suffering the great persecutions under Antiochus IV Epiphanes (and of course to us as well) is: *God is in control—do not fear*. If you faithfully continue to devote yourself to God, obeying his commands no matter the pressure from those who oppose the truth, you will ultimately be vindicated. Do not give in to fear! Whether in this life or in the next, your faith in God will have its reward. Just as God intended, Daniel's faith and courage continue to inspire those who consider the praise of God to be of greater worth than the praises of men.

## Notes

[1] One of the sub-themes of this book is how God uses historical persons as symbolic and prophetic prefigurations of the Messiah. Perhaps the most interesting example of this concept is found in Cyrus the Great. Here is a man who was not a Jew. He was not even a believer, yet God used him as a "type" of Christ. Cyrus literally saved God's people, as did

Moses, Joseph and the other Messiah "types." Cyrus, like Moses, helped God's people return to the promised land. Entering the promised land is an OT symbol of entering heaven. The writer of Hebrews specifically makes this parallel in Hebrews 3:16-4:5. The name Cyrus comes from an Elamite word meaning "shepherd." This bears an obvious relation to Jesus, who said of himself, "I am the good shepherd" (John 10:14). God says concerning Cyrus, "This is what the Lord says to his anointed, to Cyrus, whose right hand I take hold of to subdue nations before him and to strip kings of their armor, to open doors before him so that gates will not be shut" (Isaiah 45:1). Remember that the word Messiah literally means "the anointed one." In a sense, God is calling Cyrus his Messiah. One could put the name of Jesus Christ into Isaiah 45:1 and it would fit very well. There is a repeating pattern to be found here. God uses history as prophecy.

[2] A thorough treatment of this theory can be found in the book *Daniel in the Critics' Den*, (New York: Cosimo Classics, 2007—originally published in 1909).

[3] *Encyclopedic Dictionary of the Bible*, (McGraw-Hill, 1963), p. 492.

[4] Notice that in Daniel 5:30 it says that Belshazzar was killed "that very night," but it does not say that Darius the Mede began to rule Babylon that night. All it says is that Darius the Mede took over the Babylonian kingdom at some date.

[5] It is worth pointing out a few of the many examples of cities, nations and persons found in the Bible, which critics at one time claimed were biblical mistakes, but that later proved to be factual. As an example of a city whose existence was once attacked as a biblical mistake, consider Nineveh. It was once claimed that Nineveh was a mythical city, only existing in the imagination of the biblical writers. This changed when this huge city was discovered and thoroughly excavated. The Hittites could be used as an example of a nation whose very existence was once questioned. The Hittites are often mentioned in the Old Testament, particularly in Joshua and Judges. Skeptics at one time claimed that the Hittites were a mythical people. That claim fell apart when several of the major cities of the Hittites were discovered in present-day Turkey. In fact, the Hittites were the chief rival power to the Egyptians (as implied by the Bible) for several centuries. As an example of a person whose existence has been questioned by critics, Luke mentions Lysanias, tetrarch of Abilene (Luke 3:1). Luke lists Lysanias as a ruler at the time of John the Baptist's ministry, about 27 A.D. Until fairly recently, the only Lysanias known to historians was killed in 36 B.C. Many questioned the historical accuracy of Luke based on this "mistake"—that is, until an inscription was found near Damascus which describes a man as a "Freedman of Lysanias the tetrarch." This inscription has been dated somewhere between 14 and 29 A.D. Many other examples could be quoted. Sources include *Evidence that Demands a Verdict,* Josh McDowell, (Here's Life Publishers, 1979), and *More Evidence that Demands a Verdict,* Josh McDowell, (Thomas Nelson Inc. 1993). Many claim that the Bible is full of myths. The claim that the Bible is full of historical errors is itself a myth of legendary proportions.

# PART TWO

## Daniel: Prophet of Comfort

The theme of Daniel is *God rules the nations—do not fear.* In part one of this book, we looked at the portions of Daniel that depict the lives of Daniel and his friends. These stories show us in very practical ways how to deal with the pressure the world puts on us to compromise our walk with God. In part two, we will consider the dreams and visions that Daniel had. These dreams and visions are prophetic views of the future. When God's people endured the intense persecution under Antiochus IV Epiphanes, they could read in Daniel an amazingly detailed, exact foretelling of what they were going through. This foretelling, by Daniel, had been written almost four hundred years before the event! As these Jews went through agonizing decisions about whether to remain faithful to God, they could look to the book of Daniel. Not only could they find a great example of how to live, but they also found absolutely undeniable confirmation that the biblical writings were from God, and that the end result predicted in Daniel would come true. God rules the nations.

The content of Daniel to be studied in this section is found in chapters 2, 4, and 7 through 12. A sizeable portion of these chapters in Daniel contains apocalyptic writings.

The apocalyptic style is quite different from the other writing styles found in various parts of the Bible. It would be worthwhile to devote some time to explaining the nature of apocalyptic writing and how to interpret it before beginning a study of the prophetic material in Daniel.

The word apocalyptic comes from the Greek root word αποκαλυψις (*apokalupsis*), which means unveiling. The word was originally applied to the book of Revelation, which in Greek is called the Apocalypse. Eventually, because of an obvious parallel in style of writing, the word *apocalyptic* came to apply to any material written in a symbolic style similar to the book of Revelation. The list of apocalyptic writing includes most of the book of Zechariah, large parts of Joel, significant portions of Daniel, Ezekiel and Isaiah, as well as a number of non-canonical Hebrew writings, especially from the period from 200 B.C. to 200 A.D.

The essence of apocalyptic writing is a great reliance on symbolism and a very dramatic style of presentation. Apocalyptic writing uses colors, numbers and animals to represent qualities or nations. For example, a horn represents power, while the number seven will represent completeness or deity.

A rule in interpreting scripture is that one should assume that things said in the Bible are to be taken in their literal, face-value sense unless the context demands something different. This rule is reversed in apocalyptic writing. For writing in the apocalyptic style, the rule of interpretation is to assume that descriptions are intended to be symbolic unless the context indicates otherwise. For example, in Genesis 22 (not an apocalyptic passage), when it says that Abraham found a ram with its horns caught in a thicket, we are to assume that it was an actual ram with actual horns that was caught in an real bush. However, in an apocalyptic passage such as Daniel chapter eight, when one sees a ram with two horns charging, one should assume that the image is not meant to represent a literal ram or literal horns. In fact, the ram represents an empire and the two horns represent the power of the two portions of that empire.

Why did God use apocalyptic writing? To answer this requires some speculation. One possible reason is that the dramatic style is appropriate to the intense emotions involved in the persecutions and judgments being described in apocalyptic writings. Another possibility is that God used apocalyptic writing to protect the bearers of the message from unnecessary additional persecution. For example, the books of Daniel and Revelation both state, in indirect, symbolic language, that the Kingdom of God will ultimately overcome and destroy the Roman Empire. If the Bible had made this statement in more direct terms, it could have proven to be dangerous propaganda for the disciples of Christ to have in-hand. Roman officials could easily have misinterpreted this as a call for Christians to take up arms against the government of Rome. Perhaps God had these reasons in mind; perhaps he had others we have not discussed here. It is difficult to say for sure.

It is worth mentioning the significance of numbers in apocalyptic writing, as this subject will come up a number of times in studying the text of these chapters. Different authors express varying opinions, and variant contexts might demand different interpretations, but a general consensus view of the meaning of different numbers in the Bible, and especially in apocalyptic writings, could be summarized as follows:

| NUMBER | GENERAL MEANING |
| --- | --- |
| three | unity, oneness |
| three and one half (half of seven) | a limited amount of time |
| four | the world, nations |
| six | Satan, evil |
| seven | completeness, perfection |
| ten | God's revelation |
| twelve | the number of God's people |
| forty | a time of testing or preparation |
| one thousand | a great number |

This list is not comprehensive, as other numbers and other meanings could be listed. However, this list is sufficient for a study of Daniel. An example of how God uses these numbers symbolically can be cited. It is not mere coincidence that God had twelve apostles and twelve tribes, as twelve is the number of God's people. It is interesting that the number twelve in these cases is both literal and symbolic, as there were literally twelve apostles and twelve sons of Jacob. In Revelation 14, when the number of redeemed people is listed as 144,000, this is intended to be symbolic, not the literal number of saved people. This number is equal to 12 x 12 x 1000. It represents the complete number of God's people and the fact that there are a great number of them. The apocalyptic use of numbers will come up several times in the book of Daniel.

It is in general rather easy to tell when writing is apocalyptic. One reading of the book of Revelation will prepare any student of the Bible to distinguish apocalyptic writing from other styles, whether found in the Bible or outside of it. As one reads the portions of Daniel containing dreams and visions, one will find that the writing often slips back and forth between the apocalyptic and the straightforward description of events. It will be very helpful to bear this in mind when studying these passages.

In the following chapters of this book, the reader will learn about the dreams of Nebuchadnezzar and the visions of Daniel. It can get confusing trying to keep track of how the different visions fit with one another chronologically. It will be very helpful to look at the timeline in Appendix A, and to keep a bookmark there throughout these chapters. Appendix A puts all the visions and dreams into a parallel timeline, which will provide a visual basis for keeping the chronology straight.

# Chapter Seven

## A Dream in the Night

"In the second year of his reign, Nebuchadnezzar had dreams" (Daniel 2:1). These dreams occurred early in Nebuchadnezzar's tenure as king. Since Daniel was brought to Babylon in the first year of the king's reign, we can assume that he has entered service to the king fairly recently. He may even still be in the training period referred to in Daniel chapter one.

Apparently, the dreams of Nebuchadnezzar are extremely vivid. Upon awakening, he is convinced that they have some significance beyond those of ordinary dreams. He is absolutely compelled to learn the meaning of these dreams. The problem is that his customary method of determining the "truth" is unreliable. Even those who regularly rely on astrology, numerology or the psychic hotline in an attempt to gain control over a seemingly uncontrollable world eventually become aware that these methods are fallible. Nebuchadnezzar is willing to go so far as to rely on divination to determine when to go to war, because to some extent he can control a battlefield situation by gathering an army of sufficient size to overcome his enemy. In a war, he can partially rely on the diviners and partially on himself. In the case of his dreams, however, Nebuchadnezzar feels totally at the mercy of whatever divine force is causing the dreams.

For this reason, he is not content to ask his magicians, enchanters, sorcerers, astrologers and various other psychics for a simple interpretation of the dream. He wants them to tell him the details of the dream before interpreting it. Nebuchadnezzar reasons that if they can tell him what he dreamed, then he can trust their interpretation. "No fair!" the astrologers shout. "No one has ever demanded such proof that we actually have real power to determine the truth. Since when did we actually have to prove our methods really work?" Perhaps no one had ever demanded proof from these deceivers simply because they wanted to believe what the magicians had to say. The words of 2 Timothy 4:3-4 have always been true. Most people prefer having their "ears scratched" to hearing the truth about difficult things. The psychics provide us with a soothing belief that we have some control over our lives. We certainly do not want to mess up this nice feeling with questions about whether it is actually true or not: "Don't confuse me with the truth." Nebuchadnezzar has long been party to this silent conspiracy in which one does not ask for proof because one is secretly aware that it is all an illusion.

Praise God that those who believe in the Bible do not have to play this game. The Bible is the real thing. The really inspiring fact is that the more closely we examine the Bible for proofs of its divine authorship, the more confident we become that the Bible is indeed the word of God.

Under the intense pressure he feels from his undeniably significant dream, Nebuchadnezzar decides to stop the game of pretending that the religious people around him actually have some power to determine truth. If it were not a life and death matter, the scene would be comic. The magicians plead one more time for Nebuchadnezzar to recite the dream. All these psychics are completely aware that their powers are just a hoax. Notice that they do not even consider the possibility of actually trying to use their power to determine the content of the dream. Their conspiracy of silence is about to be uncovered, and they are about to be cut into pieces. The king answers, "I am certain that you are trying to gain time" (v. 8). Nebuchadnezzar levels an indictment against these religious hoaxers that applied with equal weight to today's new-age mystics, astrologers and faith healers: "You have conspired to tell me misleading and wicked things" (v. 9). Nebuchadnezzar stands his ground:

"Tell me the dream or you will be cut to pieces."

The magicians' answer reveals their deceit. They say, "There is not a man on earth who can do what the king asks....What the king asks is too difficult. No one can reveal it to the king except the gods, and they do not live among men" (vv. 10-11). They could have added: "Our claim to have access to those gods was a hoax all along, and you know it, O Nebuchadnezzar, so it is unfair for you to suddenly demand of us what you know it is impossible for us to do."

The stalling does not placate Nebuchadnezzar. A decree is issued to execute all the "wise" men in Babylon. This is where our protagonists come in. Guess who is on the list of wise men—Daniel, Shadrach, Meshach and Abednego!

Daniel's response is in diametric opposition to that of the magicians. Instead of making excuses, he tacitly acknowledges the logic in Nebuchadnezzar's demand. In faith, he simply asks for time to seek from his God the dream and its interpretation. Why have the other magicians not thought of this "delay tactic?" The idea of pretending they might actually be able to answer the question has never even occurred to them.

Please look at Daniel's instinctual first response to a very trying situation. He goes back to his house, gathers his close spiritual companions, and together they pray to God for both help and guidance in this time of trouble (v. 18). That night, God answers their prayer. Rather than immediately rushing out to tell Nebuchadnezzar the dream, Daniel first takes the time to give glory to God in prayer. He writes what could be called "the Psalm of Daniel." This psalm expresses the theme of the book of Daniel more eloquently than I could ever hope to do:

> Praise be to the name of God for ever and ever;
>     wisdom and power are his.
> He changes times and seasons;
>     he sets up kings and deposes them.
> He gives wisdom to the wise
>     and knowledge to the discerning.
> He reveals deep and hidden things;
>     he knows what lies in darkness,

and light dwells with him.
I thank and praise you, O God of my fathers:
    You have given me wisdom and power,
    you have made known to me what we asked of you,
    you have made known to us the dream of the king
(Daniel 2:20-23).

It seems that some time during that night, God has allowed Daniel to have the identical dream that Nebuchadnezzar experienced. The header to this section in the New International Version is "Nebuchadnezzar's Dream." Alternatively, we could call it, "Nebuchadnezzar's and Daniel's Dream." In a wonderful mix of both humility and confidence, Daniel goes before the king.

Nebuchadnezzar asks Daniel, "Are you able to tell me what I saw in my dream and interpret it?" (v. 26) Someone less spiritual than Daniel would have nervously blurted out, "Yes I can." The fact that that young Daniel is able to keep his head in this circumstance is a testimony to his relationship with God.

Instead, Daniel gives all the glory to God (v. 28) and none to himself (v. 30). Using the situation as an opportunity for evangelism, Daniel explains that only the true God—the God of Israel—could reveal such a mystery. Daniel pointedly reminds Nebuchadnezzar that the enchanters, magicians and diviners are powerless to reveal truth. He is aware that Nebuchadnezzar is likely to add God to the pantheon of "gods," rather than worshiping the Lord Jehovah alone. It is not surprising that Daniel's fears are later realized.

So Daniel tells Nebuchadnezzar his dream. And a truly awesome dream it was! Nebuchadnezzar (and Daniel) had seen an enormous, dazzling statue. The chief characteristic of this statue was that it was divided into a head of gold, chests and arms of silver, belly and thighs of bronze, and legs of iron. Daniel supplies additional information about the legs. The legs were made of iron, but the feet were partly of iron and partly of clay. Daniel goes on to relate to Nebuchadnezzar that at the end of the dream, a huge rock appeared suddenly out of nowhere. Unlike the statue, which apparently had been man-made, this rock was not of human origin. Daniel describes how this rock struck the statue, shattering it into dust; the dust blew away in the wind, leaving behind only this giant rock that "filled the whole earth."

At this Nebuchadnezzar is absolutely floored. Daniel has been able to describe to him in vivid and complete detail the exact dream he experienced. Probably, Daniel has even filled in details that Nebuchadnezzar is fuzzy on. Nebuchadnezzar now knows that, as he had suspected, this dream truly is a message from "the gods," or more accurately, from *the God*. Daniel immediately launches into the interpretation of the dream. There is some bad news for Nebuchadnezzar in this dream, so Daniel wisely (no one ever has accused Daniel of lack of wisdom) sets the stage by telling Nebuchadnezzar how awesome he is. "You, O king, are the king of kings.... You are the head of gold" (vv. 37-38).

What does this mean? Daniel is telling Nebuchadnezzar that the head of gold represents the Babylonian Empire. It is worth noting the courage of Daniel in telling Nebuchadnezzar that the source of his power is a foreign god—the God of Israel. "The God of heaven has given you dominion and power and might and glory...he has made you ruler over them all" (vv. 37-38). Daniel risks a prideful and violent response from Nebuchadnezzar by informing him that his success comes from the god of a nation he has conquered, rather than from Nebuchadnezzar's own strength or wisdom.

In case there is any doubt that Daniel is saying that the head represents the Babylonian Empire, rather than just Nebuchadnezzar himself, consider verse 39: "After you, another kingdom will rise, inferior to yours." The kingdom being referred to, the silver kingdom, is obviously the Persia/Media Empire. This empire did not succeed Nebuchadnezzar himself. The Persia/Media Empire succeeded the empire he helped to establish—Babylon. Again, Daniel wisely slips through a description of this second empire very quickly, perhaps to avoid raising the ire of Nebuchadnezzar. He succinctly describes this second empire (Persia/Media) as "inferior" to Nebuchadnezzar's. Surely, the Persia/Media Empire was, as Daniel describes, inferior to Babylon in some way, but Daniel does not give details. Perhaps Daniel is referring to the city of Babylon itself, which was grander than any city ever built by the Medes or the Persians. In point of fact, in almost any obvious characteristic, the empire established by Cyrus was much greater than the Babylonian. It was much greater in extent of territory (see the map in Appendix A), in wealth and in the length of duration of its power.[1] In a different context, when Daniel is not pointing out that this kingdom will destroy Babylon, God will reveal much more detail about the nature of the Persia/Media Empire.

Daniel goes on to mention the "bronze" kingdom that will rule over the whole earth. There can be no reasonable doubt that God, through Daniel, is telling us about the Greek Empire established by Alexander the Great. This is the empire which conquered and destroyed the Persia/Media Empire. Of course, Alexander's empire did not literally cover the whole earth. His armies did in fact conquer an area considerably greater than any other empire in the entire world up to that point in time (see the map in Appendix A).

Last, Daniel describes the "iron" kingdom, which is the greatest empire of them all. Like iron, it will be so strong that it will be able to break and smash every kingdom that came before it. What empire is Daniel referring to? What empire in the history of mankind could be described as an empire of iron that broke and smashed all other empires before it? Even with only a rudimentary background in history, without knowing what power had destroyed the Greek dynasties, it is easy to identify this empire. It must be Rome. Rome, without question, is the greatest empire in the history of mankind. There is not even a close second. Counting the Eastern Roman Empire, Rome was the dominant power at the crossroads of Europe, Asia and Africa for well over one thousand years.

So according to the prophetic dream, Rome is to succeed the Greek power. This vision provides very little detail about the Greek Empire. The visions recorded in Daniel chapters eight and eleven will expand greatly on this third kingdom.

In the dream, God supplies more detail to Nebuchadnezzar (and to us) about Rome. According to the dream, Rome "will be a divided kingdom" (v. 41). That is exactly what happened! It is difficult to give an exact date for the division of

Rome into East and West, as the division occurred in stages. Diocletian (284-305 A.D.) was the first to establish Western and Eastern emperors. Constantine the Great (306-337 A.D.) established a permanent eastern capital at Byzantium (later called Constantinople, now called Istanbul). The division became permanent under Theodosian after 395 A.D. This political division ultimately defined the division of the church into the (Roman) Catholic and the (Greek) Orthodox. Daniel gets this historical detail correct almost one thousand years before it occurred.

*Figure 18.*
*Alexander the Great coin image.*

But he's not finished yet! He supplies us with even more historical detail about the Roman Empire. Part of it will be brittle, like clay, and part if it will be strong, like iron. Again, that is exactly what happened. After the division, the Western Empire proved to be weak, like clay. It was able to withstand the attacks of the "barbarian" Goths, Vandals and others for only a very short time. Rome itself was sacked and the last identifiable Western Roman emperor (Romulus Augustulus) was deposed on 476 A.D.

On the other hand, the Eastern Roman Empire, later known as Byzantium, endured for over one thousand years. It definitely was the "iron" foot. This empire was not completely ended until the capture of Constantinople by the Ottomans on May 29, 1453. For eight hundred years, Byzantium stood as Christendom's eastern flank against the Moslem expansion. Could God have described this empire more accurately?

This is astounding! Using a dream that was given to both Nebuchadnezzar and Daniel, God has provided an outline of the future history of the Near East and Europe for the next two thousand years. In 603 B.C. God sent Nebuchadnezzar a dream that described the great events of history all the way through 1453 A.D.—the history of the world for the next two thousand years! Is there any other book ever written by man that can even begin to touch this great prophecy?

Perhaps you are a bit disappointed. God did not supply much detail in this particular future history lesson. Just you wait! If it is details you want, God has many of those in store for you as well.

Where is the precedent for what God did here? It would do God a disservice to even mention the names of the supposed psychics of our modern age who give vague predictions for the coming year or at most the next few years. Their predictions are occasionally vague enough to be correct, such as "I predict there will be a sexual scandal in Washington next year." The most famous supposed prophet in the United States in the recent past was Jean Dixon. Mrs. Dixon happened to predict the assassination of John F. Kennedy the year before it happened. She built an entire career on this one lucky guess. Did she ever get another major specific prediction right? The answer is no. Some prefer to mention Nostradamus, the French practitioner of "black magic" as a great prophet. Do yourself a favor and read some of his writings. You will find extremely obtuse references that have the advantage of being applicable to almost any situation in any country at any time. Unlike Nostradamus, the prophecies of Daniel make predictions which are very definite and specific in their fulfillment.

Remember the theme of Daniel—*God rules the nations—do not fear.* Is there any way God could have possibly provided stronger evidence that he rules the nations than to tell us, hundreds of years before the events, exactly what these nations will do? Is there any way he could have provided more incontrovertible proof that his Bible is inspired?

But there is one more historical prophetic detail in this dream we have not yet discussed, and it is the most encouraging of all: "In the time of those kings, the God of heaven will set up a kingdom that will never be destroyed, nor will it be left to another people. It will crush all those kingdoms and bring them to an end, but it will itself endure forever" (Daniel 2:44). "Those kings" refer to the kings of Rome. What kingdom was established during the time of Rome

*Figure 19.*
*Constantine the Great.*

that is still going strong right up to this very day? In looking at history, it is impossible to choose a physical empire that fits this description. Remember, though, that human hands did not build this kingdom. God himself will establish this kingdom (v. 44). The kingdom established during the time of the Roman kings is worldwide kingdom of God. The visible incarnation of that kingdom is the Church.

Yes, Daniel truly is a prophet of comfort. As more and more of the prophecies contained in Daniel were fulfilled in history, God's people were supplied with an ever-increasing body of evidence to convince them that eventually he would establish a kingdom on earth—a kingdom which was ushered in with the death and resurrection of Jesus; which was first publicly announced at Pentecost (Acts 2). It is true that many of the Jews misunderstood the nature of this kingdom, expecting it to be a political/military government, but God made it clear to them in the book of Daniel and elsewhere that it was to be a spiritual kingdom.

It is interesting to realize that some Jews today are still waiting for this kingdom to be established. It is a central tenet of Judaism that the Messiah will come and establish God's reign on the earth. Whether Jews will accept that Jesus is the Messiah or not, the prophecy in Daniel chapter two seems to imply that the kingdom the Jews are waiting for was to be established in the time of Rome. Rome has come and gone long ago. What are the Jews waiting for now?

What encouragement and comfort this prophecy gives to Christians! First, they can observe with retrospect the fulfillment of the entire two thousand years of prophecy. Second, they have been provided with undeniable proof that the kingdom of God is indeed *of God* and that it will ultimately overcome every power in the world. *God is in control—do not fear.* Only obey him in righteous, patient service as did Daniel, Shadrach, Meshach and Abednego, and you will be vindicated. This is the message of the prophetic parts of Daniel.

Nebuchadnezzar is totally overcome by Daniel's recital of his dream and its interpretation. He falls prostrate before Daniel, proclaiming, "Surely your God is the God of gods and the Lord of kings and a revealer of mysteries, for you were able to reveal this mystery" (v. 47). Unfortunately, Nebuchadnezzar has not quite put God in his right place yet. Thanks to this religious experience, Nebuchadnezzar admits that God is the chief of the gods. He is not quite ready to acknowledge that he is the *only* true God. Nebuchadnezzar's partial conversion is encouraging, but one should be skeptical of such emotional responses to religious experiences. It would be wiser to do as God does and look for people to "prove their repentance by their deeds" (Acts 26:20).

In gratitude, the king raises Daniel into a high position in his government and showers many gifts on him. His promotion gives Daniel a very practical reminder that his God is in control of nations and kings. In addition, Daniel's three godly friends are promoted along with him. Do you want a promotion at work, but do not want to compromise your walk with God? Follow the example of Daniel, and continued to rely Him with all your heart.

Before moving on to the next dream about the great

tree, it will be important to consider what the critics of Daniel have to say about this astounding prophecy of the four kingdoms. Those who do not accept that the Bible is from God must come up with an answer to this apparent proof that the book of Daniel is of inspired origin. In the later chapters of Daniel, Daniel describes the history of the Near East from his own day up to about 160 B.C. with such astounding accuracy that even the strongest Bible critic has no choice but to admit it is indeed reliable history.

What will the theologian do who is not ready to accept the simple truth that Daniel is from God? They will take the only available alternative. Many theologians have claimed that Daniel was written somewhere around 150 B.C. or later. In other words, these theologians claim that the book of Daniel is only accurate because it was not Daniel who did the writing. Instead, they would claim that an author posing as Daniel described events that had already taken place when the book was written. If this accusation were true, it would certainly put claims of inspiration in a bad light.

There is plenty of evidence to show that this simply cannot be the case. Some of that evidence has already been mentioned; some of it will be described later. For example, the strongest argument supposedly supporting the later date for the writing of Daniel is the language used in the book. As previously shown, the language of Daniel cannot in reality be used to support a second-century B.C. date at all.

Even if, for now, one puts aside the claim that Daniel was written in about 150 B.C., those who want to support a late date for the writing of Daniel (whatever their motivation) encounter a problem in Daniel chapter two. This chapter predicts events, including the establishment of the kingdom of God and details about Rome, which occurred much later than 150 B.C., to say the least. In order to respond to these facts, skeptics have devised the claim that the four kingdoms of Daniel chapter two are not Babylon, Persia/Media, Greece and Rome.

There are different versions of this theory. One of them holds that the four kingdoms are: 1) Nebuchadnezzar himself, 2) Babylon, 3) Persia/Media, and 4) Greece. The second theory names the four kingdoms as: 1) Babylon, 2) Media,

| Dream | "Correct" Explanation | Alternate Theory #1 | Alternate Theory #2 |
|---|---|---|---|
| Head of gold | Babylon | Nebuchadnezzar | Babylon |
| Chest and arms of silver | Persia/Media | Babylon | Media |
| Belly and thighs of bronze | Greece | Persia/Media | Persia |
| Legs of iron | Rome | Greece | Greece |

3) Persia, and 4) Greece. These views will be discussed carefully, but one must remember the purpose of these theories. They are an attempt to explain how the book of Daniel could include such accurate historical detail, without resorting to the explanation that the writing of Daniel comes from God.

The table above shows the four parts of the statue, the correct interpretation of the prophecy and the two most common alternative explanations.

There are a number of reasons to reject the first alternate theory. First, Daniel 2:39 says, "After you, another kingdom will rise." How would Nebuchadnezzar interpret this? Would he interpret his successor, his own son, as "another kingdom" from his own? In fact, all the kings of the Babylonian Empire were related to Nebuchadnezzar, either by direct descent or by marriage. If a separate dynasty had ever ruled Babylon, this might at least have the semblance of believability. Besides this, in studying the four beasts of Daniel 7, which are clearly parallel to the four parts of the statue in chapter two, it will be shown that there is no conceivable way to put Nebuchadnezzar, followed by the rest of the Babylonian Empire, in the place of the first two beasts. In addition to all this, if one were to accept theory #1, it would mean that the church had been established during the time of the Greek kings. Who can believe that explanation?

Theory #2 is the most popular explanation held by liberal theologians.[2] But this theory also has several problems that seem to make it untenable, despite the great number of well-educated people who have supported it. The Babylon-Media-Persia-Greece theory gets in trouble right away. The

Persian ruler Cyrus defeated Astyages, the last independent Median king, in 550 B.C. Babylon existed as an independent kingdom until 539 B.C. In other words, Media lost its status an independent empire *before* the Babylon rule ended. There is no way whatsoever to put Media after Babylon. Media itself was never a truly great empire, and it never had any significant impact on Israel,[3] whereas Babylon, Persia (with its subordinate Median allies) Greece and Rome represent the successive overlords of Israel. It would probably be fair to say that if a student were not predisposed to forcing the fourth kingdom to be Greece, no one would ever have proposed the Babylon-Media-Persia-Greece theory. In addition to the facts mentioned above, this theory would have the Messiah establishing the kingdom of God during the tenure of the Greek kingdom—something which is obviously impossible.

In summary, the four kingdoms of Daniel chapter two are Babylon, Persia/Media, Greece and Rome. God established a kingdom that will never be destroyed—the kingdom of God—during the time of the Roman kings. Those who hold to other theories do so not because the facts of history support them, but rather because they want to uphold a theory that can discount the divine, prophetic nature of the scripture.

In Daniel chapter two, God gives to Nebuchadnezzar every reason to believe that he truly is "the God of gods and the Lord of kings" (v. 47). We would do well to listen to this message and to take encouragement in the secure knowledge that God rules the nations.

# Notes

[1] Taking as its starting point the destruction of Nineveh (612 B.C.), and as its ending point, the Capture of Babylon by Cyrus (539 B.C.), the Babylonian Empire lasted for about 73 years. Taking as its starting point the unification of Media and Persia under Cyrus (550 B.C.) and as its ending point the destruction of the Persian armies by Alexander (331 B.C.), the Persia/Media Empire lasted about 219 years.

[2] In an attempt at an extremely informal survey, I went to the library of the religious-affiliated college where I teach. I pulled three Daniel commentaries from the shelf, which are: *Daniel*, by Norman W. Porteous, (The Westminster Press, 1965), *Daniel: Man of Desires*, by Dom Hubert Van Zeller, (The Newman Press, 1951), and *The Book of Daniel*, by Louis F. Hartman and Alexander A. DiLella, (Doubleday, 1978). All three commentaries mention a variety of theories, but hold to the Babylon, Persia/Media, Greece theory. It would be fair to say that this is the favorite theory of theologians. The theory's most influential proponent is S. R. Driver. See, for example, his book, *Introduction to Old Testament Literature*, by S. R. Driver, (T & T Clark), 1897.

[3] The point is made because all the kingdoms depicted in Daniel's prophecy had a major impact on Israel and/or the church. This is why they are included in a prophetic message to the Jews in the first place. Media does not qualify in any way as a separate empire that significantly affected Israel.

# Chapter Eight

## A King Eats Grass

Daniel chapter four contains a compelling account of how God was able to humble the great King Nebuchadnezzar. When Daniel interprets Nebuchadnezzar's dream of a great tree, he provides further proof that God promotes and demotes whomever he pleases. He shows clearly that God rules the nations. In addition, this chapter provides several practical lessons on pride and humility.

The account is presented as a letter from Nebuchadnezzar to his people. Nebuchadnezzar basically tells his people that the God of the Jews is awesome. He can and will do whatever he wants in the world: "His kingdom endures from generation to generation" (Daniel 4:34). In telling the reader this story, God is using a dramatic method common to the movies and television. The story starts with its concluding scene. The rest of the account, then, is an extended flashback in which Nebuchadnezzar explains to his people the conclusion he has reached regarding the God of Israel.

"I Nebuchadnezzar...had a dream that made me afraid" (vv. 4-5). The setting of this story is a number of years after the dream of the giant statue. Although the writer does not provide a date (such as "in the third year of..."), one can be sure that the dream of the great tree came considerably later in Nebuchadnezzar's life. One reason to believe this is that in the story, Nebuchadnezzar looks out over "the great Babylon [he has] built" (v. 30). The city of Babylon had obviously existed before Nebuchadnezzar. However, the king had overseen such extensive construction projects in his lifetime that he could with some justification describe it to himself as the city he had built. Clearly then, this dream comes somewhere toward the end of the long reign of Nebuchadnezzar (he reigned c. 605-561 B.C.). As a reasonable guess, perhaps the events of this chapter occur about thirty years after the dream of the giant statue.

In the letter, Nebuchadnezzar describes having had a dream which had terrified him. He goes on to explain to his people that, as before, he had called for his "wise men" to interpret the dream. However, this time he told them the content of the dream. Clearly, the magicians, enchanters, astrologers and diviners were now more cautious with their claims and interpretations. They knew that Nebuchadnezzar could tell false prophecy from true. Besides, this time they did not have a death penalty hanging over them if they could not interpret the dream. For these reasons, they admitted to Nebuchadnezzar that they did not know the interpretation.

As the king recalls, he finally called for Daniel, chief of the "magicians." Why hadn't he called for Daniel first? Perhaps he was testing the others, knowing that he would eventually ask for Daniel. If their interpretation conflicted with Daniel's, the king would know he had a deceiver in the ranks. Perhaps he had forgotten about Daniel, although this does not seem likely, even though it had been many years since Daniel had interpreted the dream of the giant statue.

*Figure 20. Nebuchadnezzar glazed brick facade of the palace Throne Room in Babylon, c. 600 B.C. Staatliche Museum zu Berlin.*

In the letter, Nebuchadnezzar relates how he told Daniel the dream. Nebuchadnezzar described seeing an enormous tree in the middle of the land. It was visible from "the ends of the earth" (v. 11). It had abundant fruit. The birds of the air rested in its branches, while the beasts of the field found shade under its leaves. Nebuchadnezzar described how a messenger from heaven came down and with a loud voice commanded that the tree be cut and trimmed down to a bare stump. The fruit was stripped and the birds and animals fled. Finally, the bare stump was bound with iron and bronze, sitting alone in a grassy field. Then the messenger declared:

> Let him be drenched with the dew of heaven, and let him live with the animals among the plants of the earth. Let his mind be changed from that of a man and let him be given the mind of an animal, till seven times pass by for him (Daniel 4:15-16).

Then the angel declared, in a statement sure to make any king nervous:

*Figure 21. Babylon Ishtar Gate relief.*

...The Most High is sovereign over the kingdoms of men and gives them to anyone he wishes and
sets over them the lowliest of men (v. 17).

Here one has a further hint about why the other "wise
men" had chosen not to interpret the dream. Nebuchadnezzar knew the dream was about him, and so did they. No
wonder the dream had terrified him. His astrologers were
afraid to give an interpretation in keeping with the dream
because they believed the king would become very angry.
They assumed, perhaps rightly, that Nebuchadnezzar did
not want to hear the truth.

Often when Christians share their faith, they are confronted with similar situations. Many times when we have
spiritual discussions or even just conversations of a personal
nature, difficult questions arise. One often wonders whether
the question is being asked by someone who sincerely wants
to hear the truth, or perhaps by a person who wants to have
his or her ears tickled. It would be a good idea to follow the
example of Daniel, speaking the truth to people in a loving
way, and trusting God to determine the outcome.

Surely Daniel felt fearful, but he was not overcome
by such fears, even when the question came from a king
who had the power of life or death over him. It was not that
Daniel had absolutely no fear of Nebuchadnezzar. He was
human, after all. However, his fear of God was far greater
than his fear of man.

According to the Bible, fear itself is not sin. *Giving
in* to fear is wrong in God's sight. Jesus expressed this idea
bluntly: "Do not be afraid of those who kill the body but cannot kill the soul. Rather, be afraid of the One who can destroy
both soul and body in hell" (Matthew 10:28). Another relative scripture is Hebrews 13:6 (quoting Psalm 118:6-7): "The
Lord is my helper; I will not be afraid. What can man do to
me?" When asked a difficult question, Daniel's response was
to "[speak] the truth in love" (Ephesians 4:15). The man of
God must not be controlled by sentimentality.

And speaking the truth in love is exactly what Daniel
does in Daniel 4. Daniel says, "My lord, if only the dream
applied to your enemies and its meaning to your adversaries!"

(v. 19). To his boss, who Daniel apparently loved, but who also had the power of life and death over him, Daniel says, "You, O king, are that tree!" (v. 22). As Nebuchadnezzar recounts, Daniel told him that he would be driven away from the throne. Apparently, the king would lose his sanity and go live with the wild animals, eating grass like a cow! Could there be any fate more humiliating for Nebuchadnezzar? Here is a man whom God had raised to the highest position in the world, and God was going to make him lose all he valued: fame, fortune, success and power. How would you like to hear that news? How would you like to be the bearer of such news? Daniel leaves the king with only the slightest hint of some sort of a silver lining in this cloud. After seven "times" of this discipline, if Nebuchadnezzar would acknowledge that all he had came from God, not himself, God would restore his sanity and his position. This was the meaning of the remaining stump of the tree and the iron and bronze that held it together.

At times in the Old Testament, when God announced judgment on a person or a nation through one of his prophets, he declared that it was already too late. The time to repent had passed. Judgment was at hand, and it was time to prepare to meet God. In some cases, however, God pronounced judgment as imminent, but said it was not too late to repent.[1] God declared a time of judgment and described the penalty, but then he would announce that if the person or nation would bow their heads to him and repent of their sins—deciding to obey the Lord God—then he would relent of sending the calamity.

It appears that the second description applied to Nebuchadnezzar in this case. Daniel pleaded with him to renounce his sin of pride and to show his repentance by acts of kindness to the oppressed. He implied that if Nebuchadnezzar would repent, God would not send judgment on him.

Nonetheless, Nebuchadnezzar did not take the advice. It is not that Nebuchadnezzar did not believe Daniel's interpretation of the dream. Lack of intellectual belief was not his problem. It can reasonably be assumed that Nebuchadnezzar even made some preliminary steps to comply with Daniel's advice. Perhaps he made some efforts for the first few months after the dream was interpreted to show more acts of kindness to the people in his kingdom. He may even have acted in a more "spiritual" way for a time as well. However, when the predicted calamity did not befall him for a while, the king slipped back into his prideful ways.

Nebuchadnezzar's actions in this case are certainly not unusual. It is human nature to become convinced about a need to change one's life under the pressure of some extremely stressful event, only to see that conviction gradually fade away along with the vivid memory of the event. Is that how you respond to godly advice? Is it your pattern, when offered admonition from a trusted spiritual person, to make some initial attempts to change, but then slip back into the same old habits after a short period of time? Unfortunately, I have to admit that I have fallen into this pattern a number of times. In that case, one can be sure that lack of true repentance is the problem. Nebuchadnezzar believed the message, but he lacked deep and lasting conviction about his need before God to radically change his life.

"All this happened to King Nebuchadnezzar" (v. 28). All God's promises, whether they are promises of blessings or of judgment, will come to pass just as God has said. A year after the dream and Daniel's interpretation, Nebuchadnezzar had let the initial conviction to humble himself totally slip from his mind. He looked out over Babylon, the most impressive city ever built in the entire world up to that time, and his heart swelled with pride in his work. Nebuchadnezzar had seen to the raising of the world-famous walls of Babylon. Historians have reported that three chariots could race side-by-side on top of the towering wall that encircled the city. The walls of the city were seventeen miles long and forty feet high, with towers over one hundred feet high. The temple of Bel was eight stories high! Nebuchadnezzar had built a great palace as well as the world-famous hanging gardens of Babylon, one of the seven wonders of the ancient world. He looked at these wonders and the multitude of other impressive building projects he had overseen in his life, and said to himself:

> "Is not this the great Babylon I have built as
> the royal residence, by my mighty power and for the

glory of my majesty?" (v. 30)

How prideful! What a fool! How much Nebuchadnezzar is just like us! Now, who built the city? Nebuchadnezzar could tell himself that he had built the city, and in some sense he had, but who put him into the position to build the city? God had prophesied to Israel concerning what Nebuchadnezzar would do one hundred fifty years before it happened (Isaiah 39:5-7). As can be seen from this prophecy of scripture, God had raised Nebuchadnezzar up as his instrument to judge Judah (2 Chronicles 36:15-20). It was not Nebuchadnezzar's power, but God's, which had raised Babylon. Besides, did Nebuchadnezzar really build the city? Try telling that to the workers who did the real work. How many bricks did Nebuchadnezzar lay? Where were his calluses?

Archaeologists have discovered an inscription with interesting parallels to what Nebuchadnezzar said about himself in Daniel 4:30. This inscription has been found in Babylon on what is known as the East India House Inscription. On this inscription is included a statement credited to Nebuchadnezzar: "In Babylon, my dear city, which I love, was the palace, the house of wonder of the people, the bond of the land, the brilliant place, the abode of the majesty in Babylon." Presumably, "the majesty" was Nebuchadnezzar himself. Another Babylonian inscription with parallels to Daniel 4:30 is known as the Grotefend Cylinder. On this cylinder is found this statement, in Nebuchadnezzar's name: "Then I built the palace, the seat of my royalty, the bond of the race of men, the dwelling of joy and rejoicing."

It is so easy for us to be exactly like Nebuchadnezzar. We might say to ourselves, "Look at this degree I worked so hard to earn;" or "Look at this great career I have built by my hard work and perseverance;" or perhaps, "Look at these awesome kids I have raised. Oh yes, my husband helped a bit as well;" or, "Look at this great church we have built: We have so many members and such a nice building to meet in." Another favorite is, "I have really helped a lot of people," or, "I really am a good person." Sometimes we are not so bold as to declare these words outright, as Nebuchadnezzar did, but in our hearts the thoughts are there. Where is the acknowledgement of God, who gave us the power to do what we did in the first place? To quote the apostle Paul, "What do you have that you did not receive? And if you did receive it, why do you boast as though you did not?" (1 Corinthians 4:7).

That is a good question. What good thing do any of us have—what skill, ability, good quality, accomplishment or wisdom do we have—that was not given to us by God? And if it is from God, what cause is there for boasting? The following story illustrates the impact of ungratefulness.

One day, Tim found out that his best friend, Bob, was getting married. Rather than going out and buying some boring present, Tim decided to make something with his hands. Actually, he was not much of an artist, but he was good at working with cars, so Tim found a really old, beat-up classic car. It did not cost him much, but he spent hours and hours restoring it, to the point where if he had known the number of hours it was going to take, he might not have undertaken the project. Finally, just before the wedding, Tim presented his prized work to his best friend. Of course, Bob was flabbergasted and overwhelmed Tim with thanks. "How could I ever thank you enough for this gift?" he asked.

A few years passed, and Bob and his wife had moved to another city a few hundred miles away, so Tim did not see him as often, but remained in close contact. One day, Tim was having a conversation with Joe, when they discovered that they had a mutual friend in Bob. Joe said, "Have you seen his car? He told me how he bought the car as a total junker and spent countless hours fixing it up. What an accomplishment!"

Tim was devastated. He felt his years-long friendship with Bob had been betrayed, that Bob would lie about and take the credit for what had been a profound labor of love. He felt the overwhelming thanks Bob had professed must have been a sham, and that Bob must be truly ungrateful for his friendship and for the gift that had been the expression of it. He felt so hurt that he did not know how to reveal his feelings to his friend. From that time on, whenever Bob called, Tim made excuses for how he did not have time to get together. Tim never called Bob again, and eventually Bob gave up as well, asking himself, "I wonder what happened to our friendship?"

Are we like Nebuchadnezzar—more subtle and more "spiritual," but still an ingrate? God knows our sinful nature well. He warned the Israelites: "When you have eaten and are satisfied, praise the Lord your God...do not forget the Lord your God...Otherwise, when you eat and are satisfied, *when you build fine houses and settle down*...then your heart will become proud and you will forget the Lord your God, who brought you out of Egypt, out of the land of slavery.... You may say to yourself, 'My power and the strength of my hands have produced this wealth for me.' But remember the Lord your God, *for it is he who gives you the ability to produce wealth*" (Deuteronomy 8:10-18).

Nebuchadnezzar did learn this lesson, but he was to learn it the hard way. While the words, "and for the glory of my majesty" were still on his lips, a voice rang out from heaven, interrupting the king in the middle of the conversation he was having with himself. Judgment time!

The Bible obviously does not use the terms of modern clinical psychology, making it difficult to know exactly what happened to the king, but apparently Nebuchadnezzar immediately became insane. He changed eating patterns, joining the munch-for-lunch bunch ("Nebuchadnezzar ate grass like cattle," v. 33). Perhaps in total confusion, he wandered away from the city. Or maybe his ministers covered up what was happening and hid him away in some inner area of the palace. If that is the case, then he must have been so unmanageable that they could not even cut his hair, which "grew like the feathers of an eagle," or his nails, which were "like the claws of a bird" (v. 33).

God took away from Nebuchadnezzar everything he valued: his power, his wisdom, his kingdom, and his ability to oversee great construction projects. His insanity lasted for "seven times" (v. 32). Authors have argued over the meaning of this term. It may mean seven years or it may mean seven months. Given that the number seven has the symbolic meaning of completeness in Hebrew writings, it may simply mean that the discipline of the Lord lasted until it was sufficient to accomplish what God had in mind—the humbling of Nebuchadnezzar.

What we do know is that it took a long time for Nebuchadnezzar to come to his senses and give the glory to God that he deserved. Surely, Jehovah is a gracious God. His patience is great, but it is not absolutely unlimited. Why did it take so long for Nebuchadnezzar to come to his senses? If one of us were God, our patience would have run out long before Nebuchadnezzar came around. This situation is reminiscent of Jonah in the belly of the big fish.[2] He was in there for three days before he finally got around to humbling himself and praying that great prayer (Jonah 2:1-9). What was he doing during the first two days?

So finally Nebuchadnezzar repented: "Then I praised the Most High; I honored and glorified him who lives forever" (v. 34). Nebuchadnezzar was able to say, "Now I, Nebuchadnezzar, praise and exalt and glorify the King of heaven, because everything he does is right and all his ways are just" (v. 37). Amen to that!

Now, Nebuchadnezzar is able to make the great statement that is the theme of the fourth chapter of Daniel: "Those who walk in pride he is able to humble" (v. 37). One could add that because God loves us, those who walk in pride God *will* humble. Do not be deceived: "God opposes the proud" (James 4:6); "I hate pride and arrogance" (Proverbs 8:13). No prideful person will see the face of God:

> Never again will you be haughty on my holy hill. But I will leave within you the meek and humble, who trust in the name of the Lord (Zephaniah 3:11-12).

In general, God works in one of two ways in people's lives to humble them. One way God can humble his children is by pouring out his blessings on them. This is God's preferred method of bringing his people to their knees. God wants so badly to pour out his love for his children in great and manifold blessings. His hope is that blessings will drive those who receive them to their knees to thank him for all they have received. A great example of this principle is contained in 1 Chronicles 29:10-20. All God wants is for us to acknowledge that everything we have comes from him. The only thing we have that we did not receive from God is our own sin.

Sadly, for most people, if God were to pour all the blessings on them that he would like, they would pull a Nebuchadnezzar on him. Even among disciples of Jesus, only a small fraction could handle great riches, fame and power without it going to their head. Most of us should be thankful that God has not allowed us be more wealthy than we already are. We simply cannot handle great wealth without becoming prideful. This ought to reflect humbly on his or her situation in life.

This leads to God's other way to humble his people. This is not his preferred way to humble us. God will discipline us if we walk in pride like Nebuchadnezzar. Because he loves us, as long as there is still hope that our hearts can be turned, God will allow us to face whatever trials are necessary, until we are brought to our knees. Let us be wise and help God out here. Let us get honest with ourselves, and remember the admonition of 1 Corinthians 4:7. We may have some great things in our lives, but we only have them by the grace of God. We should especially remember the message of the cross, that we are only saved by the grace of God. If we remain humble and grateful, perhaps God will be able to use the first method to humble us, rather than the second.

## Apologetics and Daniel Four

Did all this really happen? Critics of Daniel have attacked the book over the story of Nebuchadnezzar going insane for such a long time, then later regaining his sanity and being returned to power. The claim is that the story is simply unbelievable at its face value. Besides, the critics argue, there is no outside evidence to support the story. The claim that there is no outside evidence to support the story is actually not true. It so happens that the early Christian writer Eusebius described a report from the Greek historian Abydenus.[3] Abydenus was not a Jew, and presumably he was not aware of the account in Daniel. Yet he recorded that in the latter days of Nebuchadnezzar the king was "possessed by some god or other." Abydenus reported that immediately after this "possession," Nebuchadnezzar disappeared for a time. Here one has a hint from a non-biblical source in corroboration with the Biblical account. So much for the claim that there is no evidence to support the story recorded in Daniel chapter four.

Besides, who is to say that the story is unbelievable? King George III of England had on-and-off bouts with uncontrolled psychotic behavior. During his times of complete incapacitation, his ministers removed him from the spotlight and kept the wheels of government rolling without him for months and even years at a time. When George had periods of lucidity, they would prop him back up on his throne until the next time he went through a spell of insanity. It seems likely that, similar to King George, Nebuchadnezzar's chief ministers kept a form of government going, with the king as a titular head, as long as his insanity lasted. In doing so, they were able to keep their own profitable position and influence. It is interesting to speculate that Daniel himself may have served as the chief ruler of Babylon at this time. The history of Europe contains several similar examples to that of King George III. The story of the dream and its fulfillment is in fact quite believable.

A British writer Raymond Harris reports a case with remarkable similarity to that of Nebuchadnezzar's. Harris has described the case of a patient in a British mental institution with a condition that has been called boanthropy.[4]

A great many doctors spend an entire, busy professional career without once encountering an instance of the kind of monomania described in the book of Daniel. The present writer, therefore, considers himself particularly fortunate to have actually observed a clinical case of boanthropy in a British mental institution in 1946. A patient was in his early 20s who reportedly had been hospitalized for about five years. His symptoms were well developed on admission, and diagnosis was immediate and conclusive. He was of average height and weight with good physique, and was in excellent bodily health. His mental symptoms included pronounced anti-social tendencies, and because of this he spent the entire day from dawn to dusk outdoors, in the grounds of the institution....His daily routine consisted of wandering around the magnificent lawns with which the otherwise dingy hospital situation was graced, and it was his custom to pluck up and eat handfuls of the grass as he went along. On observation he was seen to discriminate carefully between grass and weeds.... The writer was able to examine him cursorily, and the only physical abnormality noted consisted of a lengthening of the hair and a coarse, thickened condition of the fingernails.

Nebuchadnezzar's symptoms are unusual, for sure, but they do not appear to be unique. In summary, through the dream and the interpretation by Daniel, as well as through the fulfillment of the dream, Nebuchadnezzar learned that God "does as he pleases with the powers of heaven and the peoples of the earth" (Daniel 4:35). *God rules the nations.* It is a big mistake to give ourselves credit for our accomplishments without giving God the glory. God can and will humble those who walk in pride. This would have been a great comfort to those who remained faithful in spite of great persecution in the days of Antiochus IV Epiphanes. It should also be a great comfort to us, if we are willing to humble ourselves before our God.

*Figure 22.*
*Bas relief of King Cyrus.*

## Notes

[1] As an example of the former, consider Jeremiah 4:11-28, especially v. 28. As examples of the latter, consider 2 Chronicles 32:24-26 and Ezekiel 18:30-32.

[2] Speaking of Jonah, is he not also a historical/prophetic type of Jesus Christ? He was in the belly of the fish for three days. Jesus used this as an anology to his being in the grave: "For as Jonah was three days and three nights in the belly of a huge fish, so the Son of Man will be three days and three nights in the heart of the earth" (Matthew 12:40). Besides this, Jonah went to a people not his own and preached repentance and salvation. The parallels to the life of Jesus are clear.

[3] Eusebius, *Praeparatio Evangelica,* 9.41.1.

[4] Raymond Harrison, *Introduction to the Old Testament*, (Peabody, Mass., Hendrickson Publishers, 2004), pp. 1116-1117.

# Chapter Nine

## A Beastly Encounter

"In the first year of Belshazzar king of Babylon, Daniel had a dream, and visions passed through his mind" (Daniel 7:1). This dream most likely occurred in the year 553 B.C., when Belshazzar became official regent to his father Nabonidus. This chapter of Daniel begins in earnest the apocalyptic parts of the book. The vision will provide the reader with a considerable amount of detail about the three kingdoms to follow Babylon, especially about the fourth kingdom: Rome. The amazing details contained in this prophecy about the distant future provide overwhelming evidence of the inspiration of Daniel. They also serve as an exclamation point to the message of Daniel: *God rules the nations—do not fear.*

After his dream, Daniel writes down the details of what he had seen. "In my vision at night I looked, and there before me were the four winds of heaven churning up the great sea" (v. 2). In apocalyptic writing, the great sea stands for the nations of mankind.[1] The winds represent the working or the power of God.[2] Here we have in prophetic vision God stirring up the nations. He is working behind the scenes to influence the great powers of the world. God does not stir up the nations merely for his entertainment—he has a plan. As the book of Daniel will reveal, the plan, ultimately, is to usher in his Kingdom and everlasting righteousness.

"Four great beasts, each different from the others, came up out of the sea" (v. 3). What an fearsome picture! Here can be seen four great beasts, representing four great nations. These beasts/nations rise up out of the sea—in other words, they distinguish themselves as much greater than all the other nations. As will be shown from a study of the text of chapter seven, these four beasts represent Babylon, Persia/Media, Greece and Rome. The four beasts in Daniel chapter seven, therefore, represent the same four empires as did the four parts of the statue in Daniel chapter two.

Why use a statue in chapter two and beasts in chapter seven? One possible explanation is that a statue is used in chapter two because in that dream God was emphasizing the fact that he had raised up these nations himself, only to ultimately have the church rise up and overcome all these kingdoms. In chapter seven, God may use beasts because he has in mind the power of these empires. The subject of the vision is largely how these nations will attack God's people, especially the fourth beast, so God is emphasizing the fearsome aspects of the beasts.

"The first was like a lion, and it had the wings of an eagle" (v. 4). This is the Neo-Babylonian Empire, whose greatest king was Nebuchadnezzar. The lion represents the strength of Babylon. In Jeremiah 48:40 one reads, "Look! An eagle is swooping down, spreading its wings over Moab." The eagle in Jeremiah 48:40 is Babylon, which destroyed the nation of Moab once and for all. While Daniel watches this lion, it loses its wings and turns from a terrifying beast into the form of a human. Surpisingly, this beast is even given a human heart. This transformation of the great beast Babylon into a human with a heart represents the transformation of Nebuchadnezzar from the greatest enemy and destroyer of Judah into a humbled supporter of the people and religion of Israel. This passage is not "prophetic" in the sense of predicting the future. Rather, it accurately describes events that had already occurred when Daniel received the vision. The description of the next three beasts, however, will be very much prophetic.

The second beast looks "like a bear" (v. 5). This bear is the Persia/Media Empire. In this fearful vision, the beast is seen to have "three ribs in its mouth between its teeth." This image puts fear into the heart of Daniel. The three ribs are what remain of three smaller "beasts" that this empire has feasted upon. In fact, after being united into a single empire under Cyrus, the Persians and Medes conquered three major powers. The first of these was Lydia, whose famous king Croesus was considered by Greek writers to be the wealthiest monarch of all history. Lydia was the inheritor of Hittite power. Cyrus destroyed this kingdom in 546 B.C. The second rib in the mouth of the bear is Babylon. Cyrus completed the destruction of Babylon in 539 B.C., as already discussed. The third great world power destroyed by the Persians (and Medes) was Egypt. The Assyrians had temporarily occupied Egypt. In addition, the enigmatic Hyskos had briefly conquered Egypt. However, it was the work of Cyrus' son Cambyses that brought the native dynasties of Egypt once and for all to an end. This feat was completed in about 524 B.C.

There you have it. That is why there were three ribs in the mouth of the bear: not two, not four, but three. How did Daniel know this? One could argue for luck or coincidence. By the time one has completed studying the predictive prophecies in Daniel chapter seven (never mind all the other prophecies in Daniel), coincidence will be eliminated as a reasonable explanation.

*Figure 23.*
*Alexander the Great.*

The third beast is one "like a leopard" (v. 6). This beast has four bird-like wings and four heads. This beast is equivalent to the bronze belly and thighs in Daniel chapter two. Why four wings and four heads? In apocalyptic language, heads represent kings or kingdoms. It so happens that the Greek Empire, after the death of Alexander, was divided into four sub-empires. More will be said about these successor-kingdoms to Alexander in the context of Daniel chapter eight, which supplies more information about these kingdoms. Should one be surprised that there were indeed four successors, not five or three, to Alexander? Is this just coincidence? God's foretelling of this event well over two hundred years in advance lends powerful credence to his claim that he himself gave Alexander and the Greek kingdoms authority to rule (v. 6).

Next, a fourth beast appears to Daniel. This beast is much more terrible than the other three. It is so "terrifying and frightening and very powerful" that no beast known to man is used to describe it. A lion or a tiger or a bear would not do it justice. The vision of Daniel chapter seven focuses primarily on this fourth beast. Consider the description of this horrible beast: "It had large iron teeth; it crushed and devoured its victims and trampled underfoot whatever was left. It was different from all the former beasts, and it had ten horns" (v. 7). The similarity to the iron part of the statue in Daniel chapter two is obvious. Both images refer to the same nation: Rome. Would you be very surprised if it is possible to identify specifically the ten horns in the vision?

After this, Daniel sees in his vision a little horn that rises up among the ten horns. For a person reading this passage for the first time, the scene with the little horn may seem like a strange prophecy. What can this small horn possibly represent? For the person not well versed in history, this prophecy and its interpretation would remain a mystery (an *apokalupsis*), but as we will see, the meaning is clear when viewed in the light of history. In verse 11, Daniel adds the detail that this small horn speaks boastful words. There is no doubt of the apocalyptic nature of this passage when one finds a horn speaking boastful words. Surely one should take this symbolically, not literally!

The task, then, is to understand the interpretation of the ten horns and the little horn that grew up among the ten. Fortunately, unlike other visions in the book, Daniel is provided with at least a partial interpretation of the dream. In Daniel 7:15-28, a being who is presumably an angel interprets Daniel's dream for him. Daniel is so troubled by the fearful vision of the fourth beast that he approaches "one of those standing there" (v. 16) to ask the meaning.

He is told, "The four great beasts are four kingdoms that will rise from the earth" (v. 17). We already knew that. The angel continues, "But the saints of the Most High will receive the kingdom and will possess it forever—yes, for ever and ever" (v. 18). This encouraging verse will be discussed shortly.

Next, Daniel asks the angel specifically about the fourth beast—the one that was almost indescribably terrifying, and about the ten horns and the extra little horn. It is interesting that in this description, Daniel adds bronze claws to the list of attributes of the fourth beast. He also adds about the little horn that, despite its size, it was more imposing than the others, and that it "had eyes and a mouth that spoke boastfully" (v. 20).[3] Next, Daniel gives a very revealing detail: The unique horn "was waging war against the saints and defeating them" (v. 21).

The explanation given by the angel concerning the fourth beast and the horns is that the fourth beast is a kingdom (Rome) that will devour the whole earth. The ten horns are ten kings in this kingdom (Rome), while the "little horn" is another king who will come after these. The last king will depose three of the other horns (kings). He will speak against God, oppress the saints, "try to change the set times and laws," and, finally, have the saints handed over to him "for a time, times and half a time" (v. 25). Whew! There is a lot there. Daniel must have been mystified by this explanation. Surely he had absolutely no idea what the angel was talking about. Fortunately, he faithfully recorded his vision, because, with historical hindsight, we can know *exactly* what God is talking about.

Before interpreting this portion of Daniel's dream, it will be very helpful to note the undeniable parallel between this vision, given to Daniel in 553 B.C., and those recorded in Revelation 13:1-10 and in Revelation 17:1-18. These latter visions were recorded somewhere around 80 A.D.—more than six hundred years after Daniel's dream. It is suggested that the reader scan the parallel passages in Revelation at this time to get a sense of the ways that they are indeed parallel to Daniel chapter seven.

Who are these kings? In looking at the history of Rome (the fourth beast) the task is surprisingly simple. The Roman Empire was originally a republic. The form of this government was a bit complicated, but to simplify, up until the first century B.C., Rome was governed by a senate, which was directly elected by the citizens of Rome.[4] In the first century B.C., a series of very powerful generals began a pattern of ruling by the force of their personal armies. The most famous of these dictators was Julius Caesar. A great number of civil wars erupted in the battle between the Roman senate and competing generals. Finally, Julius Caesar's adopted grandson Octavius, later called Augustus Caesar, seized power over Rome and the senate, once and for all. He is universally considered to be the first emperor of Rome. Although the senate continued in existence, after this point the balance of power had permanently shifted almost entirely to the emperors. Augustus is the first of the ten kings (horns) in Daniel chapter seven. He was also the emperor at the time of the birth of Jesus Christ.

Some commentators, of course, will argue with assigning Augustus as the first of the kings, but further historical detail to be offered in this chapter will confirm this identification to anyone who does not have a preconceived notion to the contrary in the matter. The successor to Augustus was his son Tiberius, who ruled at the time of Christ's death. After him, in order, came Claudius, Gaius (also known as Caligula), Nero, Galba, Otho, Vitellius, Vespasian and Titus. These are the ten kings. The "little horn" is the successor to Titus, Domitian. Domitian ruled Rome from 81-96 A.D. (see table on the next page).

Daniel chapter seven is therefore primarily about Domitian, the eleventh emperor of Rome. Think about it. That is astounding, because Domition ruled over six hundred years after Daniel received his vision. If this claim is true, it will provide quite dramatic proof of the inspiration of Daniel, to say the least. It would be difficult to overstate how strong a support to the Bible this is. The miraculous accuracy of the prophecy in Daniel seven also provided great encouragement to those going through the persecutions under Domitian (and the later Roman persecutors). If God can reveal to his people specific details about Domitian hundreds of years before he even exists—before Israel has even heard of the tiny city-state of Rome—it would provide good evidence that the judgment pronounced on Domitian in Daniel 7 would also come to pass.

## The First Eleven Emperors of Rome

| Emperor | Dates of Rule | Significance to Biblical Events |
|---|---|---|
| Augustus | 27 B.C.-14 A.D. | Birth of Christ |
| Tiberius | 14-37 A.D. | Crucifixion of Christ |
| Gaius (Caligula) | 37-41 A.D. | Attempted to put his image in the Temple |
| Claudius | 41-54 A.D. | Jews exiled from Rome |
| Nero | 54-68 A.D. | First serious persecutions; execution of Paul and Peter |
| Galba | 68-69 A.D. | One of the three overcome by Vespasian |
| Otho | 69-70 A.D. | One of the three... |
| Vitellius | 69-70 A.D.. | One of the three... |
| Vespasian | 69-79 A.D. | Attack on Jerusalem |
| Titus | 79-81 A.D. | The general who destroyed Jerusalem |
| Domitian | 81-96 A.D. | First systematic persecutor of the church |

Consider some details from the life of Domitian, the great persecutor of the church. Domitian was not actually the first Roman emperor to attack the Christian church. Nero (54-68 A.D.) deserves that distinction. Daniel's vision does not focus on Nero, perhaps because his attacks on the church were limited. The persecutions of Nero, although violent, occurred almost exclusively in Rome, and lasted for a relatively short time. They were more of a temper tantrum than a systematic policy of attacking the church. Actually, the parallel passage in Revelation 17:3-18 does deal specifically with Nero.[5] Domitian, on the other hand, was the first to institute a definite empire-wide policy of destroying the church of Christ. Compare this with the statements in Daniel concerning the little horn: "This horn was waging war against the saints and defeating them" (v. 21), and the horn would "oppress his saints" (v. 25).

*Figure 24. Domitian (c. 81-96 A.D.) with detail of a marble bust in the Palazzo dei Conservatori, Rome, Italy.*

Domitian was well known for being a braggart. Emperor-worship was begun in the eastern part of the empire under Augustus, but there is no record of Augustus encouraging the practice. Caligula was the first emperor to encourage the people to worship him as a god, but Domitian was the first to actively demand that his subjects worship him. The Roman historian Suetonius reported of Domitian:[6]

> "From his youth he was far from being of an affable disposition, but was on the contrary presumptuous and unbridled in both act and word."

When his father's former concubine was returned to Domitian, Seutonius quotes him as saying that he had "recalled her to his divine couch." Also, according to Seutonius, "With no less arrogance he began as follows in issuing a circular letter in the name of his procurators, 'Our Master and our God bids that this be done.' And so the custom arose henceforth of addressing him in no other way even in writing or in conversation."

*Figure 25. Roman Emperor Tiberius (c. 14-37 A.D.). Adopted son of Augustus in Ny Carlsberg Glyptotek, Copenhagen, Denmark.*

So Domitian was the first to demand emperor worship. This explains the statements that the little horn had "a mouth that spoke boastfully" (vv. 8, 20), and the reference in verse eleven to "the boastful words the horn was speaking." Also, the prediction that the little horn would "speak against the Most High" (v. 25) is a reference to the fact that Domitian specifically demanded of Christ's disciples that they offer sacrifice to him as a god. In fact, Domitian was so arrogant that after his death to be "a Domitian" became an idiom in Rome to denote an extremely arrogant person. Domitian was a symbol of abject pride to Rome.

The seventh chapter of Daniel supplies even more specific detail about Domitian. In Daniel 7:8, Daniel says concerning the little horn that "three of the first horns were uprooted before it." This prediction is also mentioned in Daniel 7:20. This detail refers to the three very short-lived emperors Galba, Otho and Vitellius. These three emperors all ruled during the tumultuous years A.D. 68 and 69 following the demise of the last of the direct descendents of Augustus. In fact, all three were generals who were declared emperor by their troops. The reigns of the three overlapped and none was ever able to rule the entire empire. Ultimately, the emperor Vespasian completely uprooted all three of these generals by the year A.D. 70.

*Figure 26. Roman Emperor and persecutor Nero (c. 54-68 A.D.) in the Roman National Museum, Rome, Italy.*

It is somewhat difficult to know for sure why Daniel 7 refers to the little horn as having uprooted the three, as it was actually Domitian's father Vespasian who did the primary uprooting, not Domitian. One possible answer is that when General Vespasian defeated the three pseudo-emperors Galba, Otho and Vitellius, in God's mind it was as if Domitian had done it. The defeat of the three generals by Domitian's father did indeed ultimately bring Domitian to the throne. In point of fact, Domitian was directly involved in uprooting Vitellius. While his father was on his way back to Rome to accept the throne, Domitian, his younger son, was already in the capital. Domitian took the field, helping to defeat the third of the uprooted horns, Vitellius.

For another hint as to why God, through Daniel, describes Domitian (the little horn) as if he were the one who uprooted the three, one can look to the parallel passage in Revelation 17. Revelation 17:7-8 refers to a beast that "once was, now is not, and will come up out of the Abyss and go to his destruction," and describes the beast as having "seven heads and ten horns." The ten horns in Revelation 17 are the same ten kings referred to in Daniel 7, while the seven heads are the same ten, excluding Galba, Otho and Vitellius, the three weak, relatively unimportant (especially to church history) kings. This allows the writer of Revelation to refer to Domitian using the phrase, "The beast who once was, and now is not, is an eighth king. He belongs to the seven and is going to his destruction" (v. 11).

*Figure 27. Vespasian (c. 69-79 A.D.) in Rome, Italy.*

In Revelation, then, Domitian is referred to as the eleventh king and as the eighth king. In a sense he was both. The number eight had great significance to the Christian church, as they worshiped on the eighth day. Christians traditionally called their special day of worship "the eighth day," rather than the first day of the week, to emphasize the fact that it falls immediately after the Jewish Sabbath (the seventh day). In the Sybilline Oracles, Christ is referred to numerically as 888. Revelation 17 refers to Domitian as the eighth king who belongs to the seven. In other words, he is a sub-king to the seven. This may well refer to Domitian as the successor to Nero. Although in the physical sense he succeeded his brother Titus, as far as the church was concerned, he succeeded Nero as the next persecutor of the church.

This is admittedly somewhat of a difficult argument, but to summarize, for symbolic reasons having to do with the numbers seven and ten, God chose to number the kings both with and without the three. It is interesting that the facts of history, with nearly three simultaneous semi-emperors, make it perfectly reasonable to count either seven or ten Roman emperors as having preceded Domitian. The question one can ask is, how did Daniel know about these eleven kings of Rome? And how did he get right the extremely unusual fact that the eleventh king (Domitian) helped to uproot the eighth (Vitellius); three kings before him?

*Figure 28. Roman Emperor Claudius I (c. 41-54 A.D.) in the Vatican Museum, Rome, Italy.*

Daniel chapter seven supplies a few more historical details concerning the eleventh horn. The vision reveals that he will "try to change the set times and the laws" (v. 25). Be prepared to be very impressed by Daniel's vision. Domitian, in his pride, did just what Daniel predicted. He changed the names of the "set times." He had the names of the months of his accession and of his birth changed, from September and October to Germanicus (his surname) and Domitianus. This prideful ruler "tried to change" the calendar, exactly as Daniel had described over six hundred years before! By the way, there was precedent in Rome for changing the name of a month in honor of a great ruler. Our month August is named after Augustus Caesar. Our July comes from Julius Caeser. However, there is a big difference. Augustus and Julius did not have the arrogance to change the names themselves. This was done after their deaths. Besides, they were truly great men. No one considered Domitian great, except perhaps himself. Domitian had two months named after himself while he was still alive. The Roman people showed better sense than their prideful ruler. Because Domitian was so unpopular, his attempt was unsuccessful and the calendar went back to its old names immediately after Domitian's death (noting that Daniel did not say the eleventh horn changed the set times, but that he tried to change them, which is exactly what happened).

There is more. Being the arrogant autocrat that he was, Domitian changed more than just the calendar; he also "changed the laws"—many laws, in fact. The prophecy refers to his having altered the law by which Roman senators were chosen. He passed a decree giving himself the right to choose every senator. It is not surprising that during Domitian's reign the senate was composed of many "yes men." The system of Roman law, to this day, is arguably the most famous in history. Yet, this prideful emperor tried to overthrow the entire Roman legal system. Domitian's tyrannical and cruel reign was so resented that, upon his assassination, all his laws and decrees were declared void, and all images of him were destroyed.

How did Daniel know all these spectacular details about the onset of the Roman persecution of the church and the career of its first persecutor, more than six hundred years before it happened? There is only one conceivable explanation: that he was inspired by the all-knowing God.

So far, God is presenting to his people a lot of bad news. Isn't Daniel supposed to be the prophet of comfort? The good news is about to come. Up to this point we have seen God telling Daniel (and anyone else reading the book) that at some time during the fourth empire (Rome), an eleventh king will arise (Domitian) who, in his arrogance, will attack the people of God. His attacks will appear to succeed, up to a point.

*Figure 29. Roman Emperor Trajan (c. 98-117 A.D.) after he replaced Domitian - British Museum.*

Next, however, God reveals to Daniel the good news: Ultimately, Domitian as well as the persecuting power he represents, will be judged. God's faithful people will be vindicated and the Roman persecutor will be destroyed. The Lord God Almighty enters the scene!

> As I looked, thrones were set in place, and the Ancient of Days took his seat. His clothing was as white as snow; the hair of his head was white like wool. His throne was flaming with fire, and its wheels were all ablaze. A river of fire was flowing, coming out from before him. Thousands upon thousands attended him; ten thousand times ten thousand stood before him (Daniel 7:9-10).

Here we see the throne of God described in vivid apocalyptic language. This passage has much in common with Ezekiel chapter one. God is very upset with what is happening to his people. He has allowed his people to suffer at the hands of Domitian and his successors up to a point. The limit to which God will allow his people to be persecuted has been reached. Now the books are open. By comparison with Revelation 20, we know it is judgment day.[7]

Those who are undergoing great persecution for the sake of the gospel may very well be tempted to ask God why they are suffering at the hands of ungodly people. It may not seem right to them that God would allow the unrighteous to prosper at their expense. Daniel "continued to watch" (v. 11) the boastful words of the little horn, probably thinking to himself, "When is someone going to do something to stop this?" He keeps looking "until the beast was slain and its body destroyed and thrown into the blazing fire" (v. 11). God is willing to let his people be persecuted, but only up to a certain point. There comes a time when he will no longer endure the suffering of his people and the arrogance of their enemies. Then it is judgment time, and "it is a dreadful thing to fall into the hands of the living God" (Hebrews 10:31). God is pronouncing judgment both on Domitian (and the other Roman persecutors who followed him) and on the beast (Rome). However, as John says after seeing the parallel vision in Revelation: "This calls for patient endurance and faithfulness on the part of the saints" (Revelation 13:10). Rome did not fall in a day—even when it came to God's judgment.

How long will the faithful disciples of Jesus have to endure this persecution under Domitian before God steps in to deal with the persecutor? The angel tells Daniel that, "The saints will be handed over to him for a time, times and half a time" (Daniel 7:25). The question of a "time" being a reference to a literal year will come up later in Daniel. Suffice it to say for now that in this case, it is certainly not meant to signify a literal three and one-half years. God uses the number three and one-half to symbolically describe the duration of the persecution.

A parallel example of this use of three and one-half "times" or years to represent the duration of judgment is found in Revelation 11:2, where it said that the Gentiles "will trample on the holy city for 42 months." Here one sees that "times" in Daniel 7:25 means years (even if they are not literal years) because 42 months is three and one-half years. Other biblical precedent for three and one half-years being symbolic of a limited period of persecution can be mentioned. Three and one-half is exactly half of the number seven. Seven is the biblical number of perfection or completeness. Three and one-half, therefore, represents an indefinite but limited time. This is a common figure in apocalyptic speech.[8] The implication of the three and one-half years or "times," then, is that the persecution will be intense, but will only last for a limited time.

Next, enter Jesus Christ. What a dramatic vision! Daniel says:

> ...And there before me was one like a son of man, coming with the clouds of heaven. He approached the Ancient of Days...He was given authority, glory and sovereign power; all peoples, nations and men of every language worshiped him. His dominion is an everlasting dominion that will not pass away, and his kingdom is one that will never be destroyed (Daniel 7:13-14).

Some claim that Jesus made his first appearance in the Bible in the New Testament. Could anyone question that this is Jesus himself? Consider Matthew 28:18-20, where Jesus uses the almost identical words about himself: "All authority in heaven and on earth has been given to me." Does that sound familiar? What about Jesus' command, "Go and make disciples of all nations"? Is there not a parallel here as well? "And surely I will be with you always, to the very end of the age"—Jesus' promise in verse 20 mirrors these words in Daniel 7:14, "His dominion is an everlasting dominion that will not pass away." Also consider Matthew 26:64, in which Jesus quotes Daniel, using the phrase "coming on the clouds of heaven" to refer specifically to himself. Daniel has a vision of Jesus Christ in his majestic glory!

Through Daniel, God is telling his people that it may get tough, but God rules the nations and they should not fear. In the darkest of times, it may seem that "the prince of this world" is in total control, but one should always remember that "the saints of the Most High will receive the kingdom and will possess it forever—yes, for ever and ever" (v. 17). Nations will come and go. Persecution against God's saints will at times become very intense, but ultimately, the kingdom of God will outlast them all. Praise God for these great words of comfort!

To summarize, in the seventh chapter of Daniel, God produces a miracle that defies natural explanation. In vivid detail, he describes for us the onset of the persecution of his saints under Roman domination, almost six hundred years before the kingdom of God was even begun—and well over six hundred years before the persecution actually occurred. So much for the efforts of theologians who so diligently attempt to disprove Daniel's divine inspiration by claiming the book was written after the prophesied events ever occurred! Even if Daniel were written in 150 B.C., Domitian's reign was still two hundred years in the future! How could the writer of Daniel predict, in detail, the personality of Domitian and specifics about his persecutions? The only viable explanation, even with a composition date of 150 B.C., would be that God inspired the author. Do these skeptical religious teachers have some reasonable explanation for Daniel chapter seven? Read one of their books and decide for yourself.[9]

God prophetically reveals these events in such detail, so many years before they happened, not because he wants to be a show-off, but because he wants to provide his people with the most faith-building comfort he can. He wants to give them convincing evidence that, even as they are undergoing the worst kind of persecution, if they will remain faithful, even to the point of death, he will be with them. God's righteous man or woman will never be forsaken. This should provide great comfort and assurance, not only to the early Christians, but to present-day believers as well. God rules the nations and God rules the rulers of those nations. Do not fear.

## Notes

[1] For examples, see Revelation 13:1 and Isaiah 57:20. Also, Revelation 17:15 equates "the waters" with "peoples, multitudes, nations and languages."

[2] Consider Jeremiah 49:36, Ezekiel 13:11, Ezekiel 37:9, Hebrews 1:7 and Revelation 7:1.

[3] By now, the reader has noticed that we are not analyzing Daniel 7 verse-by-verse. This is because Daniel describes the vision in the order in which it actually happened, while our analysis is being done detail-by-detail, using the vision and the interpretation.

[4] The senators were representatives of the large landowner class. In the late second century and into the first century B.C., a second body, called the equestrian order, began to share power in a significant way with the senate. This body represented the merchant class. In addition, the "People" (the plebes) shared power with the senate and the equestrian order. The plebes represented the direct will of the people. For more details, almost any book of Roman history would do. For example, see *From the Gracchi to Nero,* by H. H. Scullard, (Methuen Publishing Ltd., 1970). This title covers the period from 133 B.C. until the time of Nero.

[5] In the account, Nero is referred to as the king who "once was, now is not, and will come up out of the Abyss and go to his destruction" (Revelation 17:8). The book of Revelation was apparently written after the persecutions of Nero, but during the reign of Titus (which ended in 81 A.D.). The point of Revelation 17 is that the persecution that had begun under Nero (the one "who once was, and now is not"), but that had temporarily ceased, would be revived. It would resume under the next king after the one ruling at the time John wrote—in other words, Domitian. So Domitian would be the resurrection of Nero, only worse. Of course, the apostle and prophet John got it right. This is exactly what happened.

[6] *Lives of the Twelve Caesars,* Seutonius, Translated by Robert Graves, (Butler and Tanner, 1964), pp. 305-318.

[7] Not *the* Judgment Day, but a day of judgment.

[8] For example:

a. Revelation 11:3, where it is said that the two witnesses "will prophesy for 1,260 days." This is equivalent to three and one-half years because 1,260 days is three and one-half 360-day years. The Jewish religious year comprised twelve thirty-day months.

b. Revelation 11:3, where it is said that the two witnesses "will prophesy for 1,260 days." This is equivalent because 1,260 days is three-and-one-half 360-day years.

c. Revelation 12:6, where it says that "the woman" (in this context, the church) will be "taken care of for 1,260 days."

d. Revelation 12:14, where the Holy Spirit returns to using the phrase, "for a time, times and half a time," as an equivalent to the 1,260 days referred to in example c.

e. Revelation 13:5, which refers to the exact same persecution that is prophesied of in Daniel 7, saying that it will last "for forty-two months."

The three and one-half year symbolism will be used again in Daniel as well, as we will see.

[9] Author's personal note: Someone might say, "It sure seems like you have something against theologians. What is the deal here?" In response I would concede that this person has a good point. It is possible that, being somewhat of an intellectual, I am more sensitive to intellectual attacks on the Bible than most. Consider, however, who were the loudest and most active opponents of Jesus Christ during the time of his ministry. They were the Scribes and the Pharisees.

In other words, it was the theologians of Jesus' day who were his most vocal critics. These theologians were even in the right religion. I would claim that human nature has not changed over the last two thousand years. Yes, it does bother me that when I go into the library at my religious college and look for a commentary on the book of Daniel, every one of the so-called religious authorities takes as a given that the book of Daniel is a hoax. Even at the majority of religious colleges—never mind the public institutions—there is an extremely strong anti-Bible bias.

It may seem less intellectually sophisticated to take the view that the Bible is what it claims to be: the word of God. Those who do so will always be in the minority. One should consider, however, that Jesus reserved his harshest criticism for those who held themselves up as teachers of righteousness, but who abused their position as religious teachers to destroy the faith of those who heard them:

"Woe to you, teachers of the law and Pharisees, you hypocrites! You shut the kingdom of heaven in men's faces. You yourselves do not enter, nor will you let those enter who are trying to. Woe to you, teachers of the law and Pharisees, you hypocrites! You travel over land and sea to win a single convert, and when he becomes one, you make him twice as much a son of hell as you are" (Matthew 23:13-15).

Jesus did not mince words in dealing with the religious intellectuals of his day because they had less excuse than anyone else for their stubborn, unbelieving hearts.

# Chapter Ten

## Sheep Versus Goat

Two years after the vision recorded in Daniel 7, Daniel has another vision "in the third year of King Belshazzar's reign" (Daniel 8:1). The Babylonian Chronicle implies that Belshazzar began to rule as regent in 553 B.C., so the year of the vision is 551 B.C. This is twelve years before the feast recorded in Daniel chapter five. There are many similarities between the visions in Daniel chapters seven and eight, but their subjects are quite different. In Daniel 7, God provides much detail about the fourth beast, representing Rome. In the vision at hand, God will reveal, again in vivid, apocalyptic detail, much of the history of the Near East during the time of the kingdoms represented by the second and third beasts: Persia/Media and Greece. Together, these two visions describe the historical settings of the two greatest periods of persecution the people of God have ever had to endure. Of course, unlike other history books, Daniel's visions tell about the events before they ever happen.

*Figure 30.*
*Griffin from Susa.*

In Daniel chapter seven, God prepared the first-, second- and third-century disciples for the persecution they would experience under the Romans. He did so by giving very specific details about the nature of those persecutions more than six hundred years before the events happened. The fact that the Christians could read a description of their sufferings, written long before they ever happened, both prepared them for the actual events and gave them solid reason to believe the encouragements contained in the vision. The same prophecy that told them details of the Roman persecutions also reminded them that God is in control. The prophecy encouraged the faithful with the knowledge that God will ultimately judge both the men and the nation persecuting them. God had promised them beforehand that their faith would be vindicated if they did not give in to fear.

God certainly had the early Christians in mind when he revealed the message of Daniel. That being said, there is even greater emphasis in the book of Daniel on preparing the Jewish nation for the persecutions they were to suffer under their Greek overlords in the second century B.C. Chapters eight and ten through twelve of Daniel will provide strong support for this claim.

Daniel 7 provides details about the Roman persecution of the church, but in chapters eight and ten through twelve, one will find dramatic and detailed predictions of the future. These chapters prophesy concerning the anti-Jewish persecutions under the Seleucid Greeks, giving both the political background and the details of the events themselves.

Bible readers will most likely be less familiar with the historical background to the Greek world foretold in Daniel 8 than with the Roman world depicted in Daniel 7. An introduction to the required background was given in chapter one. More of the details needed to understand the historical context of Daniel 8 will be given presently.

One similarity between the visions of chapters seven and eight is that Daniel is given the interpretation of both dreams by an angel. The vision of the ram and of the goat in chapter eight must have been an overwhelmingly intense experience. After seeing the vision and hearing the interpretation, Daniel "was exhausted and lay ill for several days" (v. 27). Daniel was appalled at the fearful nature of what he had seen. It would appear that another of the jobs of the angel sent to Daniel was to give him the emotional and physical support he needed to handle the mind-blowing nature of the vision.

In the vision, Daniel is transported to Susa. This is the capital of the province (and former kingdom) of Elam. Cyrus eventually made it one of the two capitals of his empire. The fact that Daniel was carried to Susa provides a hint to the reader that the initial part of the prophecy deals with Persia.

*Figure 31. Susa Palace, glazed brick. Two winged lions with human heads.*

Daniel sees a ram with two horns "standing beside the canal" (Daniel 8:3). As stated previously, in apocalyptic writing, horns are symbolic of kings or national powers. The ram standing beside the canal creates the impression of an animal about to charge. The ram, of course, is the Persia/ Media Empire. In fact, the Persians took the ram as their guardian spirit. The Persian kings wore a ram's head rather than a diadem when marching at the head of their armies. And charge across the Ulai Canal (from east to west) is exactly what the Persian armies did.[1] From their homelands in the mountainous areas of modern-day Iran, the Medes and Persians under Cyrus charged westward in just a few short years to conquer almost the entire Near East.

The next detail provided to Daniel is that one of the ram's horns will grow up later, but will become longer than the other. Media is the larger horn at first, while Persia is the horn that started smaller, but eventually outgrew its partner "horn." Persia came to power later than Media did, but eventually became the much more dominant power in the dual empire. As mentioned in the historical introduction, Persia was a relatively small and weak province within the Median Empire, until Cyrus the Great rose up and, through his ability as a general and as a political leader, took the leading role in establishing the great Persia/Media Empire. Daniel gets a detail of future history right again!

According to the vision that Daniel sees, the ram will charge "toward the west and the north and the south" (v. 4). Given Daniel's track record, would anyone be surprised at this point if that was exactly what happened? The three ribs revealed in Daniel 7:5 were Babylon, Lydia and Egypt. Could it be coincidence that the three great nations destroyed by the Persians and the Medes were, in order, Babylon, to the west of Persia; Lydia to the north (actually to the northwest); and Egypt to the south (actually to the southwest)? The three directions the ram charges in Daniel 8 are the three ribs the bear ate in Daniel 7.

Last, Daniel observes in the vision concerning the two-horned ram that "no one could stand against him, and none could rescue from his power" (v. 4). For the first three generations of Persia/Media power, this proved true.

Eventually, though, the power of the Greek city-states proved too great for the Persians to completely break. This brings us to the second beast in Daniel eight: T he goat.

Now Daniel says, "As I was thinking about this..." (v. 5) Apparently, Daniel is fully aware that this is a prophetic vision, and he is considering how to interpret the meaning of what he sees. While he is taking in the vivid vision and thinking about its meaning, "suddenly" a goat with a prominent horn appears. Unlike the ram, which charged from the east, this goat charges from the west. The goat is Alexander the Great.

*Figure 32. Elamite soldier in the Persian Guard.*

Who is the greatest general and empire-builder in the history of mankind? Possible nominees include Genghis Khan, Napoleon Bonaparte and Alexander the Great. Experts in history will probably choose Alexander. Historians have written volumes about what made Alexander great. They often mention his unique background. On the one hand, Alexander was the son of King Philip, from the warlike and semi-barbaric nation of Macedon. On the other hand, he was sent by his father Philip to Athens to be tutored by Aristotle, perhaps the greatest intellectual figure in all of Greek history. His preparation, therefore, included the greatest possible military and intellectual tools of his day. Historians would discuss his blind courage, his amazing confidence, and his ability to inspire loyalty because of his love for his troops. One can list many other outstanding traits that Alexander possessed.

All of these factors could be mentioned in an attempt to explain what made Alexander great. However, we, the readers of Daniel, know who made Alexander great: God gets the credit! God told Daniel in the year 551 B.C. about the plans he had for Alexander. That was almost two hundred years before Alexander was born (356 B.C.). God is still in control, even when we are suffering,

There is an interesting parallel between what God did to prepare the way for Alexander, the conqueror of Persia, and what he did to let his people know about Cyrus, the conqueror of Babylon. In both cases, God revealed to Israel what these men would do two hundred years ahead of time.[2]

God is thus proving to the Jews that *he* has raised up Alexander to rule almost the entire known world in his day. When the Greek dynasties ultimately bring intense persecution to the Jews, God hopes that his people will still remember that, in the words of Nebuchadnezzar, "He does as he pleases with the powers of heaven and the peoples of the earth" (Daniel 4:35). God rules the nations.

Consider how God describes the career of Alexander to Daniel in the vision. This "prominent horn" (and Alexander certainly was a prominent horn!) did indeed charge from the west. In fact, Alexander crossed the straits of the Dardanelles (the narrow waterway which separates Europe from Asia), from west to east, with his relatively small army in the year 334 B.C. Alexander's army appeared "suddenly" in Asia (v. 5). Persia had been the almost unrivaled power in the entire Near East for two hundred years. At first, the king of the Persians, Darius III, did not take Alexander's invasion seriously. Alexander crossed the Dardanelles with an army of 30,000. The upstart general from Greece would have conquered the entire Persian/Median Empire with its standing army of 200,000! It truly must have appeared to his contemporaries as if Alexander was "crossing the whole earth without touching the ground" (v. 5). Exactly as Daniel saw it in the vision, the goat (Alexander) attacked the two-horned ram (Persia/Media and its king Darius III) as it lay in wait across the Ulai Canal. Alexander did indeed "attack the ram furiously, striking the ram and shattering his two horns" (v. 7).

And so, in Daniel's vision, "the goat became very great" (v. 8). That is unquestionably true of Alexander. Over a twelve-year period, Alexander followed one victory with another. After defeating the remnant of the Persia/Media Empire, a protracted siege resulted in the destruction of the city of Tyre.[3]

Next, Alexander took Palestine, including Jerusalem. Initially, the Jews feared the approach of Alexander and his troops, as did most everyone else. Some of the leaders in Jerusalem decided to appease rather than fight the Macedonians. They thought it might be wise to point out to Alexander that their scriptures had prophesied his victories. If Josephus is to be believed, they used the book of Daniel to save Jerusalem from attack. To quote Josephus, "... and when the book of Daniel was showed him, in which Daniel declared that one of the Greeks should destroy the empire of the Persians, he supposed that he himself was the person intended; and as he was then glad, he ... asked them what favours they wanted of him. The high priest requested that they... might pay no tribute on the seventh year. He granted all they desired..."[4] After taking Palestine, he conquered Egypt. Almost without pause, Alexander returned to the north and east, finishing off Darius III and conquering Bactria (more or less present-day Afghanistan), following these successes with a great victory over Indian power in the valley of the Indus River. Finally, after twelve years of nearly constant war, Alexander's troops refused to go any farther into the unknown, and Alexander was forced to turn back. Yes, it would be fair to say that the prominent horn became very great.

However, at the height of his power, in 323 B.C., after returning from India, Alexander died in Mesopotamia. As Daniel sees it, "at the height of his power his large horn was broken off" (v. 8). More than two hundred years before the event, Daniel gets it right again. Feel free to compare the specific nature of this prophecy to the vague supposed prophecies of Nostradamus.

Alexander married a Bactrian princess named Roxanna. She gave birth to a son soon after Alexander's death. Since the boy was so young, there was no obvious successor to Alexander. This led to a dynastic struggle and to the death of Roxanna and her son. To summarize a complicated series of events, within seven years, as Alexander's generals fought among themselves, four generals were left to found four dynasties. These were Antigonus, who ruled most of the Asian Greek territory, Cassander, who ruled Macedonia and much of Greece itself, Lysimachus, who ruled Thrace (northeastern present-day Greece and western present-day Turkey) and Ptolemy, who ruled Egypt and Palestine.

As Daniel describes it, "at the height of his power his large horn was broken off, and in its place four prominent horns grew up toward the four winds of heaven" (v. 8). The Bible predicted that four kings would succeed to the power of Alexander, and that is exactly what happened. Not three, not five, but four! In case there is any question about how to interpret the four prominent horns, consider the interpretation of the vision given to Daniel in 8:21-22:

> "The shaggy goat is the king of Greece, and the large horn between his eyes is the first king. The four horns that replaced the one that was broken off represent four kingdoms that will emerge from his nation but will not have the same power."

Could God have been any more specific than this? The four winds of heaven refer to the four cardinal points of the compass: Antigonus to the east of the Promised Land, Cassander to the west, Lysimachus to the north and Ptolemy to the south. And, as related in the vision, none of these successors had the same power as Alexander.

The vision continues, "Out of one of them came another horn, which started small but grew in power to the south and to the east and toward the Beautiful Land" (v. 9). The reader may ask, "What in the world could he be talking about now? What is this 'Beautiful Land' Daniel is talking about?" We know Daniel and his prophecies well enough by now to expect a very good explanation.

## The Four Horns of Daniel 7

| Horn (King) | Territory Ruled |
| --- | --- |
| Antigonus | The East: from Syria to India |
| Cassander | The West: Macedonia and Greece |
| Lysimachus | The North: Thrace and Asia Minor |
| Ptolemy | The South: Egypt and Palestine |

As mentioned previously, one of the successors to Alexander was Ptolemy Lagi. Ptolemy and his successors were to rule Egypt for just under three hundred years. Ptolemy's greatest general was Seleucus. In 312 B.C., Seleucus, under orders from Ptolemy, attacked Antigonus, seizing from him the city of Jerusalem and taking over most of the province of Syria. At this time, many Jews were taken to Alexandria, the new capital of Ptolemaic Egypt, a detail of great importance to later Jewish history. Later, Antigonus retook most of Syria, but lost Babylon to Seleucus.

This brings the story back to the vision of Daniel. Seleucus was so successful that he was able to set up his own independent kingdom, centered in the province of Babylon. So out of the Ptolemaic Dynasty came a separate dynasty, the Seleucids. In the words of Daniel's vision, "Out of one of them [Ptolemy] came another horn [Seleucus], which started small" (v. 9). And guess how this "horn" grew...It grew from Babylon, first "to the south," as the Seleucids retook Syria, this time from the Ptolemies. In addition, Seleucus and his successors grew "to the east," filling a power vacuum in the former provinces of Elam, Persia and Media. Finally, in 198 B.C., the Seleucid king Antiochus III took Palestine and the city of Jerusalem from the Ptolemies. So this late-growing horn came to occupy "the Beautiful Land"—in other words, the Promised Land. Daniel recorded this vision in 551 B.C. The prophecy was finally fulfilled to the letter in 198 B.C.

*Figure 33: Antiochus III the Great, King of Syria and father of Antiocus IV Epiphanes.*

Next, Daniel's vision turns to even more vivid, apocalyptic language. "It [the Seleucid kingdom] grew until it reached the host of the heavens, and it threw some of the starry host down to the earth and trampled on them. It set itself up to be as great as the Prince of the host; it took away the daily sacrifice from him, and the place of his sanctuary was brought low" (vv. 10-12). Clearly, the Seleucid kingdom never literally threw any of the stars in the sky to the ground.

This is symbolic language that God employs to point out the spiritual battle going on behind the scenes. This is typical of apocalyptic speech. Stars falling to the ground are used to symbolize God's coming in judgment.[5]

Daniel's vision refers (hundreds of years before it happened) to the reign of Antiochus IV Epiphanes, the Seleucid king who reigned from 175 to 163 B.C. The vision in Daniel chapter eleven will supply additional detail about the reign and the persecutions of Antiochus IV Epiphanes. More will be said about him at that time. For now, suffice it to say that Antiochus did in fact "set [himself] up to be as great as the Prince of the host," taking on many of the trappings of deity. In fact, after desecrating the temple in Jerusalem, he had a statue of Zeus placed in the Holy of Holies. The face on the statue was that of Antiochus. Antiochus literally set himself up to be as great as the Prince of the host. As prophesied in the vision, Antiochus did in fact "[take] away the daily sacrifice," and bring low "the place of his sanctuary" (v. 11). He desecrated the temple in Jerusalem and outlawed all sacrifices from 167 to 164 B.C.[6]

Now we come to the key verse in Daniel chapter eight: "*Because of rebellion*, the host of the saints and the daily sacrifice were given over to it" (v. 12). "It" again refers to the Seleucid power, specifically to Antiochus IV Epiphanes. God is telling his people about the greatest persecution that will come upon them during the time "between the Testaments." He depicts these persecutions almost four hundred years before they happen. The Lord tells "the host of the saints" that he will allow them to be persecuted, not because he has stopped loving them, but rather because of their rebellion against him. This is bad news for Israel. One would not expect that the faithful Israelites were encouraged to know that Antiochus, their greatest enemy, would prosper "in everything he did," or that "truth" would be "thrown to the ground" (v. 12).

But, as in Daniel 7, God leaves the faithful with great hope, even in the midst of the most intense suffering and persecution. At the end of the vision, as well as in the angel Gabriel's interpretation of the dream, we see God's promise that those who remain faithful will be vindicated. An angelic voice asks, "How long will it take for the vision to be fulfilled—the vision concerning the daily sacrifice, the rebellion that causes desolation, and the surrender of the sanctuary and of the host that will be trampled underfoot?" (v. 13) In other words, how long will the extreme persecution of the Jews under Antiochus continue? The answer is given in the vision: "It will take 2,300 evenings and mornings; then the sanctuary will be reconsecrated" (v. 14). The biblical pattern is that God will allow his people to be persecuted, but only for a limited time.

The duration of the persecution will be 2,300 evenings and mornings. That is 1,150 days, or just over three years. The Jehovah's Witness religious group interprets the 2,300 evenings and mornings as 2,300 years. From this assumption, and using the date of Antiochus' desolation of the temple, they calculated the end of the persecution to occur in 1914 A.D. From this, they predicted that Jesus would return to the Earth in the year 1914. How the Jehovah's Witnesses dealt with the apparent failure of this prediction is one of the interesting episodes in the history of Christianity.

But, to return to the 1,150 days, the vision of Daniel is almost certainly referring to the desecration of the temple in Jerusalem, which was perpetrated by Antiochus IV Epiphanes. This horrific event in the history of the Jews is recorded in the apocryphal books of First and Second Maccabees,[7] as well as by Josephus, a Jewish historian of the first century A.D.[8] More on this will be said later, but it will be helpful to briefly summarize the historical events relevant to the vision of Daniel chapter eight.

Unlike his predecessors, the Seleucid monarch Antiochus IV Epiphanes established a policy of systematic persecution and Hellenization of the Jewish people. As part of his attempt to suppress the unique Jewish culture and religion, Antiochus had the temple in Jerusalem desecrated in December 167 B.C. He had a statue of Zeus erected in the temple to symbolize who was now boss, and even had a pig sacrificed there, in the most blatant imaginable affront to Jewish sensitivities. He specifically outlawed sacrifice to God, as well as circumcision of male children, upon pain of death. Gross acts of immorality and drunkenness were committed on the temple grounds. Given all this, we can now see why God chose to describe these events apocalyptically by saying Antiochus "threw some of the starry host down to the earth and trampled on them." All this continued until a (partially) successful revolt, led by Judas Maccabeus, resulted in the retaking of the temple by Jewish rebels. The temple was reconsecrated on December 25, 164 B.C. The reconsecration of the temple is one of the greatest moments in Jewish history. Jews everywhere remember it in the annual festival known as Chanukah.

Returning to the vision, yes, the daily sacrifice was taken away, (vv. 11-12), but the desecration of the temple and the trampling of God's people only lasted for just over three years (2,300 evenings and mornings). Isn't that amazing? In the year 551 B.C., God revealed to Daniel specifics of a persecution that later occurred in the years 167-164 B.C. He even told Daniel how long the desecration of the temple would last. Most often, a temporary persecution is described in the Bible as lasting three and one-half years ("a time, times and half a time"), but this one is described as lasting just a bit longer than three years–1150 days. It just so happens that Antiochus defiled the temple for just over three years. The desecration of the temple began in November or possibly early December 167 B.C., while the reconsecration occurred on December 25, 164 B.C. Our imprecise historical knowledge tells us that the desecration lasted somewhere between about 1120-1150 days.

In the interpretation given to Daniel by the angel Gabriel, God provides a little more information about the end of the persecution under Antiochus. While Daniel is taking in the vision, a voice comes from across the Ulai canal, saying, "Gabriel, tell this man the meaning of the vision" (v. 16). Whose voice is this? Is it God speaking? We do not know, but we do know that Gabriel obeyed the order. Daniel is absolutely terrified at the sound of this awesome voice, so much so that he falls to the ground, prostrate.

Gabriel tells Daniel that "the vision concerns the time of the end" (v. 17). The end of what? The end of the world? From the context, apparently not. Most likely, Gabriel is referring to the judgment of Antiochus IV Epiphanes and the Greek persecutors. It is a common thing in apocalyptic language for God to refer to a judgment on a people as an "end." In fact, Gabriel reveals to Daniel concerning Antiochus:

"...A stern-faced king, a master of intrigue, will arise. He will become very strong, but not by his own power. He will cause astounding devastation and will succeed in whatever he does. He will destroy the mighty men and the holy people. He will cause deceit to prosper, and he will consider himself superior. When they feel secure, he will destroy many and take his stand against the Prince of princes. Yet he will be destroyed, but not by human power" (Daniel 8:23-25, emphasis added).

So God reveals to Daniel through Gabriel that the Lord himself will allow Antiochus to come to power and to use that power in an attempt to destroy the mighty men of God and his holy people. However, that same God will rise up and destroy the persecutor Antiochus. Here the theme of Daniel is graphically revealed once again: *God rules the nations—do not fear.*

Three purposes of this vision come to mind. First, God is preparing his people specifically to remain faithful under the persecution of Antiochus. To Jews living during the time of the temple's desecration, Daniel's vision means that the persecution will ultimately come to an end, and that Antiochus will be judged.

Second, God intends a general application to all the readers of the Bible, that they should remain faithful even when the world pressures them to betray God. The message to us is that no matter what our outward circumstances may be, no matter what difficulties we may encounter, no matter how much it may appear that God is not working in a particular situation, God is still in control. God may allow us to suffer. We might experience suffering as a direct result of our own sin. In other cases, God may allow us to suffer in order to test us and help us to grow. Or perhaps both causes may contribute to the challenges we face. However, if we will remain faithful regardless of our circumstances, in the end God will vindicate us. In his love, he will never abandon his people.

God works on both individuals and groups of people. If the church or Christian organization you are part of is experiencing struggle; if it appears that you have suffered a setback, you may be tempted to think that God is no longer with you. If we learn the lesson of Daniel chapter eight, we will understand that being attacked from outside or going through intense internal struggle does not necessarily mean God is against you. On the contrary, it may be the surest sign that God is with you. As with the Jews suffering persecution under the Seleucids, God may be judging you because of your sin, but also because he loves you.

No one appreciates being attacked. No one feels good when the number of the faithful becomes smaller. However, bear in mind what happened to the Jews because they went through the horrifying persecution of Antiochus Epiphanes. It was after this persecution that the Jews had what was probably their greatest period of spiritual growth. The persecutions pruned Israel, but it led to the formation of the Hasidim. These were a very devoted and faithful group of Jews who pursued God according to the Old Covenant with greater purity and zeal than at any other period in the history of Judaism. Let us view times of setback as an opportunity to search ourselves and repent, rather than give room for Satan to cause us to be discouraged and to give up.

Third, God is providing us with unassailable evidence that his Word is inspired. When Daniel receives a vision that describes in great detail the future of the Persia/Media Empire, of Alexander the Great, his empire and its successors, and most significantly of the Seleucid persecutors, he leaves behind marks of inspiration that only the most hardened skeptic can ignore.[9]

Here is where the cynics and many theologians will step in to protest. If there is one thing they do not want to allow to enter our minds, it is the possibility that the Bible is what it clearly says it is—the inspired word of God. They simply must come up with another explanation for all this. How could Daniel have known hundreds of years beforehand about Alexander the Great, about the four dynasties that succeeded him, and about the fifth dynasty that later arose out of the Ptolemaic Dynasty? How could he have known so much about "the distant future" (v. 26)? The prophecy is simply too specific to ignore.

The only logical alternative left to the Bible critic is to assume that Daniel was written after the event—some time after 160 B.C. It has already been pointed out that their principal argument for the late date of writing, involving the language of the book, is fallacious. The language of Daniel strongly supports the claim that it was written before 400

B.C. Let us look for a moment at Daniel 8:26 it is stated, "The vision of the evenings and mornings that has been given you is true, but seal up the vision, for it concerns *the distant future*" (emphasis added). If the book was written in about 160 B.C., then when the writer claims that the vision concerns the distant future, he is a liar, plain and simple. If that is the case, then the book of Daniel is a blatant fake. How, then, it might be asked, did the writer manage to deceive the entire Jewish hierarchy into putting it into the Old Testament canon? The book of Daniel was already part of the accepted canon of Hebrew scripture by the second century B.C.[10] Do these people really think the Jewish teachers were that gullible? In fact, one can assume that the book of Daniel was taken into the Hebrew canon as an inspired book at least in part because it predicted events in the future so accurately. The Jews loved their scripture in a way which approached worship of the very words themselves. Is it simply not believable that the teachers of the Law would allow an obviously deceitful document into the scripture.

Perhaps even more significantly, how can the critics of Daniel explain the very specific prophecies about Domitian, or about the Messiah or the kingdom of God? No one has yet had the nerve to claim that the book of Daniel was written after these events occurred. How do the skeptics, hell-bent on proving the Bible is the product of man, deal with this question? They simply ignore it. They choose to deny the obvious implications of Daniel chapters two, seven and, as we will soon see, chapter nine. Sticking one's head in the sand is a very poor way of arriving at the truth. There is only one reasonable conclusion of the matter.

After the vision, Daniel was so exhausted that he was forced to remain in bed for several days. The intensity of the apocalyptic vision was appalling to him. Let us be amazed by the vision as well, for in it God has shown once more that he rules the nations. Truly those who choose to rely on God rather than their own strength can take comfort from Daniel chapter eight.

# Notes

[1] Here we find another accurate historical detail. Susa is on the eastern side of the Ulai Canal. When the ram figuratively charged across the canal from Susa, it was in fact charging to the west, exactly as described in the vision.

[2] Isaiah (c. 750 B.C.) foretold concerning Cyrus (c. 550 B.C.), while Daniel (c. 550 B.C.) foretold about Alexander (c. 350 B.C.).

[3] Alexander's conquest of Tyre brought to completion a prophecy found in Ezekiel 26. The prophecy was partially fulfilled by the attack of Nebuchadnezzar on Tyre, but it was not fully completed until the final destruction of the city after a seven-month siege by Alexander. For a full description of the prophecy and its fulfillment, see *Evidence that Demands a Verdict,* by Josh McDowell, (Here's Life Publishers, 1992), pp. 274-280.

[4] Josephus, *Antiquities of the Jews, XI,* viii, 5.

[5] For example, see Isaiah 14:12, referring to God's judgment on Nebuchadnezzar, Matthew 24:29 (quoting Isaiah 13:10), Revelation 6:12-13 and 8:10-11.

[6] See 1 Maccabees 1:44-49 for an account of these events.

[7] The books of First and Second Maccabees can be found in any Catholic Bible, such as the *New American Bible.* Both books describe the persecutions of the Jews under Greek domination and the rise of the Maccabees. The Maccabees were the rulers of the independent Jewish monarchy, which grew up out of the rebellion against the Greek Seleucid dynasty. Of the two books, First Maccabees is by far the superior historical account. Second Maccabees contains many historical errors and is more prejudicial in its treatment of the history of Israel than First Maccabees. It would be helpful for the reader to take the time to read at least First Maccabees in order to better understand the historical context of Daniel chapters eight and eleven.

[8] *Antiquities of the Jews,* by Josephus, translated by William Whitson, (Kregel Publications, book XII), and *Wars of the Jews,* same author and publisher, Book I. Both accounts, though inaccurate in some points, and though strongly colored by Josephus' Pharisaic prejudice, provide valuable information to the interested reader.

[9] The author is running out of synonyms to describe the incredibly convincing nature of the prophecies in Daniel. Amazing, unassailable, convincing, and incontrovertible...there is only a limited vocabulary available to express the impressiveness of what God has done.

[10] Evidence to support this claim includes the fact that Daniel was included in the canonical part of the Septuagint Hebrew-to-Greek translation of the Old Testament, which was completed in the second century B.C. Further evidence is found in the fact that several fragments of Daniel were found among the Dead Sea Scrolls, which are dated in the first century B.C. It is notable that one of the Dead Sea Scroll fragments includes the transition from Hebrew to Aramaic in Daniel chapter two exactly as found in much later Hebrew manuscripts. Besides all these facts, there is the evidence that Jesus himself quoted from Daniel (for example in Matthew 24:15). Jesus never quoted from the Apocryphal books or the books of the Pseudepigrapha, as neither Jesus nor the religious leaders of Judaism ever accepted these writings as being inspired.

# Chapter Eleven

## The King Comes to Jerusalem

Chapter nine of Daniel can easily be divided into two parts. It begins with a prayer of Daniel in which he begs God, both in his own name and in the name of his fellow Israelites, to forgive the sins that had brought them into captivity in Babylon. In the prayer, he also calls for God to deliver Israel from its current bondage. In the second part of chapter nine, Daniel receives a vision concerning the future of the kingdom of God. At first glance, the two sections seem to be unrelated.

While it is easy to separate the two sections, it is wise to deal with them together. This is seen by considering Daniel 9:21-23: "While I was still in prayer, Gabriel, the man I had seen in the earlier vision...instructed me and said to me...,'As soon as you began to pray, an answer was given, which I have come to tell you, for you are highly esteemed.'" Therefore, it can be seen that the vision given to Daniel in this chapter is given to him in direct response to his prayer. Taking a cue from the Bible here, the chapter will therefore be studied as a unit.

When did Daniel offer this prayer to God and receive this vision? Note that the Bible says he prayed "in the first year of Darius son of Xerxes" (Daniel 9:1). The prayer and the vision occurred in the first year of Darius. This is either the year that Belshazzar was killed and the Persia/Media Empire came to control Babylon (539 B.C.), or possibly soon after that event, when Darius was made ruler of the province of Babylon. The wording here, "who was made ruler over

169

the Babylonian kingdom," supports the claim made earlier that Daniel views Darius, not as the ruler of the entire Persia/Media Empire, but rather as the ruler of the province of Babylon only.

Daniel is having his "quiet time" when he comes across a scripture[1] in Jeremiah. The scripture he reads is what we know as Jeremiah 25:11-12. In this passage, Jeremiah prophesied that the captivity of God's people and the desolation of the Promised Land was to last for seventy years. Jeremiah also said that, after those seventy years, Babylon would be destroyed. Can you picture Daniel observing Babylon overthrown by Cyrus and doing a little math problem? Jerusalem was defeated and the captives were taken to Babylon in 605 B.C. The year is now about 538 or 537 B.C.[2] Daniel realizes that, within a couple of years, the prophecy should be fulfilled. He decides it is time to pray.

It was the ardent desire of a great many of the captive Jews in Babylon to return to the glory days, the days when all of Israel went up to God's city Jerusalem and worshiped at God's temple on Mount Zion. Psalm 137 illustrates the feelings of many Jews at that time:

> How can we sing the songs of the Lord while in a foreign land? If I forget you, O Jerusalem, may my right hand forget its skill. May my tongue cling to the roof of my mouth if I do not remember you, if I do not consider Jerusalem my highest joy (Psalm 137:4-6).

One can assume that although Daniel was never able to return to Jerusalem, he had feelings similar to those of the psalmist. But rather than get depressed about the situation, Daniel "turned to the Lord God and pleaded with him in prayer and petition, in fasting, and in sackcloth and ashes" (Daniel 9:3). The setting and the response are similar to what is recorded in Nehemiah chapter one. The prayer in Daniel 9:4-19 is truly one of the great prayers in the Bible. In it one finds Daniel crying out to God. This is a very emotional prayer rather than a dry laundry list of requests. Daniel is certainly not going through a formula. Elements which can be seen in this prayer are:

1. Praise (v. 4, 7a, 9, 15a)
2. Confession (v. 5, 6, 7b, 8, 10, 11a, 13b, 16b)
3. Recalling the promises of God (v. 11b, 12, 13)
4. Request for deliverance (v. 17-19)

The overriding tone of Daniel's prayer is confession. Daniel does not tone down or minimize his sin or the sin of Israel. He says, "We have been wicked and have rebelled.... Lord, you are righteous, but this day we are covered with shame" (vv. 5, 7). We would do well to imitate both the emotional heart of Daniel and his humility. He could easily have said "they" have sinned against you, because he was more righteous than virtually all of God's people, but he did not.

Daniel was a powerful man, yet his success did not go to his head. "We do not make requests of you because we are righteous, but because of your great mercy" (v. 18). On the other hand, although he is humble, Daniel is very bold in making requests of his God. He cries out, "Give ear, O God, and hear; open your eyes and see the desolation of the city that bears your Name....O Lord, listen! O Lord, forgive! O Lord, hear and act!" (vv. 18-19) The words "open your eyes" could almost seem impertinent, but they are the free expression of a man who is fully confident that God wants to hear his voice. Only a true man of God can combine profound humility with such boldness in the presence of God. Those who desire to worship God are well-advised to look at their prayer life and compare it to that of Daniel, the man of righteousness.

And God hears and responds to this prayer of a righteous man. Daniel receives an answer from Gabriel while he is "still in prayer" (v. 21)! Here is great encouragement for us. How many times have we prayed and had God give the answer while we were still in prayer? Here we have a rare glance at what occurs behind the scenes when a man of God cries out to his Father in heaven. While the words are still on Daniel's lips, the angels get moving. As Daniel prays, Gabriel comes "in swift flight" (v. 21). In fact, God already knows what is on our hearts before we pray it. The angel Gabriel tells Daniel that God answered "as soon as you began to pray" (v. 23).

The answer to Daniel's prayer comes in the form of a vision. And what a vision it is! This has got to be the best news ever given to a man, at any time, in any situation in the history of the world! The Messiah is coming! Get ready! This little four-verse vision simply must be the most encouraging prophecy in the Old Testament. Let us dive in.

> Seventy 'sevens' are decreed for your people and your holy city to finish transgression, to put an end to sin, to atone for wickedness, to bring in everlasting righteousness, to seal up vision and prophecy and to anoint the most holy (Daniel 9:24).

Gabriel tells Daniel the amount of time remaining before the Messiah will come. In case there is any doubt, the word *Messiah* in Hebrew means "the anointed one." There is no question what Gabriel is talking about. So how much time remains before sin will be put to an "end?" How long before atonement for sins will be provided to mankind? What will be the waiting period before salvation comes—before God fulfills his holy word? It will be four hundred and ninety years.

Actually, Gabriel says that seventy "sevens" remain, and 70 x 7 = 490. How can one be sure he is talking about seventy sevens of years? The answer is that once a prophecy is fulfilled, then one can be sure about the meaning.[3] In this case, seventy sevens is four hundred and ninety years; no doubt about it. Consider verse twenty-five carefully: "Know and understand this: From the issuing of the decree to restore and rebuild Jerusalem until the Anointed One, the ruler, comes, there will be seven 'sevens' and sixty-two 'sevens.'"

The key to dating the coming of the Messiah (the Anointed One) is "the decree to restore and rebuild Jerusalem." At first, this presents a little bit of a problem. There are three decrees mentioned in the Bible that could at least be considered in reference to this prophecy. The first is the decree of Cyrus himself. This decree is recorded in 2 Chronicles 36:23 and Ezra 1:2-4. This decree was given "in the first year of Cyrus, king of Persia" (Ezra 1:1). Almost certainly, "the first year of Cyrus" refers to the year 539 B.C., which was not actually the first year of rule for Cyrus, but was rather the first year he ruled the province of Babylon, as well as the majority of the Jewish exiles. Cyrus had declared:

> The Lord, the God of heaven, has given me all the kingdoms of the earth and he has appointed me to build a temple for him at Jerusalem in Judah. Anyone of his people among you—may his God be with him, and let him go up to Jerusalem in Judah and build the temple of the Lord, the God of Israel, the God who is in Jerusalem (Ezra 1:2-3).

This is certainly a great moment in the history of Israel. This decree of Cyrus fulfills the prophecy given to Jeremiah that after seventy years of captivity, God's people would be freed. However, Cyrus' decree of 539 B.C. is not the one being referred to in Daniel 9. Notice that in this decree, Cyrus is allowing the Jews to go back and rebuild the temple. He is saying nothing about rebuilding the city, and especially, he is saying nothing about rebuilding the walls. There is no evidence that this decree ever led to rebuilding the wall or to a significant rebuilding of the city of Jerusalem. Soon after this decree was published, a large group of Jews did in fact return to Judah to live and to begin construction of the temple. Unfortunately, very shortly after arriving in Israel they stopped work without completing the construction. They had to be given a kick in the pants by Haggai in the second year of Darius (520 B.C.) before they finally put the building of God's temple before the construction of their fine paneled houses...but that is another story.

The second decree recorded in the Bible that should be considered is that recorded in Ezra 7:13-26. Ezra brought this decree from the king to Jerusalem "in the fifth month of the seventh year of the king" (Ezra 7:8). The king being referred to is Artaxerxes, who ruled beginning in 464 B.C. Therefore, this decree was promulgated in 458 B.C., or perhaps 459 B.C., if one allows for some time between its issuance and the time when Ezra left from Babylon and traveled to the Promised Land. Artaxerxes' letter provided a great deal of money for Ezra to improve the temple, to pay for sacrifices to God, and to provide for anything else Ezra chose to do with the contributions from the treasury (Ezra 7:21). This decree led to the return of another large contingent of Jews to Jerusalem, and ultimately led to the rebuilding of the city and its walls.

The third decree that could be mentioned is the one given by Artaxerxes to Nehemiah. This decree was given "in the twentieth year of King Artaxerxes" (Nehemiah 2:1), or 445 B.C. The decree itself is not actually recorded in the Bible, but it is significant in that it specifically authorized the building of the wall of the city. Using the power implied in the letter he received from the king, Nehemiah oversaw the actual rebuilding of the walls surrounding Jerusalem.

So *either* of the decrees of Artaxerxes—the one written in 458 (or 459) B.C. or the one published in 445 B.C.—could be described as a "decree to restore and rebuild Jerusalem." Since the second decree more or less restates the permission given to Ezra in 458 B.C., it seems most reasonable to assume that the first decree of Artaxerxes (458 B.C.) is the decree referred to by Gabriel in the vision.[4]

It is time to pull out your calculator. Taking 458 (or 459) B.C. as the starting point and adding 490 years brings one to the year 33 (or 32) A.D.[5] Now isn't that quite a coincidence? It just so happens that a man who claimed to be the Messiah was born around the year 5 B.C.[6] After creating quite a stir through his preaching and his working of many miracles, he was crucified somewhere between 28 and 32 A.D., depending on which scholars you believe. Forty days later he rose from the dead and appeared to many of his followers. Somewhere between 28 and 32 A.D., he brought in everlasting righteousness, atoned for wickedness and put an end to sin (at least for those willing to leave everything, repent and be baptized in his name).

What is the skeptic to do with this one? And what about those who attempt to date the book of Daniel at about 160 B.C. in order to prove that it is not God-inspired? How can they explain that Daniel predicted the date of the crucifixion of the Messiah? This prophecy also deserves consideration by those who are still waiting for the Messiah. According to

Daniel's vision, the Messiah was supposed to come about two thousand years ago. Any pretender to the position who came at this point in history would be unqualified. He certainly would not be able to claim, as did Jesus, "Everything must be fulfilled that is written about me in the Law of Moses, the Prophets and the Psalms" (Luke 24:44).

What is being said here? Let us get it out there in black and white. God, through Daniel, prophesied the time and place of the crucifixion more than five hundred years before it happened.

But there is quite a bit left in the prophecy, so it is time to get back to work. In Daniel 9:25 one learns that "until the Anointed One, the ruler, comes, there will be seven 'sevens,' and sixty-two 'sevens'". In other words, the Messiah would come to Jerusalem during the sixty-ninth 'seven.' That means the Messiah would show up in Jerusalem somewhere between 483 and 490 years after the issuance of the decree. In fact, Jesus came (in his ministry) approximately three years before his crucifixion.[7]

Gabriel also tells Daniel that the city "will be rebuilt with streets and a trench, but in times of trouble" (v. 25). This is probably referring to the rebuilding of the city under Nehemiah in 444 B.C. This rebuilding occurred under much pressure from the Samaritan opposition, led by Sanballat, Tobiah and others (see Nehemiah chapters four and six).

Then the angel Gabriel continues his account of the future by saying, "After the sixty-two 'sevens,' the Anointed One will be cut off and will have nothing. The people of the ruler who will come will destroy the city and the sanctuary" (v. 26). The events referred to will occur after the "cutting off" (i.e., the crucifixion) of the Messiah. At first, it may be difficult to see what this is referring to. Was Jerusalem destroyed immediately after the crucifixion of Jesus?

Actually, verse 26 is referring to the events of 70 A.D. In order to explain these events, a little background about the Roman occupation of Jerusalem is required. From the time of the Maccabees until 63 B.C., the Jewish Hasmonean Dynasty ruled Jerusalem. In 63 B.C., after a victorious campaign over the Parthian Empire (centered in present-day Iran) the Roman general Pompey attacked and took Jerusalem, ending once and for all Jewish control of the fate of Israel (that is, until 1948, when the modern state of Israel was established). Due to upheaval in Rome during the civil wars between Pompey and Julius Caesar, as well as between the successors of Caesar, the Parthians temporarily retook the city (41 B.C.). However, Mark Antony, former right-hand man to Julius Caesar, retook Jerusalem from the Parthians for good and gave the city to an opportunistic local ruler named Herod. The Idumean King Herod is referred to in Matthew 2:1 as the local king who ruled Judea at the time Jesus Christ was born.

The Jews never adapted well to Roman rule, despite the fact that Roman government was fairly tolerant of their religion. There were always a significant number of "zealots" and other groups who violently opposed Roman government. One of the apostles, Simon, was a zealot (Luke 6:15). In the year 38 A.D. the Roman emperor Gaius (Caligula) ordered that a statue of himself be set up in the temple at Jerusalem, which, as can easily be imagined, did not endear him or the empire he represented to the Jews. Fortunately, the governor of Syria interceded, or rebellion surely would have broken out that year. In the year 49 A.D., the emperor Claudius expelled the Jews from the city of Rome. During some rioting in the city of Jerusalem in 66 A.D., the Roman garrison was massacred. This was the signal for a full-scale Jewish rebellion.

The story of this rebellion is complicated,[8] but to simplify it, the Roman general Vespasian came and attacked Jerusalem in 68 A.D. Nero died during the siege of Jerusalem, and Vespasian was recalled to Rome, where he eventually became emperor. His son Titus renewed the attack on Jerusalem, surrounding the city in the year 70 A.D. Finally the walls of the city were breached, the inhabitants slaughtered, and in the process the temple was defiled and burned to the ground. The city of Jerusalem was all but leveled.

There is little room for doubt that this is the event referred to when Gabriel tells Daniel, "The people of the ruler who will come will destroy the city and the sanctuary" (Daniel 9:26). Daniel is not the only Bible prophet who predicted this momentous event. Jesus himself prophesied the destruction of Jerusalem, albeit only forty years before the event, while Daniel wrote more than six hundred years ahead of time. In Luke 21:20-22 one reads:

*Figure 34. "Romans taking spoils of Jerusalem," detail of marble relief from the Arch of Titus, Rome, Italy, c. 81 A.D. in the Roman Forum.*

When you see Jerusalem surrounded by armies, you will know that its desolation is near. Then let those who are in Judea flee to the mountains, let those in the city get out, and let those in the country not enter the city. For this is the time of punishment in fulfillment of all that has been written.

The words "all that has been written" probably refer at least in part to what is written in Daniel 9:26-27. In referring to the destruction of Jerusalem, Jesus continues,

They will fall by the sword and will be taken as prisoners to all the nations. Jerusalem will be trampled on by the Gentiles until the times of the Gentiles are fulfilled (Luke 21:24).

Matthew adds some significant additional information about the destruction of Jerusalem in 70 A.D.:

So when you see standing in the holy place "the abomination that causes desolation," spoken of

through the prophet Daniel—let the reader understand—then let those who are in Judea flee to the
mountains (Matthew 24:15-16).

When Jesus says, "spoken of through the prophet
Daniel," he is referring to Daniel 9, but also to Daniel 12, as
will be seen.

So we have Daniel and Jesus both prophesying the
same occurrence. It must therefore be a very significant
event in God's eyes. Why is that? The next words in the vision of Daniel provide a very significant clue:

The end will come like a flood: War will continue until the end, and desolations have been decreed.
He will confirm a covenant with many for one 'seven.'
In the middle of the "seven" *he will put an end to
sacrifice and offering.* And on a wing of the temple
he will set up an abomination that causes desolation,
until the end that is decreed is poured out on him
(Daniel 9:26b-27, emphasis added).

What "end" is Gabriel referring to? The words, which
are italicized in the quote above, give it away for sure. The
destruction of Jerusalem and the temple in 70 A.D. by Titus
are the "end" referred to by Gabriel. When Titus breached
the walls of Jerusalem, he did not just accept the submission
of the Jews. He leveled the temple in Jerusalem. After the
destruction ordered by Titus, the temple was never rebuilt
again. From that time on, the Jewish system of sacrifice for
the forgiveness of sins was discontinued for good. In God's
eyes, the Old Covenant had been declared null and void on
the cross. The trappings and ceremonial sacrifices of Judaism came to a formal end in the year 70 A.D.

In case there is any doubt that this is what God is telling Daniel, consider Hebrews 8:13. Here, in one of the most
significant passages in the Bible, the writer of Hebrews, referring to the distinctions between the Old Covenant (that
given by Moses) and the New Covenant, (that given by Jesus), says:

By calling this covenant "new," he has made

the first one obsolete; and what is obsolete and aging
*will soon disappear* (emphasis added).

The Hebrew writer tells us that at the time of his
writing, the Jewish religion is obsolete. He also declares
that it "will soon disappear." That is right. As far as God
is concerned, the ceremonial practices of the Old Covenant
ended on that day in 70 A.D. when God used the Gentile non-
believer Titus to burn and level the temple.

There is a somewhat difficult question raised by the
phrase "in the middle of the 'seven'" (Daniel 9:27). Does this
mean that the Messiah is to be cut off in the middle of the
last week? In other words, is the Messiah to be crucified
shortly before the end of the 490 years (i.e., shortly before a
date somewhere between 28 and 32 A.D.)? The fact that one
can only confidently date the crucifixion of Jesus somewhere
between 28 and 32 A.D. leaves this as an open question.

To be completely honest with the evidence, one can
only state with confidence that the Messiah was crucified
either 490 years after the decree to rebuild Jerusalem, or
perhaps in the three or so years before the seventieth "week"
came to an end. To put it another way, there is a slight uncertainty about how exactly to interpret the chronology of
the seventieth "week" as described in Daniel 9, which happens to correspond to a slight uncertainty about the date of
the crucifixion of Jesus Christ. Because it is difficult to be
absolutely sure whether the prophecy predicts exactly 490
years or just slightly fewer than 490 years, it would be a
mistake to be dogmatic on this point. Either way, the amazing accuracy of Daniel's prediction speaks for itself.

Besides this, there is a very subtle point here, and it
is probably the most difficult aspect to interpreting Daniel 9
correctly. The Hebrew writer says that at the time he is writing, the Old Covenant is "obsolete and aging." This brings us
back to Daniel 9. There is an apparent unexplainable gap
in the prophecy. Jesus was cut off (crucified) near or at the
end of the seventieth week (or "seven"). Yet the destruction
of Jerusalem referred to in Daniel 9:26-27 is described as
occurring at the end of the same week. In reality, this event
occurred forty years after the crucifixion. How can the forty-
year gap be explained?

The explanation reveals the inscrutable nature of God, as well as the great depth and beauty of his grace. The apparent meaning of all these scriptures, when taken together, is thus: Although the Old Covenant was essentially extinct at the time of Jesus' death and resurrection, God provided a forty-year window to the Jews, to allow them an opportunity to repent and accept the Lord and Messiah Jesus Christ. In a sense, God suspended time for forty years to allow as many of the Jews as possible to come into the kingdom. This is what the Hebrew writer is referring to when he calls the old cove-

*Figure 35. Roman General and later Emperor, Titus who destroyed Jerusalem in 70 A.D.*

nant "obsolete," but not yet dead. In (approximately) 30 A.D., God stopped the clock, both on his judgment of Israel for rejecting the Messiah, and on the prophecy of the "weeks" of Daniel chapter nine.

In his grace, God stopped the clock for forty years, but when the clock resumed, God's wrath against his people who refused the grace offered was very intense, to say the least. In Jesus' words, "If those days had not been cut short, no one would survive, but for the sake of the elect those days will be shortened" (Matthew 24:22). A subtle, but nevertheless ominous hint of this is also provided in Daniel: "Seventy 'sevens' are decreed for your people and your holy city to finish transgression" (Daniel 9:24). God is saying that only a limited time will be allotted to the Jews to take care of business. The end of this time "will come like a flood" (v. 26).

The end—the destruction of Jerusalem—truly came like a flood. During the siege of the city, wholesale massacres were perpetrated by one group of Jews on another. Death by starvation occurred on a massive scale. Josephus relates tales of murder and cannibalism. The slaughter after the breaching of the city wall took the lives of many thousands of Jewish citizens.[9, 10]

God's grace is absolutely a wonderful thing. His grace certainly finds a major part in the prophecy of Daniel chapter nine. A topic we have only briefly touched is the terrible nature of the wrath of God on stubborn and unrepentant people. But as God says in Daniel 9, "desolations have been decreed" (v. 26). And as the Hebrew writer describes it, "It is a dreadful thing to fall into the hands of the living God" (Hebrews 10:31).

There is some absolutely great news in Daniel 9. God will send the Messiah to bring in everlasting righteousness! Some devastating bad news concerning God's judgment on his people can also be found there. After giving the good and then the bad news, God chooses to end the vision with some encouragement: "And on a wing of the temple he will set up an abomination that causes desolation, until the end that is decreed is poured out on him" (v. 27). Yes, the Roman instrument of judgment on the Jews will desecrate the temple. Yes, in a manner similar to what Antiochus IV Epiphanes did in 167 B.C., Titus will come into the house of God to defile it. But in the end, God will judge the Roman power as well. Several hundred years ahead of time, God is telling his people that when they see the Romans execute judgment on Israel, they should remember that he will ultimately bring judgment on the Romans as well. This fact will also prove helpful in encouraging the disciples of Christ, as the next target of Roman wrath after the destruction of Jerusalem will be the church itself.

Josephus gives details relating to the abomination set up "on a wing of the temple." The word *wing* most likely refers to a high point in the actual structure of the temple. Josephus tells us that when the Roman legions finally breached the wall of Jerusalem, they entered the inner court of the temple, desecrating it. Either accidentally or on purpose, the temple was burned to the ground. After the temple was burned, Titus brought ensigns of war into the ruins and offered sacrifices to those ensigns right there in the temple area, committing an act of "abomination."[11] In doing so, he unknowingly fulfilled the prophecy made by Daniel more than six hundred years earlier (Daniel 9:27), showing one more time that God rules the nations.

An interesting point about the desecration of the temple in 70 A.D. is that God was not there when it happened. When the original temple was consecrated (2 Chronicles 5-7), God literally entered the temple in a very attention-grabbing fashion. As the Bible records:

> When Solomon finished praying, fire came down from heaven and consumed the burnt offering and the sacrifices, and the glory of the Lord filled the temple. The priests could not enter the temple of the Lord because the glory of the Lord filled it. When all the Israelites saw the fire coming down and the glory of the Lord above the temple, they knelt on the pavement with their faces to the ground, and they worshiped and gave thanks to the Lord (2 Chronicles 7:1-3).

After the dedication of the temple by Solomon, the temple had a checkered history, but one can be sure that God abandoned the temple once and for all on the day Jesus was killed on the cross.

Mathew 27:51 relates what happened at the moment Jesus gave up his spirit: "At that moment the curtain of the temple was torn in two from top to bottom." This was not a small tear in the temple curtain. The fabric was completely rent in half, and this was a very large curtain! The priests who observed this event must have been astounded when the curtain suddenly, without warning, was ripped in two. It would be safe to assume that they noticed the connection between the timing of the curtain's ripping and Jesus' death.

There is a double meaning to this overlooked event in the crucifixion account. First, in Judaism the curtain in the temple represented the separation between man and God. The curtain was what separated the "Holy of Holies," where God resided, from the holy place where the priests served at the altar of incense on a daily basis. Only the high priest was allowed to enter the inner sanctuary, and that only happened one time a year, on *Yom Kippur*, the Day of Atonement. Even this one entry into the "Holy of Holies" by the high priest was only allowed after the ritual slaughter of the scapegoat and the scattering of its blood. When the temple curtain was ripped in two, it represented the fact that through the blood of Christ, the separation between man and God was removed once and for all. For those whose sins are forgiven through that blood, the way into the presence of God is now open (see 1 Timothy 2:5). The high priest from the family of Aaron is no longer required to help God's people come into the presence of God. Thank God for that!

The ripping in two of the temple curtain upon the death of Christ has a second meaning as well. As has already been mentioned, when the curtain was ripped asunder, the way was opened for people to come to God through the blood of Jesus Christ. At the same time, God left the temple of Jerusalem once and for all. To the true Jews, the greatness of the temple was not found in its architecture. To the Jews, what made the temple the object of their greatest pride was the fact that in the temple, God dwelt among his people. On that fateful day in about 30 A.D., God left the temple an empty shell. For the next forty years it remained a beautiful, impressive architectural monument, but a building devoid of what had made it great. God had abandoned the temple.

So in Daniel chapter nine, one finds a prophetic hint about God's future abandonment of the temple in about 30 A.D., upon the death of the Messiah. The fact that the last "week" of Daniel nine spans forty uncounted years reveals God's grace in holding back his wrath, providing a chance for the full tithe of Jews to come into God's new kingdom.

In summary, one finds in Daniel chapter nine the prayer of a righteous man who is agonizing over the fate of God's people. In answer to Daniel's humble confession and call for help from God, the angel Gabriel is sent to Daniel to deliver the most encouraging possible message: The Messiah is coming! The final victory of God's people is assured! Everlasting righteousness will be offered to the faithful! However, the coming of the Anointed One of God will not be without trouble. It will be accompanied by great sufferings for those who do not accept the coming Messiah. Ultimately, though, the persecuting power will go the way of all those who dare to defy the living God. The message to God's people is that no matter the situation, *God is in control of the nations—do not fear,* but remain faithful to the one true God.

# Notes

[1] It is interesting to note that Daniel refers to the writings of Jeremiah as scripture. The book of Jeremiah was completed only about fifty years before Daniel received this vision. Relatively little is known about the details of how the Jews arrived at the official canon of the Old Testament. The fact that Daniel already considered Jeremiah's writings as Scripture at such an early date suggests some of the writings may have been accepted as Scripture faster than many writers would claim.

[2] Some commentators do not start the seventy-year period of captivity in 605 B.C., when Nebuchadnezzar first defeated Jerusalem and many captives (including Daniel) were taken to Babylon. Instead, they start the prophetic clock in 586 B.C., when Jerusalem was finally completely destroyed by Nebuchadnezzar. In this case, the seventy years would end in 516 B.C. This just happens to be the year that the restored Temple was completed in Jerusalem. Both interpretations are reasonable, though the author prefers the former, as it is consistent with the prophet Daniel's understanding that that the fulfillment of the prophecy is at hand as he reads it. It is quite interesting that two "destructions" and two "restorations" are both separated by seventy years.

[3] Psalm 22 provides a good example of this concept. Turn to this psalm (go ahead—it will make the illustration clearer) and imagine how you would interpret it if you had never heard any of the details of the life and death of Jesus Christ. Now, read it again, this time allowing yourself to interpret the psalm in the light of what you know about how Jesus was killed. Prophecy is most confidently interpreted in the light of its having already been fulfilled. Those who would attempt to use Daniel, or even more so, Revelation, to make detailed predictions about the end of the world would do well to remember this general rule.

[4] Those who date the decree to rebuild Jerusalem as 445 B.C. most commonly use 360-day "years" to calculate the length of the seventy sevens. They do this because in the Hebrew calendar, the length of the religious year was 360 days. Using the decree of 445 B.C. and 490 "years" of 360 days, Anderson [Sir Robert Anderson, *Daniel in the Critic's Den* (Grand Rapids, Michigan: Kregel Publications, 1990), 134] calculates the date of the crucifixion as exactly April 6, 32 A.D. It is an interesting coincidence that the two different calculations both can yield a date for the crucifixion of the Messiah as about 32 A.D.

[5] If the reader actually does the calculation they may conclude that the author is making a mistake by one year. Actually, there is no mistake. The difference is explained by the fact that there is no year zero B.C. The calendar goes from 1 B.C. to 1 A.D. directly. For example, there are only nine years between 5 B.C. and 5 A.D. This calculation is required to explain the dates used in the next footnote as well. (By the way, this is also why, technically, the millennium should have been celebrated on December 31, 2001).

[6] It is helpful to know the year of the birth of Jesus in order to attempt to date his death. This is true because the Bible gives more specific information about the year that he was born than the year he died. From the descriptions in the New Testament, it is known that he was close to thirty-three years old when he was killed. Unfortunately, it is impossible at this time to say with absolute certainty the exact year of the birth of Jesus Christ. The strongest evidence is contained in Luke 2:1, which mentions a decree of Caesar Augustus to take a census of the entire Roman world. At one time this was thought to be a historical mistake of Luke. Later it was discovered that Augustus did indeed call for such a census in the year 8 B.C. Allowing for two or three years for the decree to circulate to the provinces and to be organized and enforced, Jesus was most likely born in 6 or 5 B.C., plus or minus one year. Additional evidence for the date of Jesus' birth includes the fact that he was born before the death of Herod, which occurred in 4 B.C. The three-year window for the date of his birth, combined with about a one-year uncertainty regarding Jesus' age at death, puts the date for the crucifixion of Jesus somewhere between 28 and 32 A.D., most likely between 29 and 31 A.D.

[7] There is some question as to whether the prophecy implies that the Messiah was to be killed at the end of the seventieth week (32 or 33 B.C.) or during the seventieth week (some time during the seven years before 32 or 33 B.C.). The author would lean toward the latter, as Daniel 9:24 seems to set 490 years as the time limit by which all this must completed, while 9:25 seems to predict the time of his actually coming to Jerusalem.

[8] A thorough description of the wars of 66-73 A.D. is given by the Jewish historian Josephus [*Wars of the Jews*, Josephus, translated by William Whiston, (Kregel Publications, 1960)]. Josephus had first-hand knowledge of the wars. In fact, he actually fought on both the Jewish and the Roman sides in the war. His account is very interesting and provides useful background to the New Testament.

[9] One description from Josephus' account reads thus: "...While Manneus, the son of Lazarus came running to Titus at this very time, through that one gate which was entrusted to his care no fewer than a hundred and fifteen thousand eight hundred and eighty dead bodies, in the interval between the fourteenth day of the month Xanthicus, when the Romans pitched their camp by the city, and the first day of the month Panemus. This was itself a prodigious multitude; and though this man was not himself set as a governor at that gate, yet was he appointed to pay the public stipend for carrying these bodies out, and so was obliged of necessity to number them, while the rest were buried by their relations, though all their burial was but this, to bring them away and cast them out of the city. After this man there ran away to Titus many of the eminent citizens, and told him the entire number of the poor that were dead; and that no fewer than six hundred thousand were thrown out at the gates, though still the number of the rest could not be discovered; and they told him further, that when they were no longer able to carry out the dead bodies

of the poor, they laid their corpses therein... it was not possible to gather herbs, by reason all the city was walled about, some persons were driven to that terrible distress, as to search the common sewers and old dung-hills of cattle and to eat the dung which they got there; and what they of old could not so much as endure to see they now used for food" (Wars of the Jews, Book V, Ch. XII, v. 7).

[10] There is an interesting historical side note about the destruction of Jerusalem in 70 A.D. Tradition holds that the Christians were spared the awful carnage of this event. The disciples were well aware of the prophecies of Jesus recorded in Luke and Matthew. When the leaders of the Church in Jerusalem saw the approaching Roman armies, they understood the event to be the fulfillment of the events foretold by Jesus and Daniel. They took the advice of Jesus to "let those in the city get out, and let those in the country not enter the city" (Luke 21:21). One can assume that Christians who thus escaped the calamity in Jerusalem had their faith in the words of Jesus, as well as their respect for God's judgment, increased dramatically.

[11] Josephus, *Wars of the Jews,* Book VI, Ch. VI, v. 1.

# Chapter Twelve

## North Versus South

The last recorded vision given to Daniel spans chapters ten through twelve. This awesome vision is both the climax and the culmination of the book. It brings together, in the most amazing prophetic vision anywhere in the Bible, all the themes of Daniel. The astoundingly specific prophecies, along with the striking way that most of the Bible's great themes come together in one passage, mark this vision as perhaps the single greatest proof of the Bible's inspiration. No wonder the critics have directed their greatest efforts at discrediting the book of Daniel against this vision.

Unlike the other sections of Daniel, there is no obvious place to divide this part of the book into chapters. Daniel chapter twelve provides a very good summary of the entire book. For this reason, the current chapter of our book will address Daniel chapters ten and eleven, while the final chapter of our book will examine the twelfth chapter of Daniel.

"In the third year of Cyrus king of Persia, a revelation was given to Daniel" (Daniel 10:1). Daniel received this vision in 536 B.C. By now, Daniel is probably more than eighty years old. He is told that the revelation concerns "a great war" (v. 1). This must have been a completely overwhelming vision. Upon receiving the revelation, Daniel is so upset about what will happen to God's people that he mourns for three weeks. For those three weeks, he eats no choice food and puts no lotion on his body. Apparently, it was a big deal in the Near Eastern culture of Daniel's day for men not to put lotion on their bodies. The vision was so overwhelming that the entire tenth chapter of Daniel describes how much God had to do to encourage and strengthen Daniel so that he might receive it.

Try to picture what Daniel is going through. Imagine a person you know quite well knocking at your door without warning. You open the door to see a friend whose visage is distorted almost beyond recognition. He is so overwhelmed by some circumstance, unknown to you, that he is barely able to stand up. He is so shocked that he is completely unable to talk. He walks around in a daze, totally unaware of his environment. This behavior continues unabated for three weeks. Although you may not know what has happened to your friend, one thing you can know for sure: He has just gone through something far more overwhelming than anything you could even imagine.

The scenario just described is analogous to Daniel's condition after receiving the vision recorded in chapters eleven and twelve. It's important to note the description that Daniel was able to record once he had recovered enough to write down what he saw.

"On the twenty-fourth day of the first month, as I was standing on the bank of the great river, the Tigris, I looked up and there before me was a man dressed in linen" (v. 4). This is a flashback for Daniel. He is now describing for us what

*Figure 36. Sculpted stone lion's head from the palace of Persepolis, Iran.*

occurred before the three weeks of shock and fasting mentioned in verse 2. "His body was like chrysolite, his face like lightning, his eyes like flaming torches, his arms and legs like the gleam of burnished bronze, and his voice like the sound of a multitude" (v. 6). Could Daniel be seeing the Lord Jesus Christ himself? The parallel between this description and that given in Revelation 1:13-16 is too strong to ignore. Although it would be a mistake to state this with absolute certainty, it appears that Daniel had the privilege of meeting Jesus Christ and of receiving a direct revelation from him. The other visions in Daniel were delivered in the form of a dream or by an angel. This vision comes by direct revelation from God himself, providing further support to the idea that this vision is the climax of the book of Daniel.

The men with Daniel are unable to see the vision, but apparently they experience some manifestation of what is going on, because they are overwhelmed with terror. Perhaps they are witnesses to a great noise, or perhaps the earth shakes violently. It could be that they see a great light, but cannot make out clearly what Daniel sees. There is an obvious parallel between what happens to Daniel here and what happened, hundreds of years later, to Saul and his companions on the road to Damascus. In Acts 9:1-8, one finds the companions of Saul (later known as Paul) standing speechless because they heard a sound, but did not see Jesus. The parallel between Acts 9 and Daniel 10 provides further support to the idea that Daniel is seeing Jesus Christ in the vision being described.

Consider how intense an effect the vision has on Daniel: "So I was left alone, gazing at this great vision; I had no strength left, my face turned deathly pale and I was helpless" (v. 8). Finally, Daniel is so overwhelmed that he falls into a deep sleep with his face to the ground. After lying there unconscious for an unknown length of time, Daniel relates, "A hand touched me and set me trembling on my hands and knees." Daniel never specifies who helps him, but almost certainly Daniel is revived by the touch of an angel.

The angel goes on to tell an amazing story. God has sent him to Daniel in response to his humble prayers. "Since the first day that you set your mind to gain understanding and to humble yourself before your God, your words were heard, and I have come in response to them" (v. 12). What a great encouragement to Daniel to learn that his resolute determination to remain righteous, even while surrounded by pagan unbelievers for most of his life, has caught God's attention. And what an encouragement to modern-day disciples of Christ as well. Those who in this life make a firm decision to "set their mind to gain understanding and to humble themselves before their God" should reflect on these uplifting words. Those who have not made such a resolution would also do well to carefully consider these words. The theme of Daniel is revealed once again: Do not lose heart, disciple of Christ; do not fear, Christian, for God will reward your humble and patient service to him.

Let us get back to the story. The angel relates to Daniel that on his way to encourage him, he was held up by a spiritual battle. A protracted confrontation with Satan made him late in bringing help: "But the prince of the Persian kingdom resisted me twenty-one days" (v.13). What kind of battle is this? And who is the prince of the Persian kingdom?

Surely the angel is describing a spiritual battle. Behind the earthly battle scene that we can observe, a parallel spiritual battle is constantly being waged "in the heavenly realms" (Ephesians 6:12). The apostle Paul relates, "For our struggle is not against flesh and blood, but against the rulers, against the authorities, against the powers of this dark world and against the spiritual forces of evil in the heavenly realms" (Ephesians 6:12). This statement could either make people more confident, or it could make them more insecure than ever, depending on where their faith rests.

The entire time that Daniel is fighting his own battles with the pagan world, a parallel spiritual battle is being waged, a battle of which Daniel is normally unaware. Knowledge of this fact could make Daniel (or us) more insecure, if he worries about the battle affecting his life, even though he has no control over it. This lack of feeling in control—or more accurately, worrying about or resenting this feeling—is the root of most insecurity. On the other hand, knowledge of the spiritual battle could make Daniel (and us) feel more *secure*, if he maintains a firm commitment to take care of his own end of the battle. It is Daniel's (and our) job to make the decision to remain righteous, no matter the outward circumstances, and let God and his angels take care of the spiritual battle. It is ironic that God's way of giving us "the peace of God, which transcends all understanding" (Philippians 4:7) is to put us into situations over which we have no control, using those situations to teach us to rely on him. This reliance on God is the only source of security that will bring ultimate peace to the human soul. Whether one likes it or not, God created his people to find true peace only when their lives are entrusted to his hands.

And who is this "prince of the Persian kingdom," referred to in Daniel 10:13? Apparently this is the demonic person/power whose hand is behind the evil things that happen in Persia. No, it is not the physical king of the physical Persian kingdom. One can be certain of this by referring to Daniel 10:20-21. Here the angel speaks to Daniel of the archangel Michael as "[his] prince." Therefore, when he speaks, in the same breath, about fighting against "the prince of Persia," we can be sure that he is once more speaking about an angelic being . Thus the "prince" of Persia is a demonic angel. This may come as a revelation to the reader.

Apparently, from the vision of Daniel, one can conclude that specific angels act as the defenders of individual nations. Besides that, it would appear that specific demonic beings lurk behind the scenes to lead individual nations astray. The implication of Daniel chapter ten is that, even now, there are spiritual battles being fought. These battles, which rage on even without our awareness, have dramatic implications for our personal lives.[1] One can assume that Daniel takes comfort in this fact, but for those who have not put their complete faith in God, this revelation could be very disconcerting.

This brings to mind another question: Who is the unidentified angel who is speaking to Daniel in this vision? It would be difficult to say for sure, since this angel is not identified by name. The most reasonable conjecture would be that the angel speaking to Daniel is the other "archangel" spoken of in the Bible. It is most likely Gabriel himself. Looking back at Daniel 8:16 and Daniel 9:21 gives a lot of credence to this idea. One is left with the impression that Michael and Gabriel are the archangels who were given special responsibility to watch over the nation of Israel.[2]

Back again to the story. Gabriel tells Daniel that he was delayed because he had been battling the prince of Persia for the past twenty-one days. This apparent standoff was only settled when Michael came to assist Gabriel in his battle against the evil powers. In heaven, Michael and

Gabriel will have some great war stories to share with us! Interestingly, later in Gabriel's conversation with Daniel, the angel declares that he is off next to continue the battle with the prince of Persia. During this battle against Persia, "the prince of Greece will come" (v. 20). This may be a reference to the future historical attack of Alexander against the Persian Empire, or of the Greek kingdoms against the Jews (the subject of Daniel 11), or it may refer to some other unknown spiritual battle. It would be fascinating to have more insight into the nature of these spiritual battles, but Bible students must content themselves with speculating on this subject, because God chooses to give only a very sketchy description.

Gabriel tells Daniel, "Now I have come to explain to you what will happen to your people in the future, for the vision concerns a time yet to come" (v. 14). Of course, the skeptics would claim that the writer of Daniel is actually writing *after* the events about to be described. The great majority of theologians would tell us with confidence that the claim to foretell "a time yet to come" is a mere deception created by a pious Jew posing as Daniel. They would claim that this deception was thrust upon the gullible Jewish rabbis during the second century B.C. The internal evidence in the book, however, does not support this claim. Besides, the theologians' claim asserts that Jewish teachers of the second century B.C. were so gullible that they were fooled into believing that a spurious writing of one of their contemporaries was actually written four hundred years before. This accusation is so outrageous that it barely deserves mentioning.

Daniel is so overwhelmed by the explanation given to him by Gabriel that he bows to the ground, completely unable to speak. "Then one who looked like a man touched my lips, and I opened my mouth and began to speak" (v. 16). This is Gabriel again, giving him strength. Daniel is now able to speak, but he is still so devastated by the vision that he is physically exhausted to the point that he can barely even breathe. In verse 18, Gabriel touches Daniel for the third time. One can see a parallel with Jesus' need in the garden of Gethsemane (Matthew 26:36-46) to return to the Father in prayer three times in order to gain the strength to face the crucifixion. Finally, Daniel is strengthened enough for the vision to continue. This must be quite a vision!

Before proceeding, Gabriel informs Daniel that what he is telling him "is written in the Book of Truth" (v. 21). This revelation comes straight from the word of God.[3] Finally, the prophetic vision begins:

"Three more kings will appear in Persia, and then a fourth, who will be far richer than all the others. When he has gained power by his wealth, he will stir up everyone against the kingdom of Greece" (Daniel 11:2). The three more kings referred to in the vision are Cyrus and his successors, Cambyses (530-522 B.C.) and Darius I (522-486 B.C.). The fourth king Daniel is told about is Xerxes I (486-465 B.C.). The reign of Xerxes I represented the zenith of Persian power. The only remaining rival to Persian power in the Near East was that of Greece. Xerxes staked the entire wealth and prestige of Persia on a huge campaign to conquer unified Greek military power under the leadership of Athens. He actually had a great canal built across the cape of Athos in Greece in preparation for his naval assault, in order to avoid the stormy peninsula. Xerxes spent three years building up provisions at strategic locations. He recruited soldiers from forty-six nations ("he will stir up everyone against the kingdom of Greece," as Daniel's prophecy describes it) and employed twenty-nine generals to command his army. Perhaps most incredible of all, he had a bridge built across the straits of the Dardanelles, which separate Asia from Europe. He did this by connecting a great number of ships to one another, allowing his army to march directly from Asia to Europe. To this day, no other bridge has been built across the Dardanelles. This was one of the greatest military campaigns of all time. Daniel tells us in detail about this great battle 56 years before it occurred (in 480 B.C.). Is any believer in God surprised that Daniel got it right?

What the angel does not tell Daniel is that after some initial successes, Xerxes' campaign was to be a failure. This defeat of Xerxes marked the turning point in the back-and-forth conflict between Persian and Greek power. At this point, the vision leaps forward to the next significant conflict between the Greeks and the Persians: "Then a mighty king will appear, who will rule with great power and do as he pleases" (Daniel 11:3). This is Alexander the Great. A gap of one hundred and thirty years spans between the reigns of Xerxes and Alexander.

*Figure 37. Tomb of Cyrus in Iran.*

The skeptics have tried to claim that this represents a "mistake" in Daniel. They claim that Daniel only knew of four kings of Persia, when in fact, there were a total of ten emperors in Persia between the ascension of Cyrus and the death of the last Persian emperor, Darius III, in 330 B.C. In response, one could ask, "Where in Daniel does it say that there were only four kings in Persia?" It is true that Daniel only mentions four kings. The fact is that in the period between the defeat of Xerxes and the conquests of Alexander, there was relative peace between Greece and the Persian Empire. Besides this, it was a time of relative stability in the Holy Land as well. There was no single event in this rather long period worth mentioning by the Biblical prophet. Therefore, God chooses to leave out mention of this period. Where is the mistake here? It simply does not exist.

At this point in the prophecy and in history, Alexander, son of Philip of Macedon, bursts onto the scene. In case there was any doubt about his identity, the angel continues by telling Daniel that after this king leaves the scene, his kingdom will be parceled out into four pieces. This is undeniably a reference to the four successor kings who followed Alexander. Any remaining uncertainty about the identity of the mighty king who will appear is removed when Gabriel gives a few more details. He tells Daniel that the power of this king will not go to his descendants and that the kingdom will not be as great as it was under him. This is a clear reference to Alexander.

Up to this point, the prophecy in Daniel 11 has provided the reader of this book with no major new information. All that will change presently. The angel continues, "The king of the South will become strong, but one of his commanders will become even stronger" (v. 5). Now, the main body of the prophecy will begin. In Daniel 11, the king of the South is the empire of the Ptolemaic Dynasty, centered, as mentioned before, in Egypt. The king of the North in this prophecy is the empire of the Seleucid Dynasty, centered in Syria/Mesopotamia. Perhaps the reader has previously studied Daniel chapter eleven but thought this prophecy had nothing to do with any actual historical event.

The statement that the kings of the South are the Ptolemies and that the kings of the North are the Seleucids is no idle claim. In fact, the reader will find from the following discussion that there can be absolutely no doubt about what the prophecy means. It is very interesting to remember that Daniel has absolutely no way of knowing what the angel is talking about, because all the events Gabriel describes will take place well over two hundred years after Daniel's death. Daniel has no idea at all who the kings of the North and of the South are.

The angel is about to describe in painstaking detail the future history of the wars between the Ptolemies and the Seleucids, over a period spanning from about 315 B.C. to about 160 B.C. Rather than go through the account verse-by-verse, the author will provide a loosely paraphrased re-translation of the text, inserting the actual historical facts, including names, dates and places where the biblical prophecy leaves them out. The reader should peruse the following account with the biblical version in one hand and the retranslation given here in the other. Remember that the series of historical events described here comes from historical accounts external to the Bible.

(v. 5) By 315 B.C., Ptolemy I Soter, the founder of the Greek Ptolemaic Dynasty, will establish himself in Egypt. In a battle in 312 B.C. with his strongest competitor, Antigonus, he will rise to become the predominant successor to Alexander. However, Ptolemy's greatest general, Seleucus, the one who had defeated Antigonus, will break away from him to establish an independent dynasty in Mesopotamia. Eventually, his kingdom will become even greater than the southern kingdom of the Ptolemies.

## The Kings of the South and the Kings of the North in Daniel Eleven

| Kings of the South | Kings of the North | Daniel 11 Verse |
| --- | --- | --- |
| Ptolemy I, 323-283 B.C. | Seleucus I Nicator, 321-282 B.C | Daniel 11:5 |
| Ptolemy II Philadelphus, 283-247 B.C. | Antiochus I Soter, 280-261 B.C. | Daniel 11:6 |
| | Antiochus II Theos, 261-246 B.C. | Daniel 11:6 |
| Ptolemy III Eugertes, 247-221 B.C. | Seleucus II Callinicus, 246-226 B.C. | Daniel 11:7-8 |
| | Seleucus III Soter, 226-223 B.C. | Daniel 11:8 |
| Ptolemy IV Philopater, 221-203 B.C. | Antiochus III "The Great," 223-187 B.C. | Daniel 11:9-19 |
| Ptolemy V Epiphanes, 203-181 B.C. | Seleucus IV Philopator, 187-175 B.C. | Daniel 11:20 |
| Ptolemy VI Philometor, 180-146 B.C. | Antiochus IV Epiphanes, 175-164 B.C. | Daniel 11:21-35 |
| | Antiochus V Eupator, 164-162 B.C. | |

(v. 6) After some early, indecisive struggles, the Ptolemaic kingdom and the Seleucid kingdom will agree to share power peacefully. In order to seal the deal, Ptolemy II Philadelphus will send his daughter Berenice to marry Antiochus II Theos, the heir to the northern, Seleucid throne. This marriage in 252 B.C. will serve to make the two empires political allies. After both the kings of the North and of the South (Antiochus I and Ptolemy II) die in 246 and 245 B.C., respectively, the alliance will break down. Laodice, the half-sister and wife of Antiochus II will have Berenice and her son (the heir to the throne) poisoned.[4] Because of this murder, Antiochus II will succeed to the throne of the Seleucids.

(v. 7) In revenge, Berenice's brother, Ptolemy III Eugertes, will take the Egyptian throne and use it to attack Seleucus II Callinicus (successor to Antiochus II) in what will be known as the "Laodicean War," gaining much territory from Seleucus in Syria. (v. 8) Ptolemy III will return to Egypt in 240 B.C. with much booty, to live out his reign in peace.

(v. 9) Later, Antiochus III, sometimes known as Antiochus the Great, will take the throne in the Northern Kingdom. He will attack the Southern Kingdom in 221 B.C., with some success, but will be forced to retreat by the Ptolemaic general Theodotus. (v. 10) Undaunted, Antiochus III will return to the attack in 218-217 B.C., taking the strongholds of Tyre, Gaza, and even Raphia, a fortress on the border of Egypt proper. (v. 11) However, this particular victory will be short-lived as Ptolemy IV Philopater will raise an army and visit a disastrous defeat on Antiochus III, retaking all the conquered territory.

(v. 12, 13) After the death of Ptolemy IV, Antiochus III will raise an even greater army and attack the Southern Kingdom in 202-198 B.C. (v. 14) During this drawn-out campaign, many of the Jews will rebel against the Southern Kingdom and ally themselves with Antiochus III. (v. 15) Antiochus III will defeat the Egyptian general Scopas, who will retreat to Sidon. At Sidon, Scopas will be besieged, and ultimately forced to surrender in 198 B.C. (v. 16) As a result of this victory, Antiochus III will take all of Syria and Palestine from the Ptolemaic kingdom, including the Promised Land ("the Beautiful Land"). (v. 17) In order to secure his victory, Antiochus will send his daughter, Cleopatra, to marry the young Ptolemy V, but this marriage alliance will not prove to be successful. (v. 18) Antiochus will reach a great height of power, as he will go on to conquer the coast of Asia Minor (196 B.C.) and even the margins of Greece (192 B.C.). However, at the height of his power, the new power in the Mediterranean comes into the picture: Rome. In two battles at Thermopylae and Magnesium, the Romans, bringing to an end the expansion of Seleucid power, decisively defeat Antiochus III. (v. 19) Antiochus will suffer the humiliation of paying a huge indemnity. He will be forced to send his son (the later Antiochus IV Epiphanes) as a hostage to Rome. After these events, he will return to Syria to die.

(v. 20) His successor, Seleucus IV Philopater, will send his prime minister, Heliodorus, throughout the Northern Kingdom to collect exorbitant taxes (this event is recorded in 2 Maccabees 3). For political reasons, Heliodorus will have Seleucus IV killed (i.e., Seleucus IV will not die in battle, but will be assassinated). (v. 21) The successor to Seleucus IV will be the despised Antiochus IV Epiphanes. Antiochus IV Epiphanes will not be the presumed heir, but he will use political intrigue to gain political allies in the kingdom and illegitimately seize the throne of the Northern Kingdom.

The paraphrase will be continued below, but it is appropriate to stop the story briefly at this point to explain some of the background to the arrival in Jerusalem of Antiochus IV Epiphanes. The prophecy of Daniel 11 focuses primarily on the reign of this much-despised ruler. In fact, verses 21 through 35 will be about the unfortunate relationship between this radical Hellenizer and the Jews.

The rule of the Greek/Egyptian Ptolemaic Dynasty over Jerusalem had been relatively benign. The Jews were allowed to pursue their own religion relatively unfettered. They also were allowed to appoint their own high priest and were given a good deal of local autonomy under the Ptolemaic governors. It is ironic that the Jews supported Antiochus III in his battles against the Ptolemies. They welcomed him into Jerusalem with open arms. The irony exists because under the Seleucid kings, the fairly benevolent policies of the Ptolemies were overturned in favor of a much harsher policy towards the native Jewish population. This was to prove especially true when Antiochus IV Epiphanes took the throne.

Antiochus IV had been born in Athens, and had spent twelve years in Rome as a hostage. As a pun on his official royal name of Antiochus IV Epiphanes (meaning "the manifestation of the gods"), the Jews sarcastically called him "Antiochus IV Epimanes" (meaning "the madman"). He became convinced that the Greco/Roman culture should be the only acceptable culture for the people throughout his empire. Therefore, Antiochus set out on a policy to systematically Hellenize the Jews. He forced them to accept the cosmopolitan Greek lifestyle, with its mode of dress, political life, and—most significantly—its religion. Many of the liberal Jews actually embraced this change, but the core of conservative, nationalistic, faithful Jews were determined to oppose the Hellenizing policies of Antiochus IV Epiphanes at any cost whatsoever.

In the process of Hellenizing Israel, Antiochus had a gymnasium built in Jerusalem. At this gymnasium, athletes competed in the nude. This was obviously extremely offensive to the conservative Jews. In his arrogance, Antiochus forbade the circumcision of Jewish children under penalty of death. This foolish policy pushed the faithful Jews beyond their limit of toleration. Open rebellion was the result. The intense persecutions that Antiochus IV Epiphanes committed on these faithful Jews, and the determination of this Jewish remnant to remain faithful no matter what the opposition, is the primary subject of this prophecy. The reader should be reminded that Daniel is telling the story approximately three hundred and fifty years before it happened!

It is time to return to the running commentary on chapter eleven. (v. 22) Antiochus IV Epiphanes will ally himself with the liberal Jewish leader Jason to attack and defeat the strictly orthodox high priest (i.e., the "prince of the covenant") Onais. (v. 23) Because of a bribe, Antiochus will appoint the Hellenizing Jason as the high priest, but he will deceive Jason and use him to establish his power over the Jews. Eventually, he will accept a bribe from another pretender, Menelaus, and give the high priesthood to him. (v. 24) Antiochus will be a master of intrigue, attacking provinces when they are least prepared to defend themselves. He will use monies taken from one province as booty to bribe others to support him. This deceitful policy will succeed for Antiochus up to a point.

(v. 25) After establishing his hegemony throughout Palestine and Syria, Antiochus will attack Ptolemy VI in 170 B.C. Antiochus will succeed in this campaign as much because of disunity in the Egyptian camp as because of his overwhelming power. (v. 26) Because of a plot against Ptolemy VI by some of his closest allies, Antiochus IV will defeat Ptolemy VI. (v. 27) They will meet to sign an armistice and to make many agreements, but both rulers will act hypocritically and break their agreements. Ultimately, at least in part because of their dishonesty, God will bring both kingdoms to ruin. (v. 28) After this victory, Antiochus will pass through Jerusalem. He will be welcomed by his puppet high-priest Menelaus. At this time, he will confirm and extend his persecutions against the Hasidim (the pious Jews). He will then return to Syria.

(v. 29) After a very short truce, Antiochus IV Epiphanes will renew the attack on Egypt in 168 B.C. Probably this attack would have resulted in the final destruction of the Ptolemies by the Seleucids. (v. 30) However, seeing the potential rising of a great power in the east under Antiochus IV Epiphanes, the Romans will decide to intervene. They will send a fleet of ships from Cyprus to support the flagging Ptolemaic power. This move will lead to the defeat of Antiochus IV. In a fit of rage, Antiochus IV Epiphanes will return to Jerusalem to vent his anger on his enemies, the non-conforming Jews.

(v. 31) In what will be the most outrageous attack on true Jews in the entire history of the nation, Antiochus will send his soldiers to desecrate the temple. He will outlaw the Jewish system of sacrifice in the temple at Jerusalem. He will also outlaw circumcision and Sabbath-observance. He will tear down part of the wall of Jerusalem. He will order the ceremonial worship of Greek deities by everyone. He will have an image of the Greek god Jupiter hung in the temple (setting up "the abomination that causes desolation"). Greek soldiers will perform disgusting pagan sexual ceremonies right there in the temple! He will even sacrifice a pig on the altar where sacrifices had been made to God. Antiochus will enforce laws promulgating Hellenism and outlawing Jewish observance with the utmost cruelty. One of the most respected of the Hebrew scribes, Eleazar, will be publicly flogged to death for refusing to eat pig flesh. A mother and her seven children will be publicly murdered, one at a time, for refusing to sacrifice to a Greek god.

(v. 32) The victory of the Hellenizing party under Menelaus may seem sure, but the barbaric attacks of Antiochus will inspire the religious zeal of the minority of Jews who refuse to submit to the persecutions of the "madman" Antiochus. Those who truly have a relationship with God will firmly resist Antiochus. (v. 33) Many courageous Jews will continue to observe the Sabbath, to circumcise their sons, and to teach about God. For a period of time, their faithful attempts to obey God will result in many of these faithful Jews being slaughtered. The pious Jew Mattathias will rise in revolt against the Greek persecutors. (Mattathias and his five sons will ultimately establish an independent Jewish nation in Israel. The family will be called the Maccabees, and they will establish the Hasmonean Dynasty) (v. 34). Mattathias and his son Judas Maccabeus will experience some success in their rebellion, but some insincere Jews will join them. Traitors to the Jewish cause will help Antiochus temporarily overcome the rebellion. During this time, the true believers of God will have their faith "refined and made spotless." Those who remain faithful will ultimately see the end of the persecution. At the appointed time, Judas and his army will move on Jerusalem and defeat the Greek sympathizers there. They will enter the temple grounds, and in one of the most celebrated moments in all Jewish history, they will destroy the "abomination that causes desolation" and reconsecrate the temple to the true and living God.

This momentous event is what Jews celebrate as the feast of Chanukah. Ever since the rededication of the temple, Jews have remembered the event with one of their greatest feasts. In the ceremony, they remember not only the rededication of the temple, but also the refusal of their fathers and mothers to compromise their commitment to the one true God. Although this persecution was truly a fearsome thing, the recommitment to the basics of Judaism that it inspired resulted in one of the greatest revivals in the history of God's people. It is a great historical irony that Antiochus IV Epiphanes' attempt to annihilate Judaism only resulted in its purification. Thanks to the persecutions of Antiochus, the Jews were forged into a nation that was overall considerably more devoted to God than ever before.

As the famous saying goes, "History repeats itself." In the first three centuries, as Nero, Domitian and their followers attempted to destroy the church of Jesus Christ, they only succeeded in purifying and strengthening the religion they sought to rub out. Those who experience persecution for their faith today would do well to bear in mind these examples.

Think for a moment how encouraging the book of Daniel must have been to the faithful and righteous Jews as they endured the outrageous attacks of Antiochus. They were able to read a detailed account of their sufferings as recorded in the book of Daniel hundreds of years earlier. When God told them, through Daniel, that ultimately the end would come for their persecutor, this must have given many of them the strength they needed to hold up under the ferocious attacks against their faith. Is it any wonder that Daniel became one of the most revered books in the Hebrew canon?

What about the theologians who attempt to attack the inspiration of the Bible by claiming that the book of Daniel is a forgery, written in about 160 B.C.? It seems reasonable to ask at this point how they can support their view with a clear conscience. They would claim that just a few years after the momentous events of Antiochus' persecution—events that left an indelible mark on the national memory of the Jewish nation—some deceitful author was able to produce a spurious historical and religious romance containing the prophecy in Daniel 11. They would claim that this forger was able to convince the Jewish teachers and scribes that it was actually written by Daniel four hundred years earlier. This unsupportable theory flies in the face of the historical fact that Daniel was already a part of the Jewish canon before the persecutions of Antiochus even happened. It is refuted by the undeniable fact that the events during the Seleucid reign solidified forever, not only the place of Daniel in the Hebrew canon, but also its place as one of preeminent honor in the Bible. Can anyone believe the claim that the Jewish leaders in the second century B.C., most of whom were alive during these great persecutions, were fooled into accepting a recent forgery as if God had inspired it? This claim proves the desperation of Satan's attack on the living word of God. It also shows the great gullibility of the supposed Bible scholars who are willing to honor such unsupportable notions.

Remember, though, that this is the last line of defense for those who are unwilling to accept the miraculous inspiration of the Bible. By now the reader is well aware of the extremely specific nature of the prophecy in Daniel chapter eleven. Daniel 11 is a point-by-point, detailed chronological history of the Near East over about a two-hundred-year period leading up to the reign of Antiochus IV Epiphanes. It contains specifics about places, people and events, all of which can be verified from outside historical sources. Daniel recorded each of these historically verifiable facts hundreds of years before the events occurred.

As mentioned previously, the first scholar on record to point out the extremely specific nature of the account in Daniel 11 was the third-century A.D. philosopher Porphyry. Porphyry was well aware of the detailed nature of the prophecy. Porphyry was faced with two possible conclusions: Either Daniel is genuine, and therefore the Bible is without question an inspired book, or Daniel is a forgery, and the Bible has no credibility at all. Unfortunately, being a pagan philosopher, he chose to conclude that the book was a forgery, making himself the vanguard of modern theology. From all the evidence we have examined, one can assume Porphyry reached this conclusion not because the evidence backed it up, but because he was unwilling to accept the implication of the Bible's inspiration (and hence its authority in his life). With all the evidence now available to modern scholars, they are left with even less excuse than Porphyry had.[5]

Besides, the prophecy is not yet complete. The angel continues his description of future events to Daniel. The rest of the vision concerns events which actually occurred after the supposed date of authorship of the book as claimed by the skeptics. It concerns the fulfillment of God's judgment on the Greek power mentioned in Daniel 11:35 as well as in Daniel 8:25: "Yet he will be destroyed, but not by human power." How are the skeptics to explain the rest of the vision, which describes incidents that eventually led to the complete destruction of the Greek kingdoms in the year 31 B.C.? The critics, understandably, are silent on this point because there is no reasonable answer to this question.

Unlike the first thirty-five verses of Daniel 11, which all the commentators agree refer to the conflict between the Ptolemies and the Seleucids, there is virtually no agreement among scholars about the specific interpretation of Daniel 11:36-45. To the author, this is a very curious fact, as a fairly straightforward study of the history of the Near East provides an obvious interpretation. One author[6] has claimed that "no commentator claims to find precise fulfillment in the remainder of this chapter." I'm convinced that I would be an exception to this statement. Let the readers decide for themselves.

In a change of temporal scene similar to the one between Daniel 11:2 and Daniel 11:3, the vision now takes a leap forward in time. The change is signaled by the statement in Daniel 11:35, where the angel tells Daniel that the righteous should be patient "so that they may be refined, purified and made spotless *until the time of the end*, for it will still come *at the appointed time*" (emphasis added). The end of the Greek persecutors will come at the appointed time, but the faithful Jews must be patient, allowing themselves to be refined and purified by their persecutors. The "time of the end" finds its fulfillment in Daniel 11:36-45. Beginning in Daniel 11:36, the scene fast-forwards about one hundred years. The king of the North is now Rome, while the king of the south is now the nearly extinct Ptolemaic Dynasty. This switch may seem somewhat hard to follow, but the description of the vision about to be given will prove the point.

In Daniel 11:36-39 one reads :

> The king will do as he pleases. He will exalt
> and magnify himself above every god and will say
> unheard-of things against the God of gods. He will be
> successful until the time of wrath is completed, for
> what has been determined must take place. He will
> show no regard for the gods of his fathers or for the
> one desired by women, nor will he regard any god, but
> will exalt himself above them all. Instead of them,
> he will honor a god of fortresses; a god unknown to
> his fathers he will honor with gold and silver, with
> precious stones and costly gifts. He will attack the
> mightiest fortresses with the help of a foreign god
> and will greatly honor those who acknowledge him.
> He will make them rulers over many people and will
> distribute the land at a price.

The king in this passage is Rome! It is the legs of iron
in Daniel chapter two and the indescribable beast of Daniel
chapter seven. In other words, in this passage, the king of
the North has become Rome.

How can one be sure of this identification of the king
of the North in Daniel 11:36-45? Two reasons for identifying
the king of the North in this passage as Rome should be
mentioned. First, God is revealing to Daniel (and to us) how
the persecutor of his people will be avenged. Historically, the
destroyer of Greek power was Rome. Second, the description
in the passage fits extremely well with what is commonly
known about the history, religion and culture of the Roman
Empire.

Unquestionably, Rome "did as he pleased" throughout
the Mediterranean region for several centuries. The power of
Rome "exalted and magnified itself above every god," to say
the least. In fact, although Rome began with a traditional
belief in a number of gods, somewhat similar to the more
familiar Greek pantheon, eventually the chief "god" of Rome
became Rome itself. The Romans called this god "Roma." The
people throughout the far-flung Empire of Rome literally
worshiped the Roman power. From the time of Augustus on,

the Roman people began to worship the emperors themselves rather than the less well-defined Roman war-god. To a large extent the Roman people abandoned the traditional gods of the past. This fits exactly the prediction that "he will show no regard for the gods of his fathers" (v. 37). The description, "he will honor a god of fortresses," again, is an apt description of Rome's worship of the national god of war.

What about the phrase, "He will attack the mightiest fortresses with the help of a foreign god and will greatly honor those who acknowledge him" (v. 39)? Again, this description fits the Roman power with uncanny accuracy. In achieving its unprecedented world domination, Rome would find powerful local rulers to act as allies in defeating whatever state it was attempting to subdue. For example, when Rome, under Pompey, defeated the Parthian Empire, the local Hasmonean Dynasty (the dynasty that held power in Jerusalem) was recruited in the effort. At the end of the war, the Romans left an independent client king from the Hasmonean power in charge. Through the remainder of the first century B.C. and well into the first century A.D., Roman power was largely administered through the client-kings established as allies of Rome in this way. This is how the famous king Herod, the one who attempted to kill Jesus when he was a child, came to power. He was a client-king of the Romans. This well-known Roman policy matches in an uncanny way the description, "He will make them rulers over many people and will distribute the land at a price" (v. 39).

The Roman policy of expansion also involved incorporating the unfamiliar foreign gods of the conquered or the soon-to-be-conquered nations into the Roman pantheon of gods. For example, many Romans followed the cult of the Egyptian god Isis even before Egypt was subdued. This explains the phrase in the vision predicting that Rome would gain power "with the help of a foreign god" (v. 39). These policies of Rome are well known to historians, but one might ask how Daniel could have known about them in 536 B.C.?

The angel continues by relating specific information about the Roman power (the king of the North): "At the time of the end the king of the South will engage him in battle, and the king of the North will storm out against him with chariots and cavalry and a great fleet of ships" (Daniel 11:40). In this statement, Gabriel is describing to Daniel the final end of

the Ptolemaic Dynasty (the king of the South). The battle being described by the angel is the famous battle of Actium. In this battle, which took place in the year 31 B.C., Octavian, the adopted son of Julius Caesar, fought and defeated Mark Antony and his ally Cleopatra. The battle was fought on land ("with chariots and cavalry"), but the decisive conflict was actually a huge naval battle ("and a great fleet of ships"). This was one of the greatest

*Figure 38. Mark Antony, the "Avenger."*

naval battles in history. In the battle of Actium, the Ptolemaic power was finally broken forever. Mark Antony committed suicide after hearing a false rumor that his lover Cleopatra had been killed. Later, after attempting and failing to win the affections of Octavian, Cleopatra committed suicide as well by exposing herself to an asp. Notice that according to the prophecy, this battle will occur "at the time of the end"(v. 40). The prophecy is exactly correct. In 31 B.C., on God's timetable, the Greek power, as prophesied in the book of Daniel, was finally brought to an ignominious end.

However, Gabriel is not done yet. He supplies even more information about the battle and about what the Roman victor will do to follow up his victory:

> He will invade many countries and sweep through them like a flood. He will also invade the Beautiful Land. Many countries will fall, but Edom, Moab and the leaders of Ammon will be delivered from his hand. He will extend his power over many countries; Egypt will not escape. He will gain control of the treasures of gold and silver and all the riches of Egypt, with the Libyans and Nubians in submission. But reports from the east and the north will alarm him, and he will set out in a great rage to destroy and annihilate many. He will pitch his royal tents

between the seas at the beautiful holy mountain
(Daniel 11:40b-45).

This is *exactly* what happened to Octavian after the
battle of Actium! Is the Bible believer surprised at this? After the battle of Actium, Mark Antony's army soon dissipated. King Herod, who had been an ally of Antony, decided to
humble himself before Octavian, frankly pointing out that
he had been a loyal servant of Antony, and proposing that he
would be an equally faithful servant of Octavian. With the
help of Herod's mainly Jewish army, Octavian consolidated
his victory by taking most of the territory of the remnant
Ptolemaic Dynasty, including the rest of Palestine ("the
Beautiful Land") and Egypt, as well as the upper reaches of
the Nile (the Nubians) and the coast of Africa west of Egypt
(the Libyans).

Actually, Octavian (later the first emperor of Rome,
known as Augustus) failed to take one significant part of
the former Ptolemaic territory. He did attack the Arab ter-
ritories of Edom, Moab and the Ammonites, but was unable
to bring them into submission. In fact, the Romans were unable to conquer the Arabs until the reign of Trajan, well over
one hundred years later. How did Daniel know this detail
back in 536 B.C.? A casual look at a historical map showing
the territory controlled by Rome in the time of Augustus will
show that there was a noticeable tract of unconquered territory in the area south and east of Palestine. This is the exact
territory described by Daniel five hundred years earlier.

Octavian (Augustus) was unable to complete his victory over the Arabs at least in part because he was called
away to defend the empire against a renewed Parthian
threat. The Parthians were a reconstituted Persian power.
This is the "report from the east" that Gabriel tells Daniel
about. Historical records show that when Octavian heard
about the threats from the Parthians, he immediately sent
his armies to defend against attack from the east. On his way
to fight the Parthians, Octavian passed through Palestine,
pitching "his royal tents between the seas" (i.e., between the
Mediterranean and the Dead Seas) in the Holy Land.

*Figure 39. Octavius (later Augustus Caesar, who reigned c. 27 B.C.-14 A.D.) in Rome, Italy.*

The skeptics would claim that Daniel was written in about 160 B.C. They do so in an attempt to prove that an all-powerful God did not inspire the book. That explanation, although inconsistent with many facts about the book, would at least explain how Daniel 11:2-35 could have been written, because it describes events which occurred before 160 B.C. The argument completely falls apart, however, in light of Daniel 11:36-45. How could the supposed author in 160 B.C. have been able to produce detailed information about the battle of Actium and its aftermath? These events did not occur for another 130 years. How could he have been privy to such detailed information about the end of the Greek persecuting power? The answer, of course, is that he could not have known about the battle unless, by inspiration, he had been given a vision from God—the same God who chose to bring the kings of the South to judgment through the power of Rome.

The second half of Daniel 11:45 provides the perfect ending to the historical/prophetic part of this great vision. Concerning the Roman power that brought into judgment the kings of the South, God declares, "Yet he will come to his end, and no one will help him." God tells his people to bear in mind that the Roman power will be judged as well. There is an unmistakable parallel between Daniel 11:35, describing the fate of the Greek power, and Daniel 11:45, predicting the downfall of Rome. The great persecutor, Antiochus IV Epiphanes, went the same route as the Greek power that he represented. God is telling his people that the great Roman persecutors—Nero, Domitian, Diocletian, and all the other Roman princes—will go the same way as well. They and their ungodly power will come to an end, and no one (especially their almighty "god of war") will be able to help them. Do not be afraid; remain righteous no matter what the circumstances, because God rules the nations!

# Notes

[1] Frank Perretti has written a series of books that puts this battle into a present-day context: *This Present Darkness, Piercing the Darkness* and *Prophet*, (Crossway Books). These books are a bit overly dramatic, and should be taken with a grain of salt. Nevertheless, they may help the reader to a greater appreciation of the nature of the unseen spiritual battle that is always being waged over the souls of men. Another book that the author would recommend is *The Screwtape Letters,* by C. S. Lewis. This book is not intended by Lewis to be taken literally, but it does provide a great insight into how Satan works in the lives of people.

Parallel passages in the Bible would include Ephesians 6:10-18, 1 Corinthians 10:20, and Isaiah 24:21.

[2] All this discussion about angels may be a bit hard to swallow for those who are not used to thinking of angels as having an impact on their everyday lives. In fact, it may sound at first like a bunch of fairy-tales. The marks of inspiration that pervade the book of Daniel should cause one to carefully consider this view. The place of angels in Daniel is developed more thoroughly in Appendix C.

[3] In a parenthetical aside, Gabriel tells Daniel, "In the first year of Darius the Mede, I took my stand to support and protect him" (Daniel 11:1). Comparison of this verse with Daniel 10:1 strongly implies that the third year of Cyrus was the first year of Darius the Mede. Although the identity of this Darius remains uncertain, this passage implies that he took the governorship of the province of Babylon in 536 B.C.

[4] There is some doubt about the Hebrew text in Daniel 11:6, as noted in most Bibles. Some manuscripts have the words "power" and "father" in this verse, while others have "son" in both places. In fact, it was Berenice's son who was killed, not her father.

[5] There are many modern incarnations or of Porphyry. Unfortunately, most of them are supposed Christian theologians. For example, consider a statement from the theologian F. W. Farrar, *The Book of Daniel*, F. W. Farrar, (Hodder & Stoughton, 1895), p. 299, commenting on Daniel chapter eleven: "If this chapter were indeed the utterance of a prophet in the Babylonian Exile, nearly four hundred years before the events—events of which many are of small comparative importance in the world's history—which are here so enigmatically and yet so minutely depicted, the revelation would be the most unique and perplexing in the whole Scriptures. It would represent a sudden and total departure from every method of God's providence and of God's manifestations of His will to the mind of the prophets. It would stand absolutely and abnormally alone as an abandonment of the limitation of all else which has ever been foretold." To paraphrase Farrar: *If Daniel 11 is not a second-century B.C. forgery, then the "minutely depicted" events would be such an amazing prophecy that I would have to accept that the Bible is a miraculously inspired book. I am not prepared to do that, so I will conclude that it is a forgery.*

[6] It is difficult to be sure what the phrase in verse 37 "or for the one desired by women" refers to. It may refer to the lack of Roman regard for worship of the mother goddess, the most ancient of all religions.

# Chapter Thirteen

## End Times

Chapter twelve of Daniel makes for a very fitting climax and conclusion to the book. Through the angel Gabriel, God tells Daniel about the time of the end. There is great encouragement here. Daniel learns about the ultimate fate of both the enemies of God and the faithful allies of God. This short chapter contains the strongest hints contained anywhere in the Old Testament about the resurrection of the dead and about the judgment of all people that will happen at the end of the ages. It is certainly no coincidence at all that the last chapter of Daniel, the great apocalypse of the Old Testament, has much in common with the last three chapters of Revelation, the great apocalypse of the New Testament.

When studying the twelfth chapter of Daniel, it will be helpful to bear in mind that there is no real break between what preceded it in chapters ten and eleven. Chapter ten is the lead-up to the last great vision of Daniel: Chapters eleven and twelve.

"At that time Michael, the great prince who protects your people, will arise" (Daniel 12:1). Again, one can see that the archangel Michael, and by implication, the archangel Gabriel, were assigned as specific angels to fight for God's people. Can it be assumed that these two great archangels are still out there, fighting to support the kingdom of God against its spiritual enemies? This certainly seems like a reasonable conclusion. What an encouragement!

Gabriel's speech continues, announcing that he will arise to protect God's people because "there will be a time of distress such as has not happened from the beginning of nations until then" (v. 1). Gabriel is describing the great tribulation that would accompany the destruction of Jerusalem in 70 A.D. These events are the same as those described in greater detail in Daniel 9:25-27.

If this is true, then the vision has taken another leap forward between Daniel 11:45 and 12:1, similar to the fast-forward between Daniel 11:35 and Daniel 11:36. Daniel 11:35 mentions "the time of the end" of the Greek power. It is followed by an immediate jump of about one hundred years to the actual events of that end, as described in Daniel 11:36-44. Similarly, Daniel 11:45 talks about the time of the end of the Roman power, followed by a leap of approximately one hundred years to the events surrounding the end of the Jewish sacrificial system.

Gabriel describes to Daniel a time of distress for God's people, greater than any other before it. He is referring to the destruction of Jerusalem and the systematic persecutions of the church by the Roman power, which began at about the same time. It is easy to imagine that this could cause the follower of God to experience great fear, but God provides the best possible encouragement to those who suffer for the name of Jesus Christ. There will be great distress, "but at that time your people—everyone whose name is found written in the book—will be delivered"(Daniel 12:1). The people of God say "amen" to that. The book referred to in Daniel 12:1 is the same book described in Revelation 20:12-15.

Actually, in Revelation 20, one learns about two books. The first is the book containing a record of all the acts committed by all the people—whether good or bad—awaiting judgment. This is not the book Daniel is learning about. The second book found in Revelation 20 is the Lamb's book of life. This is the book that lists all those saved by the blood of Jesus Christ. Considering what is written in Daniel chapter twelve, it would be a very good idea to make sure that one's name is written in this book! If the reader has any doubt at all about their inclusion in the book of life, they would do well to clear up those doubts! Sit down with a person who knows the Bible, study out the subject of salvation in the Bible, and make sure to get signed up in the book of life as soon as possible.

If the angel is describing for Daniel the Judgment Day, then the vision has leaped forward in time, all the way from the tribulation surrounding the destruction of Jerusalem, to the final Judgment Day. This should not come as a great surprise, because that is exactly what Jesus did in his great discourse on the destruction of Jerusalem and on the resurrection of the dead (Matthew 24:3-35, Mark 13:3-31 and Luke 21:5-28). In all three of the passages referred to, Jesus begins by prophesying concerning the events of 70 A.D., but then he seamlessly slips into prophesying about the time of the end of the world, when he will return with a trumpet call from heaven.

This is an easy transition in time for God to make because, in the dispensation of God, the stretch of time from the destruction of Jerusalem in 70 A.D. to the end of the world—the "second coming of Jesus"—is one uninterrupted period. There has been no new revelation from God to his people for almost two thousand years. God is now waiting for the full number of those to be saved to come into his kingdom.[1]

Gabriel is describing to Daniel the awesome scene that will occur at the end of time. This is the most detailed description in the Old Testament of what Christians call "Judgment Day." Perhaps somewhat surprisingly, the Old Testament provides relatively little information about the resurrection of the dead, about the final Judgment Day, or even about heaven and hell.

The casual Bible reader might not notice that the resurrection of the dead, a very common topic in the New Testament, is in general either not referred to in the Old Testament, or only mentioned indirectly. The exception to this rule is the book of Daniel! This is one reason that the book of Daniel is so important to a study of the Old Testament. Consider the NT scene in which Paul comes before both the Sadducees and the Pharisees after being arrested in Jerusalem (Acts 23:1-10). At that time, he says that he is on trial "because of my hope in the resurrection of the dead." This leads to a great argument between the Sadducees, who do not believe in the resurrection and the Pharisees, who do.

This argument between the two power groups within Judaism is easier to understand if one bears in mind that, unlike the Pharisees, the Sadducees tended to acknowledge only the Pentateuch, the first five books of the Bible. These books contain no direct mention of the resurrection of the dead at all. It is not surprising, then, that the Sadducees rejected the doctrine of the resurrection of the dead, so clearly spelled out in Daniel; whereas the Pharisees, who accepted as scripture the entire Old Testament, believed in the resurrection of the dead.

The resurrection is referred to in other places in the Old Testament, but in a way that is less direct than in Daniel. For example, when Peter explains to the crowd in Jerusalem at Pentecost that Jesus' resurrection from the dead was prophesied in the Scriptures, he uses Psalm 16:10: "... because you will not abandon me to the grave, nor will you let your Holy One see decay" (Acts 2:27). For a student of the New Testament reading Psalm 16, the resurrection of the dead is easily detected. However, for a person not familiar with the New Testament (or with Daniel), it would be hard to establish a doctrine of the resurrection of the dead from Psalm 16 alone. If fact, the word *resurrection* does not appear in the Old Testament at all, whereas it appears in the New Testament forty times.

This is not to say that the resurrection of the dead was an invention of the NT writers—not at all! However, until the writing of the book of Daniel, the doctrine of the resurrection was not clearly revealed by God to his people. Again, one can see the importance of Daniel to the OT canon.

We find a similar situation regarding the concepts of heaven and hell, as well as the doctrine of a Judgment Day, in which each person's eternal destiny is determined. Although these concepts are certainly not absent from the rest of the Old Testament, they are in general only referred to in an indirect way. Again, the exception to this pattern is the book of Daniel. One can easily see, then, that Daniel is an extremely important book connecting the Old Testament to the New. For example, David and others refer to *Sheol* and *Abaddon* in the Psalms and in Proverbs.[2] These terms are generally translated as "the grave" and "Destruction." The New Testament reader will read these as "Hades" (or "Paradise") and as "hell,"[3] but someone reading only the Old Testament would cull a somewhat loosely defined doctrine of eternal judgment from such passages. This is not to say that judgment, heaven and hell are completely absent from the rest of the Old Testament. It is true, however, that Daniel chapter twelve contains what is easily the clearest reference to these doctrines, doctrines that are so important to the teachings of Jesus Christ.

While describing the Judgment Day, Gabriel goes on to make one of the most encouraging statements in the book of Daniel: "Those who are wise will shine like the brightness of the heavens, and those who lead many to righteousness, like the stars for ever and ever" (Daniel 12:3). What a great picture of the resurrection and of heaven! Consider what an encouragement this statement would be to the Jews during the great persecutions of Antiochus IV Epiphanes, or to the disciples of Jesus, suffering under the devastating attacks of the Roman princes. In this passage, "those who are wise" could be interpreted as those who are righteous. For the Jews, the book of Proverbs had made the word *wisdom* essentially synonymous with righteousness. Those who will be righteous to the very end will shine like stars forever and ever. Those who would follow Jesus Christ would do well to remember these words.

There is more reason for encouragement here. Gabriel provides great motivation for those who "lead many to righteousness." The work of leading people to heaven is extremely strenuous. Great stores of energy are required to achieve the goal, but leading people to God is the passionate desire of all followers of Jesus Christ. It is their "Great Commission" (Matthew 28:18-20). Here is great encouragement to those who devote themselves to making others disciples of Jesus. Keep it up. In the end, your efforts will definitely prove worthwhile. In fact, you will shine like a star forever and ever.

The writer of Daniel 12:3 is employing the familiar Hebrew poetic technique of producing two parallel equivalent phrases for emphasis. That being true, then, "those who

are wise" (the righteous) are the same as "those who lead
many to righteousness" (the evangelistic). What better way
for a man or woman of God to remain faithful than to continue to lead others to God? And what better reward than to
shine forever in heaven?

Finally, the main body of the great vision is concluded
with the next verse:

> But you, Daniel, close up and seal the words of
> the scroll until the time of the end. Many will go here
> and there to increase knowledge (Daniel 12:4).

God is telling Daniel to "seal up" the prophecy. What
does this mean? Since we can read it, it does not seem to
have been sealed very well. The phrase "seal up" probably
means that Daniel should preserve the words of the prophecy as a whole. The interpretation of the words will only make
sense once the times of the end have been reached. When the
events prophesied occur, the scroll will have been unfolded.
"The end" could refer to the end of the Greek persecuting
power when Mark Antony and Cleopatra were defeated in
31 B.C., or to the end of the Hebrew worship in 70 A.D., or it
could refer to the destruction of the Roman power. Each of
these three events is referred to as an "end" in Daniel, and
all three, when they occurred, revealed the meaning of the
scroll. But is difficult to be sure which specific event God
is referring to in this part of the prophecy. In any case, the
point is that many men and women will look all around for
portents concerning the future (for example, see the appendix on premillennialism), but when the events are fulfilled,
then people will see for themselves that when God speaks,
he will act.

Now that the vision has ended, Daniel sees two "others" on either side of the river (i.e., the Tigris River; see Daniel 10:4). It is difficult to know for sure who these two are,
but they ask questions that both Daniel and the reader of
the book would naturally be asking at this point. Certainly
the Jews who read the words of Daniel—for whom these
words represented the future—would be asking, "How long
will it be before these astonishing things are fulfilled?" (v.

6) In a gesture meant to reveal the solemn intent of God, "the man clothed in linen"—in other words, Jesus (see the description of Daniel 10:4-6)—points towards heaven. He swears by God, saying, "It will be for a time, times and half a time. When the power of the holy people has been finally broken, all these things will be completed" (v. 7). In Hebrew tradition, the raising of the right hand denotes the taking of a solemn oath. In this case, the man dressed in linen raises both his right and his left hands, again showing the importance of the oath, as well as the depth of God's commitment to carrying it out. Besides this, he makes the oath in front of two witnesses (or three, counting Daniel). The presence of two—or preferably three—witnesses is an OT requirement for confirming a solemn oath (Deuteronomy 19:15, 31:28, 2 Corinthians 13:1). God is really trying to reassure Daniel and his people with this oath.

To which of the great events described in Daniel's many visions is Jesus referring? The answer is that when he mentions "astonishing things" that will occur at a time "when the power of the holy people has been finally broken," he is referring to the great events surrounding the destruction of the temple and the city of Jerusalem in 70 A.D. Satan and his allies will have power over God's people for a limited time, represented by three and one-half years—an amount of time equal to half of seven years, where the number seven represents the fullness or perfection of God. The point is not that the duration of any specific tribulation will literally last for an exact three and one-half years. Rather, the point is that God is in control, and he will be sure to limit the time of stress so that his people can stand up under the trial. This is obviously intended as a word of comfort to Daniel, to the two hearers, and of course, to the reader of the book of Daniel.

Daniel is still confused, however. He asks the Lord for himself about the outcome of all the terrible events that have just been described to him. Despite all God's efforts to reassure Daniel that he is in control, and that he will protect his people, no matter how intense the persecutions or times of difficulty, Daniel still feels insecure. The same is true for us. The followers of God sometimes find themselves in situations in which they say to God, "What will the outcome of all this be?" This may happen despite all the assurances of the word of God; regardless of all the examples of righteous men prevailing over temptation; and despite all the wonderful biblical illustrations proving that, whatever the struggle, God will never abandon or forsake his children. Most faithful disciples of Christ will find themselves in a situation like this at some point in their lives. What should a righteous man of God do when he is at his spiritual wits' end?

God's answer to Daniel and to us may not be what we would want to hear. God says to Daniel, "Go your way, Daniel, because the words are closed up and sealed until the time of the end" (v. 9). In other words, *Daniel, you are just going to have to trust me on this.* In essence, God is saying to Daniel, and to anyone else feeling insecure despite all of God's assurances, *I am in control. You need to decide to trust in my providence. Go your way, Daniel, and let me handle the tough stuff. In my own good time, I will reveal to you what I have in mind. Your job is simply to continue living the righteous life I have commanded, and trust in me.*

Jesus continues his reply to Daniel by saying, "Many will be purified, made spotless and refined, but the wicked will continue to be wicked. None of the wicked will understand, but those who are wise will understand" (v. 10). Through Jesus, God tells Daniel one more time to trust in his providence. Although the great persecutions of his people may seem at the time to be a tragic event, God will use these times of struggle to purify, make spotless and refine his faithful people. The readers of Daniel would do well to remember this lesson. This passage is strongly reminiscent of 1 Peter 1:6-7: "In this you greatly rejoice, though now for a little while you may have had to suffer grief in all kinds of trials. These have come so that your faith—of greater worth than gold, which perishes even though refined by fire—may be proved genuine and may result in praise, glory and honor when Jesus Christ is revealed."[4]

God is also urging Daniel not to worry about those who will be unwilling or unable to understand his message. The wicked will remain wicked, and there may be nothing Daniel can do about that. The message to Daniel, then, is that God is in control of the wicked as well. Daniel should try to reveal the truth to everyone, but he should realize that many will choose not to accept the message.

The Lord is also encouraging Daniel that "those who are wise will understand." No matter what critics say against his message or how much they scoff at the Bible, God is reassuring Daniel that the righteous, those who are willing to obey the will of God, will understand the prophecy. The fact that only a small minority will understand and be able to accept the message requires a great deal of trust on the part of Daniel. Jesus provided a similar statement in John 8:31-32. To paraphrase, he said that although his message may be veiled to those who are unwilling to obey it, those who are willing to follow the commandments of God will definitely be able to understand it.

On a personal note, I can certainly relate to the point being brought up by Daniel and answered by God. I have studied the Bible with many people on a personal level over the years. Many times, I have reviewed passages of scripture with people who are willing to study, but are still hesitant about accepting the implications of the Bible in their life. It has been my experience that even with passages that are so clear that a child could easily understand them, those who are still unwilling to obey the will of God will come up with the most off-the-wall misinterpretations of scripture. The amazing thing is that when these same people finally surrender, deciding to accept God's will in their lives, all of a sudden the same passages suddenly become extremely easy for them to understand. When I ask myself how the theologians could make such a mess of understanding the book of Daniel, I am reminded of Daniel 12:10 and John 8:31-32.

The statement that "those who are wise will understand" can certainly can take a load off the mind of those who seek to share the Bible with their friends. When sharing the Word with people, one should remember that many will not accept it. In many cases, there is nothing that can be done about people who refuse to accept the message. However, for those with a good heart, for hearers who are "wise," the message will pierce right to the heart.

Despite having told Daniel to relax and trust in his providence, God decides to provide one last specific assurance to him: "From the time that the daily sacrifice is abolished and the abomination that causes desolation is set up, there will be 1,290 days. Blessed is the one who waits for and reaches the end of the 1,335 days" (vv. 11-12). At first glance it may seem that God is repeating himself. He had already declared in verse 7 of the chapter that the great tribulation would only endure for three and one half years. It just so happens that 1,290 days is three and one-half years (see below for a more thorough explanation). The fact is, though, that Jesus is not talking about the same thing here. In verse 7, he was reassuring Daniel that the trials in the time of the destruction of Jerusalem would be only for a limited time. In this passage, God is telling Daniel that the great persecutions under Antiochus IV Epiphanes will also only be for a limited time. God will only allow the times of great stress for his people to endure for a pre-determined amount of time, after which he will "return" to bless his people.

One can be made sure what God is referring to by looking at the wording of the passage in question. The abolition of the daily sacrifice has to be a reference to what happened under Antiochus IV Epiphanes, when he abolished the Jewish worship. A temporary abolition of the daily sacrifice in the temple would not fit the events of 70 A.D. The phrase "the abomination that causes desolation is set up" almost certainly refers to the statue of Jupiter that the abominable Antiochus had set up in the temple. Therefore, one can know God is assuring Daniel that the great persecutions of Antiochus against God's people will only last as long as God allows them. God is in control, even if outward appearances will appear otherwise.

The reader is probably ready to ask about the difference between the 1,290 days during which the daily sacrifice will stop, and the 1,335 days through which the faithful will have to wait before seeing the blessing of God. It so happens that the 1,290 days is equivalent to forty-three thirty-day months (one month more than three and one-half years). The Hebrews kept track of their years using lunar months of thirty days. To the Jews, then, a year was twelve thirty-day months, or 360 days. In order to keep their calendar in line with the solar cycle, so that annual events like harvest festivals could actually occur during the harvest or other appropriate time, they had to add one thirty-day month (known as an intercalary month) to the year about every six years.[5] Forty-three months, then, is three and one-half years if one of the years contains an intercalary month. Of course, the next question is, what is the significance of the extra forty-five days (one and one-half months) that make up the 1,335 days? Unfortunately, at this time, I'm at a loss to interpret its significance or meaning.

Bear in mind that this is an apocalyptic passage. The prophecy is not talking about an exact and literal three and one-half year duration for the attack of Satan on God's people. The three and one-half years represents the temporary and limited nature of Satan's attack. In point of fact, the time of the actual desecration of the temple was about three years (December 167 B.C. until December 164 B.C.). It is entirely possible that the extra one and one-half months refer to some detail in the actual events during the attacks of Antiochus. In other words, there may be some actual event which occurred after the reconsecration of the temple (1,290 days), but before the blessing on those who waited (1,335 days). Surely by now, the reader would not be in any way surprised to learn that even the smallest detail in these visions can correspond to an actual event in history. Unfortunately, I'm not aware at this time of the passage's meaning when referring to the extra forty-five days. If any of the readers of this book are able to shed light on this text through their own study, please let me know!

In asking about the 1,290 and the 1,335 days, it would be a good idea not to miss the forest for all the trees. The big picture is that for those who remain faithful through the dark days when God's purpose in this world is under attack—when it will seem as if Satan is winning the victory—the time of great stress will end at God's predetermined time. In the end, those who endure the trials patiently and faithfully will be blessed. In the words spoken by the angel to John, "This calls for patient endurance on the part of the saints who obey God's commandments and remain faithful to Jesus" (Revelation 14:12).

God's final words to Daniel are the same he would

give to any faithful disciple of Jesus, as they look forward to the life in front of them: "As for you, go your way till the end. You will rest, and then at the end of the days you will rise to receive your allotted inheritance." During a time of great trial (and all faithful disciples will endure many trials in the name of Jesus Christ), a follower of Jesus may lose sight of the blessings of God in their life. They may instead focus on all the hard work for God ahead of them. They may begin to feel overwhelmed when considering all the future trials and persecutions, all the late nights and personal sacrifices. Although the life of a disciple of Jesus is great, it certainly is not easy, to say the least.

As Daniel considers the overwhelming immensity of the trials God's people would go through—as he begins to even doubt if God would really take care of him—God gives him a simple answer: *Daniel, mind your own business, and let me take care of mine. Keep your life's energy focused on the task I have given you, and keep your eyes fixed on the end of the journey. No matter how hard it gets, do not ever forget that at the end of your life there will be a great Sabbath rest in store for you.*

Probably the writer of Hebrews had Daniel 12 in mind when he wrote, "There remains, then, a Sabbath-rest for the people of God; for anyone who enters God's rest also rests from his own work, just as God did from his. Let us, therefore, make every effort to enter that rest, so that no one will fall by following their[6] example of disobedience" (Hebrews 4:9-11). Jesus said, "Trust in God; trust also in me. In my Father's house are many rooms; if it were not so, I would have told you. I am going there to prepare a place for you" (John 14:1b-2).

Could God have offered any more comforting words? To those who will put their trust in him, God is saying that it will be very much worth the effort to remain faithful. Each righteous man or woman of God will receive an inheritance specifically allotted for him or her. Will life be hard? Yes. Will there be temptations to take one's hand from the plow (Luke 9:62)? No doubt. Will there be times when things get so difficult that the man of God will feel overwhelmed? Probably. Will it be worth it? The answer from God is a resounding and unqualified *yes*. Do not give up. Do not fear. God rules the nations.

## Summary

In the end, the two parallel strands of the book of Daniel come together. The lives of Daniel and of his friends Shadrach, Meshach and Abednego provide practical examples of how to lead a righteous life while living among unrighteous people. They show the reader of Daniel how to "go your way till the end." The prophetic parts of Daniel provide the evidence required as a foundation for faith, a faith that helps the righteous to keep on that narrow way. They give unassailable proof that God is not lying when he tells us, "at the end of the days you will rise to receive your allotted inheritance."

It has been my job to fill in the historical background, thus revealing the powerful nature of the historically specific prophecies in Daniel. It is my hope that the reader's faith has been increased by a close inspection of the visions in this great book. Ultimately, though, the goal is for the reader to combine the *faith*—gained from the prophecies—with *deeds*—inspired by the righteous example of Daniel and his friends—to produce a life more pleasing to God. If that is the case, then to God be the glory!

## Notes

[1] For a good passage about the patience of God as he waits for the last days to end, see 2 Peter 3:1-18.

[2] For example, *Sheol* is found in Psalms 16:10, Psalm 88:3, Proverbs 15:11 and many others. *Abaddon* is found in Psalm 88:11, Proverbs 15:11 and others.

[3] Or possibly as the aspect of Hades referred to as "hell" in Luke 16:23.

[4] See also James 1:2-4 and Romans 5:3-4.

[5] For example, this is why the date of the Jewish Passover celebration, and therefore the traditional date of Easter in Western Christendom, moves around in a cycle between late March and late April. These dates follow the lunar calendar.

[6] "Their" refers to the Israelites who rebelled against God while wandering in the desert. The Israelites did the exact opposite of what God is asking Daniel to do, which was to keep marching and trust in him.

# Appendix A

### 🐚

## Maps and Timelines

The historical background to the book of Daniel was described in chapter one of the book. The purpose of this appendix is to provide a big-picture background to the historical aspects of the book of Daniel, since Daniel discusses more than six hundred years of prophecies. Now that the reader has been given a detailed account of the fulfillment of the prophecies in the book, it will be helpful to see how they overlap and complement one another.

Included in this appendix is a timeline relating biblical events to the specific prophecies in Daniel, as well as maps, which will help the reader to picture the kaleidoscope of nations found in the prophecies of Daniel.

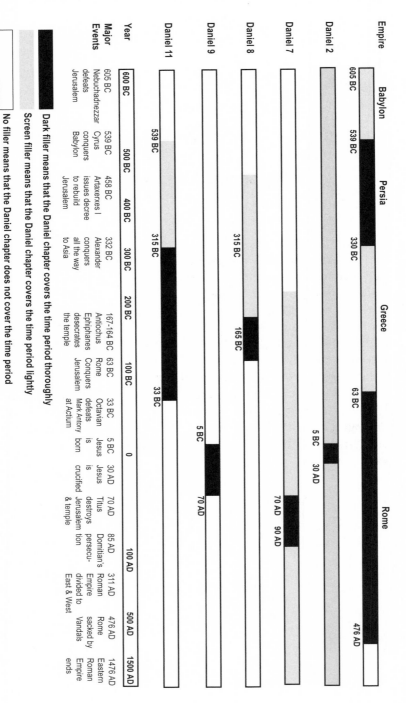

# DANIEL TIMELINE

| Empire | Babylon | Persia | Greece | Rome |
| --- | --- | --- | --- | --- |

Dark filler means that the Daniel chapter covers the time period thoroughly

Screen filler means that the Daniel chapter covers the time period lightly

No filler means that the Daniel chapter does not cover the time period

| Year | 600 BC | 500 BC | 400 BC | 300 BC | 200 BC | 100 BC | 0 | 100 AD | 500 AD | 1500 AD |
| --- | --- | --- | --- | --- | --- | --- | --- | --- | --- | --- |
| Major Events | 605 BC Nebuchadnezzar defeats Jerusalem | 539 BC Cyrus conquers Babylon | 458 BC Artaxerxes I issues decree to rebuild Jerusalem | 332 BC Alexander conquers all the way to Asia | 167-164 BC Antiochus Ephiphanes Conquers desecrates the temple | 63 BC Rome defeats Jerusalem | 5 BC Jesus is born | 30 AD Jesus is crucified | 70 AD Titus destroys Jerusalem & temple | 85 AD Domitian's persecu- tion |

| | | | | | | | 33 BC Octavian defeats Mark Antony at Actium | | 311 AD Roman Empire divided to East & West | 476 AD Rome sacked by Vandals | 1476 AD Eastern Roman Empire ends |

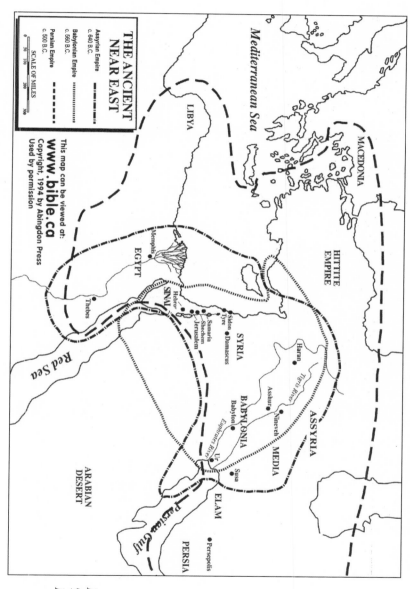

Figure 40.
The ancient
Near East.

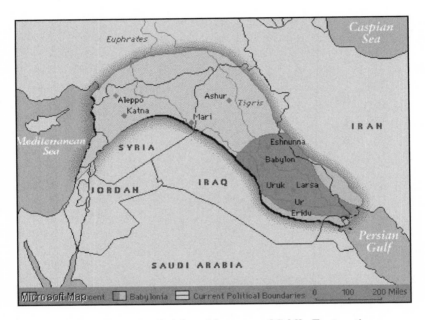

*Figure 41. Babylon at its height with current Middle East nations.*

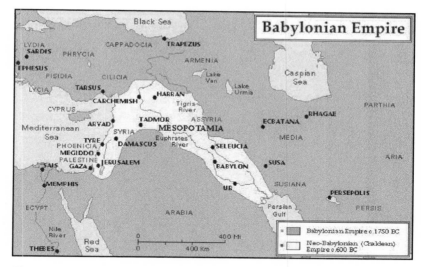

Figure 42. Babylonian Empire, c. 1750 B.C. and c. 600 B.C.

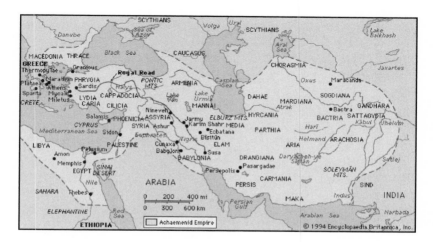

Figure 43. Achaemenid Persia/Media Empire at its height, c. 450 B.C.

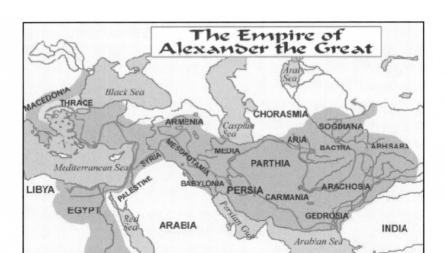

*Figure 44. Empire of Alexander the Great, c. 330 B.C.*

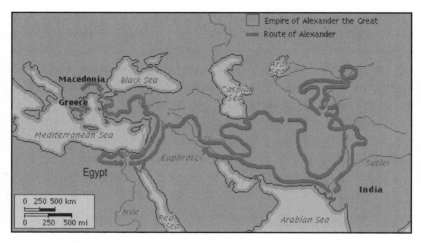

*Figure 45. Alexander the Great's travels.*

*Figure 46. Palestine during the Maccabean Period.*

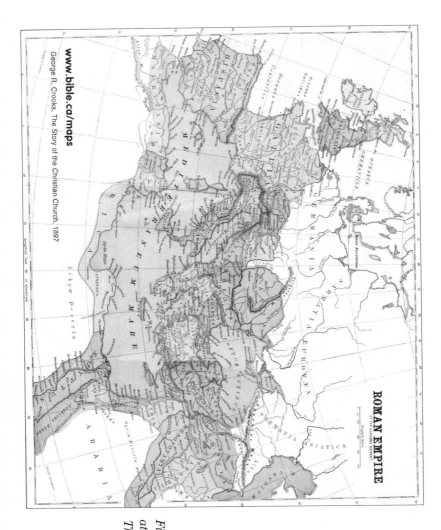

Figure 47. Roman Empire
at its height,
Third Century A.D.

# Appendix B

### Daniel and the Premillennial Doctrine

A whole school of thought exists with respect to the interpretation of the book of Daniel which has been left unexplored until now. This school of thought and the doctrine associated with it are known as premillennialism. The premillennialists are definitely not liberal theologians. In general, they would hold strongly to belief in the inspiration of the Scriptures. However, in their overly literal interpretation of apocalyptic passages in the Bible, they would support a view of the kingdom of God radically different from that described in this book (and in the Bible, in my opinion). The favorite Bible books used by the premillennialists in supporting their doctrine are Revelation and its nearest Old Testament cousins, Daniel and Ezekiel.

So what is the premillennialist doctrine, and why was consideration of this viewpoint held off until an appendix? Of course, there are a wide variety of viewpoints represented by those who could be called premillennialists, but the main thrust of their interpretation of the Bible can be stated fairly simply. The premillennialists hold to the belief that the kingdom of God did not come at Pentecost. They believe that the kingdom of God will be ushered in at some date in the future. According to this doctrine, the arrival of the kingdom of God will herald a literal thousand-year reign of Jesus Christ in the literal city of Jerusalem.

Another important teaching of the premillennialists is that the millennial reign of Christ will be preceded by the rapture of the Christians as well as a great tribulation. Most premillennialists believe that this tribulation will last for seven years, and that it will culminate in a giant battle, which they would identify with Armageddon. The great majority of premillennialists believe that the rapture, tribulation, and reign of Christ in Jerusalem are events which will occur in the very near future. As a corollary, they (incorrectly) assert that the "last days," as mentioned in a number of OT prophecies, have not yet begun. The great majority of premillennialists believe that the last days will start with the tribulation and associated events. For example, Hal Lindsey predicted in 1973, in the most well-known of premillennialist books, that the rapture would occur some time around 1988![1] One can assume that he has since backpedaled on this claim.

There are a couple of reasons that the issue of premillennialism and its refutation were postponed until the end of this book. First, the passages of relevance to the premillennialist view are scattered throughout Daniel. By dealing with the relevant passages collectively, in this appendix, we can see a coherent overall picture of the arguments for and against the premillennial doctrines. Second, to pause our other studies in order to address the premillennialist view every time a relevant passage appeared would have detracted from the main thrust of this book, which is to bring out the message of Daniel and to use Daniel to dramatically prove the inspiration of the Bible.

This appendix is not in any way intended to be an exhaustive analysis of premillennialism, but only a brief introduction to make the reader aware of the issue. There are a great number of works that address the premillennialist doctrine much more thoroughly than we will attempt here. Besides, I freely admit that I'm not an expert in this area! A couple of excellent sources are recommended in the notes. I would especially acknowledge reliance on Jim McGuiggan's book on Daniel as a source in this section.

Which are the passages in Daniel that are used to support the premillennial doctrine? The first example is found in the prophecy of the great statue in Daniel chapter two. As mentioned earlier in this book, the four parts of the statue are the head of gold (Babylon), the chest and arms of silver (Persia/Media), the belly and thighs of bronze (Greece) and the legs of iron (Rome).[2] The premillennialists would agree with this outline. It is definitely not their goal to disprove the inspiration of Daniel. However, they would claim that there are two aspects to the Roman Empire involved in the leg part of the prophecy. The premillennialists would claim that the legs of iron imply both the historical Empire of Rome, and a revived Roman Empire in the late twentieth century. Daniel says, "In the time of those kings, the God of heaven will set up a kingdom that will never be destroyed, nor will it be left to another people. It will crush all those kingdoms and bring them to an end, but it will itself endure forever" (Daniel 2:44). As discussed previously in this book, God is describing through Daniel how the kingdom of God, the church, will be established during the time of the Roman Empire. However, Hal Lindsey, John Walvoord and other premillennial teachers claim instead that in this prophecy, Daniel is predicting the establishment of the kingdom of God after the appearance of a revived Roman Empire some time near the end of the twentieth century.

The premillennialists would get the same sense out of Daniel chapter seven's vision of the four beasts. In referring to this vision, Lindsey, popular leader of the modern-day premillennialist movement, makes the following statement:

> This verse (Daniel 7:19) speaks of the first phase of this fourth kingdom. In phase 1 this kingdom gains world authority (as Rome did), and then disappears to merge again just before Christ returns to establish the Kingdom of God. In phase two of the fourth kingdom, Rome, the kingdom will be in the form of a ten-nation confederacy.[3]

Lindsey uses Daniel 7:20 to support the idea of a separate Roman ten-nation confederacy. Note that Lindsey is very specifically stating here that the kingdom of God has not yet been established. In all the varying statements of the premillennialists, this is one unanimous theme. Another quote to give the reader the flavor of premillennialist thinking on this subject comes from Walvoord's commentary on Daniel:

> By its terminology, the interpretation of verses 23-27 demands that, for the fifth kingdom to overcome the fourth, the fifth kingdom must be basically a sovereign and political kingdom, whatever its spiritual characteristics. By so much, it also demands that it be a future fulfillment, inasmuch as nothing in history corresponds to this.[4]

Here Walvoord is claiming that the fifth kingdom, the kingdom of God, is a sovereign, political nation. This claim is made despite the clear statement of Jesus Christ, "My Kingdom is not of this world" (John 18:36).

The reader may be asking where the idea of the ten-nation confederacy came from. The premillennialists find a ten-nation confederacy in Daniel 7:7, 20 and 24. To quote Daniel 7:24, "The ten horns are ten kings who will come from this kingdom." The angel tells Daniel that the horns are *kings*, but the premillennialists believe they are ten *kingdoms* which will unite to form a revived Roman Empire in our own day. To quote Lindsey again,

> We believe that the Common Market and the trend toward unification of Europe may well be the beginning of the ten-nation confederacy predicted by Daniel and the Book of Revelation.

What was known as the Common Market in the 1970s is now known as the EEU, or European Economic Union. It is a common belief of premillennialists that the EEU will produce a ten-nation confederacy that the Antichrist will eventually come to rule in Rome. In March, 1999, Poland, Hungary and the Czech Republic were added to the EEU, with a number of East European nations, as well as Malta and others ready to follow. The ten-nation Common Market has become the fifteen-member EEU, and so this theory has lost some of its luster.

The premillennialists see a ten-nation confederacy

in Daniel chapter two as well. Many of them have pointed out the feet and toes, made partly of clay and partly of iron (Daniel 2:41), and noted that the statue had ten toes. This has been quoted as further evidence for a ten-nation confederacy! To quote Walvoord,[5] "the ten toe stage of the image has not yet been fulfilled in history and is still prophetic." It is almost certainly true that the statue had ten toes, but it seems unreasonable to pull a biblical prophecy out of ten toes that were not even mentioned in the biblical text. Besides, what will these people do with the eleventh king in Daniel 7? Did the statue have eleven toes?

A question must be asked at this point: If students were to simply read Daniel chapter two and Daniel chapter seven for themselves, is there any chance that they would find two separate fourth (Roman) empires, separated by about one thousand five hundred years? Is there any chance they would envision a ten-nation confederacy coming back to revive a kingdom that had been dead for over a millennium? The answer is that they certainly would not. The only way to find two different Roman Empires in Daniel is to read them into the scripture because of some pre-conceived notion. Besides, in what sense is the EEU a Roman Empire? To answer this question, Lindsey claims in *The Late Great Planet Earth* that "Daniel says that *out of the culture* of the first Roman Empire ten kings shall arise"[6] (emphasis added). Where does one find an empire emerging *out of the culture* of Rome in Daniel?

The biggest problem with the premillennialist idea is not what seems like a convoluted misinterpretation of Daniel. The greatest problem with premillennialism is that it promotes a false idea of the kingdom of God. There was indeed a kingdom established by God "in the time of those kings," and it will indeed "endure forever" (Daniel 2:44). The church of Christ is the kingdom of God on the earth, and it was established in the time of the Roman kings, just like Daniel prophesied. The ten horns are in fact ten kings (not ten nations), just as Daniel was told. They were kings of Rome, as described in the chapter on Daniel 7. And as Daniel was told in the prophecy in Daniel 7, the kingdom of God, the church, was established during the Roman Empire, and it will endure forever and ever.

Despite the false claims of the premillennialists, God's kingdom is not now and never will be a physical kingdom. Jesus himself said, "My kingdom is not of this world. If it were, my servants would fight to prevent my arrest by the Jews. But now my kingdom is from another place" (John 18:36). The premillennialists repeat the error of the Jews, who believed that the Messiah would reign on this earth at the head of an earthly kingdom. Jesus said, "The time has come. The kingdom of God is near. Repent and believe the good news!" (Mark 1:15). Jesus said that the kingdom was at hand during his lifetime. But the premillennialists say that the kingdom was still very far off from Jesus' day— about two thousand years from the time Jesus said it was at hand. Who should one believe, Jesus or the premillennialists? Every single biblical hint points to the Day of Pentecost as recorded in Acts 2, as the day the kingdom of God came in its full power. The complete proof of this claim is outside the scope of this book, but it just so happens that Daniel provides some of the strongest evidence to support this claim. As it says, "In the time of those kings...."

Several other scriptures in Daniel are favorites of the premillennialists. One example is found in Daniel chapter nine. Members of the premillennial school have their own special interpretation of the seventy-week prophecy. Typically they would claim that the seventy weeks (490 years) began in 445 B.C., and that Jesus was killed at the end of the sixty-ninth week (483 years later). There is nothing too controversial here so far. The next part is where the premillennial doctrine takes a radical turn. They would claim that the prophetic clock stopped ticking at this point (the death of Jesus). Lindsey, Walvoord and premillennialists in general teach that the prophetic clock stopped ticking for about two thousand years. The last week, according to them, is the seven-year period called "the tribulation," which is to occur in our very near future. In Daniel 9, one can read, "After the sixty-two 'sevens,' the Anointed One will be cut off and will have nothing. The people of the ruler who will come will destroy the city and the sanctuary.... He will put an end to sacrifice and offering. And on a wing of the temple he will set up an abomination that causes desolation, until the end that is decreed is poured out on him" (Daniel 9:26-27). It has already been shown that this is exactly what happened in 70 A.D. when Titus overcame Jerusalem, destroyed the temple and the city, performed abominations on the site of the temple, and so forth, exactly as predicted in Daniel.

The premillennialists, however, insist that there is an approximately two-thousand-year gap spanning Daniel 9:26a and Daniel 9:26b. They insist that the temple will be rebuilt in Jerusalem—that a revived Jewish/Christian church will reestablish the sacrificial system there. To quote Walvoord,

> A careful study of these passages [referring to Daniel 12:4] indicates that before the second coming of Christ, the dictator in the Mediterranean will desecrate a future Jewish Temple and stop the sacrificial worship of God being carried on in this temple.[7]

When I study Daniel 12:4 carefully, I certainly do not see a modern-day dictator of the Mediterranean area, or a revived Jewish practice of animal sacrifice near the end of time. I trust that the reader will not find these things there either, but the premillennialists do.

The premillennialists also believe that the Antichrist will come into this rebuilt temple to perform abominations: an event which will signal the start of the tribulation and bring on Armageddon. To quote Lindsey,

> Obstacle or no obstacle, it is certain that the Temple will be rebuilt. Prophecy demands it.[8]

The obstacle Lindsey is referring to is the Dome of the Rock, the second most holy site of Islam, which happens to be built on what many believe is the approximate site of the former temple in Jerusalem. For political reasons, it seems extremely unlikely that the Jews will be able to tear down the Dome of the Rock. However, even if they did, that would not be a fulfillment of Daniel chapter nine. Daniel 9:26-27 was fulfilled in 70 A.D. The Jewish system of sacrifice is over in God's eyes, and that is the end of the story.

Besides, why would God want the Jewish temple sacrificial system to be reinstituted at this point? The day Jesus died on the cross, the temple curtain was torn in two. Spiritually, only a shell of the former temple remained from that point until the building was finally destroyed in 70 A.D. Temple sacrifices would avail nothing at this point. For God to reestablish the sacrifice of animals in the temple for the forgiveness of sins would be very confusing, to say the least. Jesus died so that we no longer need to make sacrifices again and again: "But now he has appeared once for all at the end of the ages to do away with sin by the sacrifice of himself. Just as man is destined to die once, and after that to face judgment, so Christ was sacrificed once to take away the sins of many people" (Hebrews 9:26b-28).

Premillennialists do not necessarily see things this way. For example, in referring to the cross of Christ, Walvoord says, "While the *basic provision for reconciliation* was made at the cross, the actual application of it is again associated with the second advent of Christ as far as Israel is concerned"[9] (emphasis added). What does Walvoord mean by basic provision for the forgiveness of sin? Is there some other requirement on God's part for forgiveness of sin? This teaching is treading on thin ice.

The premillennialist group sees a bit more in Daniel 9 as well. They interpret "the ruler who will come" (Daniel 9:26) as being the Antichrist, rather than Titus. They would claim that this ruler, the Antichrist, is the eleventh king in Daniel 7 as well. Can one find the word Antichrist in Daniel 9? Is there even the slightest hint that the ruler who will come and destroy the temple is the Antichrist? No, it is not there at all.

But that leads the discussion right into Daniel chapter eleven. The premillennial view of Daniel 11 would more or less parallel that described in this book until one comes to verse 36. Daniel 11:5-35 prophetically describes the history of the conflict between the kings of the North (the kings of the Greek Seleucid Empire) and the kings of the South (the kings of the Greek Ptolemaic Empire). At verse 36, the prophecy takes a dramatic turn. It begins describing the death-throes of the Ptolemaic Dynasty in Egypt during its conflict with Rome. That is not how these passages would be viewed by the premillennialists. Daniel 11:36 mentions a king who "will do as he pleases," who will "magnify himself above every god and will say unheard-of things against the God of gods." This refers to the Roman power, as described earlier in this book.

The premillennialists claim that the king referred to in Daniel 11:36 is the Antichrist. They typically identify him with the eleventh horn in Daniel 7 as well. The premillennialists would insert approximately twenty-two hundred years between Daniel 11:35 and Daniel 11:36 (a leap from 165 B.C. to sometime in the very near future). According to the premillennial view, the battle described in Daniel 11:36-45 will occur during the time of the tribulation. Here there will be some variation, as the premillennialists attempt to jibe their theories with the latest news events. The king of the South may be an Egyptian/African coalition, while the king of the North may be Russia. Or the king of the North may be the revived Roman Empire, headed by the Antichrist. A few years ago, I was listening to a Christian radio broadcast during the Desert Storm crisis in which the preacher was confidently proclaiming that the conflict with Iraq was a fulfillment of Daniel 11. The Arab/Israeli conflict or the Middle Eastern oil conflicts are also variously interpreted as being the fulfillment of Daniel 11.

There are a few problems with all these attempts at interpreting modern-day events as fulfillments of Daniel 11. Perhaps the greatest problem is the fact that the events described in Daniel 11 have already happened! They were fulfilled in exact detail in the conflict between Rome and the decaying Ptolemaic Dynasty, as was described carefully in this book. Walvoord, on the other hand, says, "The entire period from the death of Antiochus IV Epiphanes to the time of the end is skipped over with no reference to the events of the present church age, and the second section, verses 36-45, deals with the last Gentile ruler who will be in power when Christ comes in his second advent."[10] A few questions are appropriate at this point: Is the word "Armageddon" in Daniel 11? Is the word "Antichrist" there? Are these concepts in any way even implied in this prophecy? The premillennialists would answer yes! The truth is that these concepts are not found in Daniel 11 at all.

An excerpt from Lindsey's book will serve as a typical example. In referring to Daniel 11:40, he says: "We have identified the characters in this passage. The Arab-African confederacy headed by Egypt (King of the South) launches an invasion of Israel. This fatal mistake spells their doom and begins the Armageddon campaign." Paraphrasing Daniel 11:40b, he continues, "But the king of the North shall rush upon him (the Israeli leader) like a whirlwind with chariots (mechanized army) and horsemen (cavalry) and with many ships."[11] In Lindsey's description, the Israeli leader is in coalition with the Antichrist, headquartered in Rome, and the king of the North is a Russian army. Later, when the king of the North heads east (Daniel 11:44), Lindsey brings an army from China into the conflict as well!

In a more recent book, Walvoord sees the Middle East oil crisis as being key to understanding Daniel 11:36-45: "The prosperity of the world depends on some mechanism to guarantee peace and the continual flow of oil from the region. This is precisely what Biblical prophecy predicts."[12] Precisely which passage of Daniel chapter eleven predicts the Middle East oil crisis in the twentieth century?

As another example, one can find in Daniel 11:44 a prophecy concerning the response of Octavian to a Parthian threat from the east (as described earlier in our book). Some premillennialists interpret this same passage as predicting the coming of an army of two hundred million Chinese soldiers to the Middle East to fight a battle sometime in the near future.

Again, this ever-changing premillennial injection of present history into Daniel 11 may seem ridiculous (it certainly does to me anyway), but the biggest problem with this approach is not its silliness. The biggest problem is the false concept of the kingdom of God that it supports. The premillennialists interpret Daniel, Revelation and other books in support of the false idea that Jesus Christ will come back to the earth to reign at the head of an earthly, physical kingdom in Jerusalem. To quote from Lindsey:

The sequence is clear in the last chapters of Revelation. First there is the return of Christ at the climax of the greatest war of all time. Second, Christ separates the surviving believers from the surviving unbelievers; the unbelievers will be judged and cast off the earth. Third, Christ establishes the millennial kingdom and the surviving believers go into it as mortals and repopulate the earth. Fourth, at the end of a thousand years the unbelieving children rebel, Christ judges them, then He completely changes the old heaven and earth and creates a new one.[13]

There you have it. The fact is that no one simply reading Daniel chapter eleven would ever interpret it as premillennialists do. The only way to find in Daniel 11 a modern-day revived Roman Empire, ruled by the Antichrist, fighting a great war in the Middle East (and so forth) is to read it into the text by cruising the Bible in search of scriptures to stuff into a pre-conceived doctrine.

A legitimate question to ask at this point is whether the premillennial doctrine is really a big deal to get worked up about. That is a good question. It does not seem likely that a false understanding about the details of how the world will end could be a matter of salvation. As far as one can tell, the details of the second coming of Christ were not a major part of Peter's first gospel sermon in Acts 2.

A more difficult question to ponder is whether an incorrect understanding of the nature of the kingdom of God is a serious issue. One might argue that all the attention given by some people to end-time predictions may distract hearers from the weightier matters of biblical basics such as faith, repentance and baptism. Distraction from the most important teachings of Jesus may lead to an unhealthy feel-good approach to one's spiritual life. The readers are left to consider for themselves whether or not premillennialism is a dangerous, heretical doctrine.

The apostle Paul had to deal with a similar situation, in which some people had a wrong concept about the Scriptures that was not a matter of salvation. It may be wise to consider his attitude toward those people:

All of us who are mature should take such a view of things. And if on some point you think differently, that too God will make clear to you. Only let us live up to what we have already attained (Philippians 3:15-16).

Paul trusted God to work out the details. His main concern was regarding the basic teachings: things that he assumed they had "already attained." These things would include the lordship of Jesus, repentance, the grace of God, the message of the cross, and the like. Nevertheless, one can assume that at whatever opportunity he had, Paul instructed people more fully and carefully, even about these non-salvation issues.

There are several questions which have been raised by this short section on premillennialism and the book of Daniel. What about the thousand-year reign of Christ, depicted in Revelation 20? What about the Antichrist? What about Armageddon? These are very good questions, but they are outside the scope of this work, because this book is about Daniel, and Daniel simply does not discuss these issues at all. The interested reader should consider consulting some of the references already mentioned.[14]

In summary, the efforts of the premillennialists to insert present-day history into the prophecies of Daniel are doomed to failure. As already shown in this book, with the slight exception of Daniel 12:2-4, which is a picture of the judgment at the last day, all the prophecies in Daniel have already been fulfilled. They have been fulfilled in a way that provides the most dramatic possible support to belief in the inspiration of the Bible. These fulfilled prophecies provide the disciple of Jesus with great confidence because they prove that God rules the nations, and therefore we should not fear!

# Notes

[1] Hal Lindsey, *The Late Great Planet Earth* (Grand Rapids, Michigan: Zondervan, 1973), 54. To quote from Lindsey, "...Within forty years or so of 1948, all these things could take place. Many scholars who have studied Bible prophecy all their lives believe that this is so."

[2] Books to be recommended would include *Mine Eyes Have Seen the Glory*, by Gordon Ferguson (Discipleship Publications International, Billerica, Mass., 1995), as well as three books by Jim McGuiggan: *The Book of Daniel, The Kingdom of God and the Planet Earth,* and *The Book of Revelation* (all available from Star Bible and Tract Corporation).

[3] Hal Lindsey, *The Late Great Planet Earth* (Grand Rapids, Michigan: Zondervan, 1973), 92.

[4] John F. Walvoord, *Daniel, the Key to Prophetic Revelation* (Chicago, Ill.: Moody Press, 1971), 175.

[5] John F. Walvoord, *Daniel, the Key to Prophetic Revelation* (Chicago, Ill.: Moody Press, 1971), 72.

[6] Hal Lindsey, *The Late Great Planet Earth* (Grand Rapids, Michigan: Zondervan, 1973), 105.

[7] John F. Walvoord, *Oil, Armageddon and the Middle East Crisis* (Grand Rapids, Michigan: Zondervan, 1990), 104.

[8] Lindsey, *The Late Great Planet Earth,* (Grand Rapids, Michigan: Zondervan, 1973), 56.

[9] Walvoord, *Daniel, the Key to Prophetic Revelation* (Chicago, Ill.: Moody Press, 1971), 222.

[10] Walvoord, *Daniel, the Key to Prophetic Revelation,* (Chicago, Ill.: Moody Press, 1971), 252.

[11] Lindsey, *The Late Great Planet Earth* (Grand Rapids, Michigan: Zondervan, 1973), 153-154.

[12] John F. Walvoord, *Oil, Armageddon and the Middle East* (Grand Rapids, Michigan: Zondervan, 1990), 15.

[13] Lindsey, *The Late Great Planet Earth* (Grand Rapids, Michigan: Zondervan, 1973), 178.

[14] One excellent reference not mentioned previously is *Revelation,* by Jim McGuiggan (Lubbock, Tex.: International Biblical Resources, 1976). This book deals with some of the same questions as they relate to the book of Revelation.

# Appendix C

## Daniel and Angels

Recently, there has been a great revival of interest in angels. Hollywood has certainly gotten in on the act. The bookstores have dozens of titles exploring the theme. Angels are in the outfield, intervening in baseball games, they are touching people. Some are really good and some have just a little of the devil in them. But what is the real scoop on angels? One place to go to find out is in the book of Daniel.

Some would scoff at the whole idea of angels, and who could blame them? It is not as if angels are making public appearances (that we know of, anyway!). There certainly is not any scientific evidence to support the belief in angels. From the skeptic's point of view, angels are the result of wishful thinking and an overly inventive imagination. Yet angels are an inescapable part of the book of Daniel. What is one to do about that?

The angelology of Daniel has given the critics cause to attack the book as well. The basis for this attack is two-fold. First, they claim that angels were virtually non-existent in the Old Testament outside of the book of Daniel. They would mention that there are no examples of angels identified by a personal name, like Gabriel or Michael, anywhere else in the Old Testament. These people would go on to imply that the Jewish people developed the idea of angels to the extent found in Daniel only much later (in the second and first centuries B.C.). Their conclusion, not surprisingly, is that Daniel was written in the second half of the second century B.C.

The second angle of critics' attack on the angels in Daniel is the claim that there are simply no such beings as angels. Following this view, the entire book of Daniel becomes a fairy tale, with absolutely no claim to inspiration or to moral authority at all. Both of these anti-Daniel complaints will be dealt with in this chapter.

There is at least a small grain of truth to the first "criticism." Angels certainly do play a prominent role in the book of Daniel. However, the claim that there is a sudden and inexplicable increase in the presence of angels in Daniel is patently false. Angels are referred to directly in the books of Genesis, Exodus, Numbers, Judges, the Samuels, Kings and Chronicles, Job, Psalms, Isaiah, Ezekiel, Hosea, and, most notably, in Zechariah. They are referred to indirectly in several other OT books as well. The book of Zechariah was written after Daniel. One could argue that angels play an even greater role in Zechariah than they do in Daniel.

What one is left with, then, is the fact that Daniel is the only book in the Old Testament that refers to angels by name.[1] Specifically, Daniel mentions the archangels Michael and Gabriel. One could reasonably ask the critics of Daniel what that proves. Daniel never mentions cherubim, a kind of angel that Ezekiel saw. He also never mentions seraphim, a kind of angel mentioned in Isaiah. The reality is that God has chosen to reveal to his people knowledge about angels gradually. It is true that one can learn more about angels in Daniel than most of the other OT books. For reasons known to God alone, he chose to reveal more information about angels toward the end of the OT period, in Daniel and Zechariah. It is also true that God reveals even more to us in the New Testament regarding angels, especially in the book of Revelation.

There is much precedent for this gradual revelation of truth by God to his people. One can certainly learn about God's grace in the Old Testament. However, a case could be made that God's grace was gradually revealed more fully as the Old Testament developed. Only in the New Testament is the full glory of God's grace revealed to his people. The same could be said about the biblical doctrines of salvation and of heaven and hell, and many others. In each case, God progressively reveals these glorious doctrines to his people throughout the Old Testament. He then brings the ideas out in full in the person of Jesus Christ and in the New Testament. This pattern is repeated in the way God reveals knowledge of angels in the Bible.

What about the other criticisms against the presence of angels in Daniel? What about the claim that the very idea of angels is right up there with unicorns, elves and the tooth fairy?

Can the Bible believer refute this claim with any solid evidence? Do we have any bona fide angel wings to present in a court of law? The answer, clearly, is no. The answer is that we have just about as much reason to believe in angels as we do to believe in heaven, in hell, in Satan, in a final judgment day, in the "second coming" of Jesus Christ, or in the saving power of the blood of Jesus. There are many things in the Bible that one can be sure of because of the evidence. The inspiration of the Bible, the miracles of Jesus, the resurrection of Jesus, the existence of God, the historical accuracy of the Bible, along with many other truths, are all provable by direct means. Whether one likes it or not, God has left certain things to be believed, not by empirical evidence, but by faith in the integrity and inspiration of the Bible. This book has already shown that if there were any writing in the entire world with the marks of divine inspiration it would be the book of Daniel. Let the skeptics say what they will; I believe Daniel when he says he saw the archangels Michael and Gabriel. Daniel's integrity is above reproach. Those who would call him a liar had better be prepared to defend their libel.

So what does one learn about angels in Daniel? For one thing, one learns from Daniel that angels are messengers from God. In fact, the word *angel* means "messenger." The Bible contains several examples of God communicating with a person or group of people through angels. One instance of this phenomenon is found in Genesis 19, in which the angels warned Lot to flee from Sodom and Gomorrah. Another example is found in chapters one and two of Luke, which have several examples of angels being used as messengers of God to both individuals and to groups of people.

Another thing one can learn about angels from Daniel is that they are not physical beings, bound by the normal physical laws humans are subject to. In Daniel we find Michael and Gabriel whizzing around from place to place, not on wings,[2] but by a means left to the imagination of the reader. It would appear from Daniel that Michael is a sort of guardian angel for the nation Israel. In fact, from the conflict referred to in Daniel chapter ten, one can reasonably conclude that there are specific fallen angels with a great amount of influence over pagan nations like Persia and Greece. When Michael defeated the bad angel of Persia, as recorded in chapter ten, that victory may well have been what opened the way for the open-heartedness of Cyrus and his successors towards the Jewish cause.

In the book of Daniel, one can see that angels are very powerful![3] Gabriel comes to Daniel after fighting with the prince of the kingdom of Persia (Daniel 10:13). He also will join the battle, along with Michael, against "the prince of Greece" (Daniel 10:20). Angels are involved in fighting spiritual battles of which we are normally unaware. One finds that angels fight spiritual battles, but at the same time, they are able to take time to comfort those God has assigned them to help. Gabriel takes time out from a great battle over the souls of the Persians to comfort and strengthen Daniel (Daniel 10:10-14 and Daniel 9:20-23), as well as to instruct him and bring him a message. Apparently, angels have a number of talents.

Another thing one can learn about angels from Daniel is that they are persons. They are not humans, but they definitely are individual persons. They even have specific names, like Michael and Gabriel. They are not simply some sort of impersonal force working as a direct extension of God's power. These facts set the stage for Jesus, who went on to declare that children have angels in heaven specifically watching out over them (Matthew 18:10). Speaking of angels watching over specific people, this concept is first introduced to the Bible reader in Daniel as well.

In Daniel, one discovers that God has specific angels in charge of watching out for the nation of Israel: Michael and Gabriel. Besides this, there appears to be an angel (who is unnamed) watching over Daniel. This angel comes to the rescue when Daniel is in the lions' den, shutting the mouths of the lions. Shadrach, Meshach and Abednego are not without personal ministering angels either, as can be seen by their heavenly visitor in the fiery furnace. The one "like a son of man" who shares their time in the fire is most likely an angel.

God reveals much about angels in Daniel, but he does not provide the complete revelation about their nature. For example, God does not share through Daniel the part that angels will play in the judgment day (Matthew 13:49). Other examples could be given. The fact is that even with the completion of the New Testament, there is a great deal about angels that God has decided not to reveal to his people. Many questions could be asked about them that God chooses to leave to our imagination. What is the difference between cherubim and seraphim? Are Michael and Gabriel in a completely different category of angels than these? What will our relationship to the angels be like in heaven? It is fun to speculate on these questions, but revelation is silent about them. The readers of Daniel will have to content themselves with what God has chosen to reveal about angels, and wait for the rest of the answers until reaching heaven, when all will be revealed.

## Notes

[1] Isaiah 14:12 is a debatable exception. Some versions have the word "Lucifer" in this verse. The NIV reads, "How you have fallen from heaven, O star of the morning, son of the dawn! You have been cut down to the earth, You who have weakened nations!" More likely, Isaiah 14:12 refers to the fall of Assyria.

[2] The only angels with "wings" as described in the Bible are the cherubim (for example, in Ezekiel 1, and as represented in the cherubim above the ark in the temple) and the seraphim (as described in Isaiah 6). There is a somewhat obscure reference to a woman with wings in one of the visions of Zechariah (Zechariah 5:9). This is an apocalyptic passage, so it is difficult to know what to infer from it.

[3] The book of Daniel does not provide the prime example in the Old Testament of angelic power. For example, consider 2 Chronicles 32:20-21, in which an angel destroyed the entire army of the Assyrians as they lay siege to Jerusalem. Another example is 2 Samuel 24:15-16, in which an angel destroyed seventy thousand men of Israel and was about to destroy Jerusalem when God stayed his hand.

# Appendix D

## Daniel and the Apocrypha

A study of the book of Daniel would be incomplete without mention of its relationship to the Apocrypha. There are a few reasons the Apocrypha of the Old Testament has relevance to a study of the book of Daniel. First, many of those who would attack the inspiration of Daniel are, in essence, claiming that the book is apocryphal (this term will be defined shortly). It is therefore worthwhile to understand what the claim that Daniel is apocryphal would imply about the book. Second, many of the books of the OT Apocrypha were written in more or less the same time period that the critics claim Daniel was written (i.e., in the second century B.C.). For this reason, a brief study of the writings in the Apocrypha will provide a context for considering the claim that Daniel was written at this late date. A third reason that knowledge of the Apocrypha is relevant to a study of Daniel is that one section of the OT Apocrypha is actually attached to the original book of Daniel. When one reads Daniel in a Catholic version of the Bible, there are a number of extra verses! A fourth reason that a study of the Apocrypha is important to a full appreciation of Daniel is that the Apocrypha contains historical accounts, specifically in First and Second Maccabees, which are very much relevant to the predictive prophecies of Daniel. The last reason to be mentioned for looking at the Apocrypha has nothing to do with the book of Daniel at all. The Apocrypha is simply an interesting topic that many Christians know little or nothing about. If a study of Daniel gives one a good excuse to learn a little about this very interesting topic, so much the better!

So what is the Apocrypha? Actually, there are two separate terms which must be defined. First, there is *the Apocrypha*. The term *the Apocrypha* refers to a very specific list of additions to the Old Testament that was brought into the Latin Vulgate translation made by Jerome in the fourth century A.D. It would appear that these additions to the Old Testament were an accidental result of the work of Jerome. The bishop of the Roman Church, aware that the various Old Latin versions then in use by the Western churches were not of the best quality, asked the renowned scholar Jerome in about 370 A.D. to produce a brand new Latin translation of both the Old and the New Testaments. The translation that Jerome produced was generally of excellent quality because he attempted to use the best Greek and Hebrew manuscripts available. The version prepared by Jerome was far superior to any available in Latin at that time. His translation eventually became the standard Latin version of the Bible. It was the King James Bible of its day. This explains why it is called "the Vulgate version" (in Latin, the *versio vulgata*). The Latin word vulgata means "common." In fact, the English word *vulgar* comes from this Latin root word for "common."

When Jerome made his translation of the Old Testament, he made much use of the Greek version of the Old Testament, commonly known as the Septuagint. This Greek translation was already over five hundred years old at the time Jerome made his translation. It had considerable authority both to Christian and to Jewish scholars at the time. It would appear that, for reasons that are now obscure, Jerome translated significant parts of the non-canonical Greek texts of what we now call the Apocrypha, and included them in his edition of the Old Testament. It is important to note that these Greek translations of Hebrew writings were never considered canonical (in other words, they were never accepted as legitimate scripture) by any of the Jews. From what is known of Jerome as a scholar, it is extremely unlikely that he was confused about the non-canonical nature of these writings. He studied Hebrew under Jewish rabbis. He actually openly disparaged the worth of the Apocrypha even as he translated it. Jerome is the person who actually coined the word *apocrypha* to refer to these spurious writings.

Despite Jerome's apparent intentions, once the additions to the Old Testament were included in his Vulgate translation, they took on a life of their own. Ultimately, as what we now call the Roman Catholic Church came to increasingly rely on the Vulgate translation, the distinction became blurred between the non-canonical books (the Apocrypha) and those accepted as legitimate by the Jews. This process did not occur with the Eastern Church (later known as the Orthodox Church). The Eastern Church, with its capitals in Byzantium and Alexandria, relied on Greek rather than Latin versions of the Bible. For this reason, Jerome's translation did not have a significant effect on the Eastern Church. Therefore, the Apocrypha were never accepted at all by the Eastern Christians. Despite the fact that there is literally no support whatever for the inclusion of the Apocrypha in the Old Testament, the tradition of the day ultimately won out. To this day, when one reads a Roman Catholic translation of the Bible, one will find the writings commonly called the Apocrypha included.

It would be appropriate at this point to list these writings, but not before defining a second important term. One must make the distinction between *the Apocrypha* and the term *apocryphal*. The word apocryphal originates from the Greek word "ἀποκαλνψιζ," which is the same root word from which we derive the word *apocalyptic*. Any writing that is claimed by some to be legitimate scripture, but which was not considered legitimate by the great majority of the Jews when the OT canon was established, would be apocryphal. In the case of the New Testament, any book that was not accepted by general consensus of the early church, but which some might claim to be inspired, would be called apocryphal. There are a number of apocryphal books that some have claimed to be "lost" books of the New Testament, such as the "Gospel of Thomas." Besides these, there are still other books that some have claimed to be "lost" books of the Old Testament, but which were not included in Jerome's Vulgate translation, and are therefore not part of "the Apocrypha" as defined above. For the sake of simplicity, in this appendix the term "the Apocrypha" will be used to refer only to the additions to the Old Testament that appeared in Jerome's Vulgate translation, and which are therefore included in the Roman Catholic Bible. Other unaccepted books will simply be referred to as apocryphal.

The writings of the Apocrypha are listed below in the order in which they appear in the Roman Catholic Bible.

Tobit
Judith
Additions to Esther
First Maccabees
Second Maccabees
Wisdom
Sirach (Ecclesiasticus)
Baruch
Additions to Daniel:
    The Prayer of Azariah and The Song of the Three Children
    Susanna
    Bel and the Dragon

The writings of the Apocrypha are of varying quality, especially in their historical validity. It will be worthwhile to consider each of the books of the Apocrypha individually.

The books of Tobit and Judith are moralistic and romantic folk tales with very dubious historical accuracy. The book of Tobit includes such quaint details as using the smoke from the liver and heart of a fish to drive off a demon. A simple reading of the text marks it as vastly inferior to the inspired writings of the Bible. The book of Judith includes the most obvious historical blunders. These would include having Nebuchadnezzar listed as a king of the Assyrians! Even an avowedly Roman Catholic edition of the Bible[1] includes as an introduction to the book the statement, "Any attempt to read the book directly against the backdrop of Jewish history in relation to the empires of the ancient world is bound to fail." Despite their failings and obvious non-inspired nature, these stories make for interesting reading. The reader is encouraged to get hold of a Catholic Bible and carefully read these stories for themselves. The inspired nature of the OT books is made more obvious when they are read in comparison to the writings of the Apocrypha.

The additions to Esther are a Greek interpolation into an original Hebrew text. They were clearly added at a considerably later date, and are intended as a commentary on the original. It was the tradition of the Jewish rabbis to write commentaries on the Hebrew texts and include them in parallel with the original Biblical writings. The Talmud would be an example of this type of Jewish commentary. The fact that the additions were never even written in Hebrew makes the claim that they are spurious appear undeniable. These additions are not significant enough to deserve much comment here.

Of more interest are First and Second Maccabees. Both are primarily historical accounts of the events that occurred in the time between the Testaments. They cover the time of the Greek kingdoms, especially the time of the Seleucid domination of Palestine, and of the early Jewish/Maccabean Dynasty. The two are of greatly different value.

First Maccabees is a remarkably accurate historical account of the same events that Daniel prophesied about, especially in Daniel chapters eight and eleven. The biggest difference between the two accounts is that Daniel wrote about four hundred years before the incidents happened, whereas the writer of First Maccabees had the advantage of writing a generation or so after they occurred.

The quality of First Maccabees is such that, if it were slipped in amongst the inspired books of the Old Testament, it would not stick out as clearly not belonging there (unlike the other books of the OT apocrypha), at least in the opinion of this author. It contains no serious historical errors and no statements that would be in obvious doctrinal or theological contradiction to the Bible. One might ask why it was not included in the Hebrew canon of scriptures. Perhaps it was not included in the Hebrew canon because, despite its high quality, it is simply not inspired. It is also possible that the Jews excluded it from the Old Testament because it puts the Roman Empire in a relatively favorable light (when compared to the Greek persecutors).[2] The Jews in the time of

Christ would have struggled greatly to see anything good in their Roman overlords, and might have excluded First Maccabees from the Old Testament on that account. It is strongly recommended that the reader find a Catholic version of the Bible and read First Maccabees. Reading this account in light of the prophecies of Daniel can be a real inspiration. First Maccabees expands greatly on the persecutions of Antiochus IV Epiphanes and the righteous acts of those who refused to compromise their faith in God.

The book of Second Maccabees is of considerably lesser quality. It covers a similar period of history as First Maccabees. However, it contains some historical errors, including mistakes in chronology and obvious exaggerations in numbers. It does contain some additional historical details not found in First Maccabees, such as the story of the martyrdom of a mother and her seven sons under Antiochus IV Epiphanes for refusing to eat pork (2 Maccabees 7). The book describes a number of other very inspiring incidents of faith under extreme persecution. Despite these strengths, the book contains such colloquialisms as that found in 2 Maccabees 6:17, "Without further ado, we must go on with our story..."[3] Most interesting is the author's quote at the end of the book: "I will bring my own story to an end here too. If it is well written, and to the point, that is what I wanted; if it is poorly done and mediocre, that is the best I could do" (2 Maccabees 15:37-38). Can one imagine such a quote at the end of the book of Acts, or of Second Kings? Clearly, this is not an inspired book.

The books of Wisdom and Sirach (also known as Ecclesiasticus) are written in styles that are obvious imitations of the book of Proverbs. Both are essentially a list of wise sayings. The writer of Wisdom pretends to be Solomon himself in some sections. Because this book was written in about 100 B.C., one can see the analogy to what the critics claim (wrongly) is the case with Daniel: that it was written by a pretender. There was a well-established tradition of Hebrew writers ascribing a false authorship to a book to give it greater moral weight. This tradition gave rise to the collection of pre- and post-Christian writings known as the Pseudepigrapha (or "false letter").[4] The problem, in hindsight, with the attempt to give greater moral weight by using a false authorship is that, in the end, it actually undermines the document's credibility, unless the reader is successfully deceived.

There are, in fact, a good number of very wise sayings collected in these books. For example,

> What good is an offering to an idol that can neither taste nor smell?
> So it is with the afflicted man who groans at the good things his eyes behold (Sirach 30:19-20).

> Envy and anger shorten one's life,
> Worry brings on premature old age.
> One who is cheerful and gay while at table benefits from his food (Sirach 30:24,45).

> If there are many with you at table,
> Be not the first to reach out your hand (Sirach 31:18).

A great number of other examples could be cited. One can assume that the writers of these books were sincerely trying to impart morality and wisdom to their Jewish readers. However, if a person reads Wisdom or Sirach as scripture, they will run into trouble. Consider such passages as those quoted below, which have a dubious doctrinal or theological basis.

> Tell nothing to a friend or foe;
> If you have a fault, reveal it not (Sirach 19:7).

This passage seems to be in conflict with the strong advice in Proverbs and elsewhere that those who love God should not hide their faults and sins, but rather should confess them and bring them out into the light in order to find healing in their lives.

There are a number of passages in these books that seem to defend the idea of works salvation. For example:

> Before you are judged, seek merit for yourself,
> and at the time of visitation you will have a ransom
> (Sirach 19:19).

> For kindness to a father will not be forgotten,
> it will serve as a sin offering–it will take lasting
> root.
> In time of tribulation it will be recalled to your
> advantage, like warmth upon frost it will melt away
> your sins (Sirach 3:14-15).

This passage should raise some eyebrows, but now consider Sirach 3:29:

> Water quenches a flaming fire and alms atone for
> sins.

One can see some justification for the Medieval Roman Church practice of selling indulgences here. This church policy involved people giving money to the church and receiving the promise of forgiveness of their sins in proportion to their contribution. One should be aware that when the official Catholic Church quotes Scripture to support various teachings, it uses the Apocrypha freely.

The books of Wisdom and Sirach take a dim view of the relative worth of women. For example, consider:

> For he who despises wisdom and instruction
> is doomed.
> Vain is their hope, fruitless are their labors,
> and worthless are their works.
> Their wives are foolish and their children are
> wicked; accursed is their brood (Wisdom 3:11-12).

Those Christian wives who have difficult situations with non-believing husbands, yet remain faithful, are certainly not fools; neither are their children necessarily wicked or accursed. Consider also:

Worst of all wounds is that of the heart, worst of all evils is that of a woman....

There is scarce any evil like that in a woman; may she fall to the lot of the sinner (Sirach 25:12,18).

If these books contained similar strong words about the evil tendencies inherent in men, perhaps it might give some perspective to such statements about women, but both Sirach and Wisdom are one-sided in their view of women, reflecting the prejudice of Hebrew men in the second century B.C. This very dim view of women may have provided some of the justification to the Catholic Church for eventually excluding married men from the priesthood.

More examples could be mentioned, but the point is made. These books do indeed show some wisdom, but they definitely are not inspired books.

The next item in the Apocrypha is the book of Baruch. This book is pseudepigraphical, in that it pretends itself to have been written by Baruch, the scribe to Jeremiah. The book is generally of greater quality than some of the others in the Apocrypha, because it is a relatively accurate account from a historical perspective. Besides this, it does not contain such theological or doctrinal inconsistencies as do the books of Wisdom and Sirach. The sixth chapter purports itself to be a letter from Jeremiah to the exiles in Babylon. One cannot absolutely rule out the possibility that this letter is genuine. It is a stinging rebuke of idolatry, much in the style of Jeremiah's writings. Despite the quality of this book, there is no evidence that the Jews ever considered it to be part of the OT canon.

The last section of the Apocrypha is the part that is actually included as if it were part of Daniel in the Roman Catholic Bible. These "additions to Daniel" include two prayers in the form of psalms, which are inserted into chapter three of Daniel, as well as two fable-like stories added at the end of the book.

The first of the additions to Daniel are known as "The Prayer of Azariah" (i.e., of Abednego) and "The Song of the

Three Holy Children." The Prayer of Azariah follows Daniel 3:23. It begins with the phrase, "They walked about in the flames, singing to God and blessing the Lord. According to this section of the Apocrypha, in the fire, Azariah stood up and prayed aloud,

> "Blessed are you, and praiseworthy, O Lord, the God of our fathers... " (Daniel 3:26 in the Catholic Bible).

What follows is a psalm of praise to God, of confession of Israel's sins and a plea for deliverance from the Babylonian captivity. The poem itself contains no obvious false teachings. The only problem with the poem is the dubious claim that Abednego actually recited the psalm while in the flames of the furnace. Certainly the Jews themselves believed the poem to be pseudepigraphic. In other words, they believed that it did not contain the actual words of Azariah. This is shown by the fact that they never included it in the accepted text of Daniel.

Following the poem comes an interlude including the statement that "the king's men who had thrown them in continued to stoke the furnace with brimstone, pitch, tow and faggots. The flames rose forty-nine cubits above the furnace...But the angel of the Lord... drove the fiery flames out of the furnace and made the inside of the furnace as though a dew-laden breeze were blowing through it." It seems extremely unlikely that the servants of Nebuchadnezzar would have continued to stoke the fire after their compatriots had already been consumed by its intensity. The forty-nine-cubit flame height and the dew-laden breeze comment all make one think that the quality of this supposed passage of scripture is very questionable.

After the interlude mentioned above, the apocryphal addition to Daniel continues with a second psalm, commonly known as "The Song of the Three Children." Again, this is a nice spiritual poem, but it is very unlikely its authors were Shadrach, Meshach and Abednego, as claimed. The Jewish teachers in the time before Christ—God's chosen arbiters of what became part of the OT canon—never included this poem.

In the Catholic Bible, what is known as Daniel chapter twelve is followed by two stories. The first of the stories is known as "Susannah." In the story, two hypocritical judges attack Susannah (a beautiful and righteous Jew) after they are overcome with their lust when they see her bathing. When they attempt to rape her, she screams. The servants come rushing in and the wicked judges accuse Susannah of lying with another man. In a trial, the judges accept the story of the wicked judges because they are highly respected. Susannah is condemned, but as she is led off to execution, Daniel, who is described as a young boy, stops the procession. He accuses the judges of lying and demands a continuance of the trial in which he tricks the men into revealing their lie.

In the end, Susannah is exonerated, the wicked judges are cut in two, "and from that day onward, Daniel was greatly esteemed by the people" (Daniel 13:64). This is a nice fable with an obvious moral, but it cannot be taken seriously as belonging to the inspired book of Daniel!

Next comes the story of Bel and the Dragon. In this story, Bel is the chief god of Babylon, and the dragon is an idol in the shape of a dragon, which the Babylonians supposedly worshiped. This story appears so far from being believable that it does not even seem worth relating the details to the reader. It might work fairly well as a moral fable to be told by Jewish parents to their children. This may very well have been the original intent of its author. Suffice it to say that in this absolutely unbelievable story, Daniel uses his wisdom to prove to Cyrus the king that both Bel and the dragon are in fact not gods at all. It must be an embarrassment to anyone who attempts to pass off the entire Bible as inspired, yet must defend this fable as being among those inspired books.

Remember that those who would attack the authenticity of Daniel would seek to put it in a group of books along with Tobit and the additions to Daniel. They would claim that Daniel is, in essence, apocryphal. From the simple descriptions given here, it is not difficult at all to see that this claim is outrageous. Daniel contains none of the blatant historical blunders, quaint moralizing fables, or teachings that obviously conflict with basic Bible truths, as do the books of the Apocrypha.

In summary, the writings that were included in Jerome's translation of the Bible into Latin, which later came to be known as the Apocrypha, include a number of books and parts of books that vary greatly from one another in quality. They span the range from poorly written fables to very valuable historical documents that can supplement our understanding of some of the prophecies of Daniel. In the final analysis, despite the fine quality of some of the writings, there is no justification for including any of these into the officially accepted canon of scripture. Claims that the traditional book of Daniel is in fact apocryphal do not hold up to careful scrutiny. This is made especially true when the generally low quality of the apocryphal writings are compared to the clearly inspired writing in Daniel.

## End Notes

[1] *The New American Bible,* Catholic Bible Press, 1987, Introduction to Judith, p. 446.

[2] See especially 1 Maccabees 8.

[3] Quotes from the Apocrypha are taken from *The New American Bible,* Catholic Bible Press, 1969.

[4] There are a number of these "pseudepigraphical" books, such as First, Second and Third Esdras, The Book of Enoch, The Apocalypse of Moses, The Testament of Job, and others. These are all apocryphal, but not part of the Apocrypha.

To get the latest news from the ministry of John M. Oakes go to:

# www.EvidenceForChristianity.org

**Science and the Bible**
Author: Dr. John M. Oakes
Price: $5.00
1-CD (with downloadable outlines)
Available at: www.ipibooks.com

**From Shadow to Reality**
Author: Dr. John M. Oakes
Price: $5.00
1-CD (with downloadable outlines)
Available at: www.ipibooks.com

**Judas: Another Gospel?**
Author: Dr. John M. Oakes
Price: $5.00
1-CD (with downloadable outlines)
Available at: www.ipibooks.com

**The Problem of Pain and Suffering**
Author: Dr. John M. Oakes
CD Price: $5.00   DVD Price: $8.00
1-CD (with downloadable outlines)
Available at: www.ipibooks.com

**Freedom For What?**
Author: Dr. John M. Oakes
Price: $5.00
1-CD (with downloadable outlines)
Available at: www.ipibooks.com

# From Shadow to Reality
A Study of the Relationship Between the Old and the New Testament

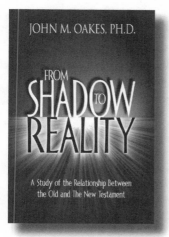

The purpose of this book is to show the historical, doctrinal and prophetic relationship between the Testaments. The conclusion is that in its essence, from Genesis to Malachi, the Old Testament is a foreshadowing of the New Testament. The theme of the entire Bible is God's desire to have a relationship with us.

Chapter subjects include: Prefigures of the Messiah; The Earthly Tabernacle and the Heavenly Tabernacle; Old Testament Ritual Sacrifice points to New Testament Sacrifice; The Old Covenant Feasts Prefigure Specific Aspects of the Christian Life; Prophecies in the Old Testament Predict Events in the Life of Jesus Christ and much more. This book clearly shows the undeniable unity of the Bible.

ISBN: 0-9745342-3-4, Author: Dr. John M. Oakes
Price: $15.00, 288 pages, Available at: www.ipibooks.com

# Is There A God?
Questions About Science and the Bible

The need for biblical evidence is greater in our generation than ever before. Secularism and humanism are rampant, the media and the educational system bombard us with half-truths and untruths about the meaning of life, and multitudes are confused about the fundamentals of human existence. So profound is the confusion today that many ask not, "What are the answers?", but rather, "What are the questions?" We in Western society are in a bad way indeed! The need for scientifically current apologetic books—well thought out, well written, and well adapted to our generation—is great, I believe that with this volume, you will have such a book. Every reader will want to follow the flow of John Oakes' reasoning and master the arguments, in order to be better equipped to convince others about the truth of God's Word.

ISBN: 0-9776954-2-5
Price: $14.00, 196 pages
Available at: www.ipibooks.com

## Lessons from Daniel: Prophet to the Nations

This audio series by Dr. John Oakes will make the book of Daniel come alive for you. The series is divided into two parts. In Part 1, John relates the practical lessons of staying pure in a corrupt world. He looks at the examples of Daniel, Shadrach, Meshach and Abednego and makes application to our Christian walk.

In Part II, John examines the prophecies of Daniel and how they were fulfilled. Your faith will increase as you see vision after vision fulfilled and learn that God controls the nations and can control the circumstances of our lives. Also included on CD 1 are classroom notes on Daniel, Prophecies in Daniel (word documents and PDFs) and also a PowerPoint presentation on the book of Daniel.

CD 1: Staying Pure in a Corrupt World
CD 2: God Rules the Nations: Do Not Fear

ISBN: 978-0-978803906
Author: Dr. John M. Oakes
Price: $10.00
2-CDs in hard case
Available at: www.ipibooks.com

## Reasons For Belief: A Handbook of Christian Evidence

Without a doubt, faith is at the heart of Christianity. *"Without faith it is impossible to please God"* (Hebrews 11:6). This book is intended to provide a basis in fact for belief in the Bible as the inspired word of God. It will be helpful, both to deepen the faith of those who already believe and to establish a factual basis for belief to those who do not yet accept that the Bible is the inspired word of God.

ISBN: 0-9767583-3-4
Author: Dr. John M. Oakes
Price: $14.00, 256 pages
Available at: www.ipibooks.com

# That You May Believe
### Reflections on Science
### and the Miracles of Jesus

In Acts 2, there are three words used to define supernatural works: "Miracles" is the Greek word *dunamis*, defined as "power, ability, physical or moral, as residing in a person or thing." "Wonder" is the rendering of the Greek noun *teras*, literally, "something strange." The emphasis is on events that cause the beholder to marvel. "Signs" is the Greek word *semeion*. The word means "sign or signal". It implies a thing which can be used for identification. The emphasis is that miracles and wonders are signs of divine authority.

There are unbelievers who deny miracles ever happen. Even among liberal "believers," the miracles of Jesus are doubted or explained away. But none of those who spent time around Jesus, even among his enemies, ever denied his miracles. Instead, they sought to discredit him in various ways, attributing his miraculous power to Satan or demons. The records we have in the New Testament accurately document what Jesus accomplished in the realm of the miraculous.

You will marvel as you meditate on his miracles, watch him create the universe, heal the human body, bend the laws of physics, manipulate creation, read the thoughts of others and resurrect the dead. Think beyond the doubt and absurd fantasies of unbelieving scholars, and understand what he accomplished. Apply these ruminations to your own life, and come to believe, in a fuller and more mature way, what he is capable of achieving in and through you. "The work of God is to believe," so strap in, observe, marvel, and be prepared to believe as never before!

ISBN: 978-0-9797886-6-8     Authors: Dr. John M. Oakes and David Eastman
Price: $14.00, 184 pages     Available at: www.ipibooks.com

To get the latest news from the ministry of John M. Oakes go to:
# www.EvidenceForChristianity.org

# Illumination Publishers International

Toney Mulhollan has been in Christian publishing for more than 30 years. He has served as the Production Manager for Crossroads Publications, Discipleship Magazine/UpsideDown Magazine, Discipleship Publications International (DPI) and on the production teams of Campus Journal, Biblical Discipleship Quarterly, Bible Illustrator and others. He has served as production manager for several printing companies. Toney serves as the Executive Editor of Illumination Publishers International. Toney is happily married to the love of his life, Denise Leonard Mulhollan, M.D. They make their home in Houston, Texas along with their daughters, Lyndsey and Audra Joan.

For the best in Christian writing and audio instruction, go to the Illumination Publishers International website. We're commited to producing in-depth teaching that will inform, inspire and encourage Christians to a deeper and more committed walk with God.

You can reach Toney Mulhollan by email at: toneyipibooks@mac.com or at his office phone (832) 559-3658, or cell (713) 376-8803.

# www.ipibooks.com

www.ipibooks.com